The Hollywood Musical

Other Books by Ethan Mordden

Better Foot Forward: The History of American Musical Theatre
Opera in the Twentieth Century
That Jazz!: An Idiosyncratic Social History of the American Twenties
A Guide to Orchestral Music
The Splendid Art Of Opera
The American Theatre

The Hollywood Musical

by ETHAN MORDDEN

ST. MARTIN'S PRESS
New York

Library of Congress Cataloging in Publication Data

Mordden, Ethan
The Hollywood Musical

Discography: p.
Bibliography: p.
1. Moving-pictures, Musical—History and
criticism.   2. Moving-pictures—United States—
History.   I. Title.
PN1995.9.M86M6   791.43′09′09357   81-8738
ISBN 0-312-38835-7   AACR2

Design by Dennis J. Grastorf

10 9 8 7 6 5 4 3 2 1

FIRST EDITION

Frontispiece: Ginger Rogers and Fred Astaire in the "They All Laughed" number
in *Shall We Dance.*

To my students in CSSM 190b:

*Vicky, Tom, Stephen, Ethan, Michael,
Liza, David, Carl, Susan, Tommy, Bill,
Donna, Christian, David, and Laurie*

Table of Contents

	Preface	xi
	Acknowledgments	xiii
1:	The Texture of Sound	1
2:	What's a Musical?	17
3:	The Early Musicals	24
4:	The First Stars	50
5:	The Texture of Popular Music	66
6:	The Allure of Genre	79
7:	The Dance Musical	109
8:	Opera Versus Croonbelt	122
9:	The Comedy Musical	135
10:	The Stars of the Late 1930s	142
11:	Fantasy and the Story Musical	153
12:	The Texture of Swing	160
13:	Wartime People	165
14:	Americana	174
15:	The Inertia of Genre	180
16:	The Energy Peters Out	186
17:	Economics of a Stereo Era	194
18:	The Big Broadway Roadshow	201
19:	The Texture of Rock	209

20: Interesting Times   217
21: Rest in Peace   224
A Selective Discography   233
A Selective Bibliography   239
The Ethan Mordden Hall of Fame and Disrepute   243
Index   251

☆ ☆

Preface

I OVERTRAINED FOR THIS BOOK. Reviewing classics and tracking down rarities, I filled notebooks with data that would have made this volume unreadably comprehensive. I apologize to *Reckless, Sweetheart of the Campus, Something to Shout About, Two Girls and a Sailor, Look for the Silver Lining, The Kissing Bandit, Show Business, Rhythm on the River*, and the many other films that didn't get into the first draft, and to others that were dropped at the second cut. I apologize also to readers who were hoping to hear of Jean Harlow's musical, of Ruby Keeler's last musical, of Janet Blair's best musical, and other fine notes of the canon. Less is never more; less is less. But it does make for a trimmer read.

This survey is limited to the American film musical: no foreign works are covered unless they had some impact here. All those that did are British, and often take in major American participation, in director (the first two Beatles films), songwriters and biggest international star (*The Slipper and the Rose*), or in financing. But I have tried to make the book comprehensive within its limits, starting with the first sound films and taking the musical up to the present writing, omitting nothing that is generally thought important or that I find amusing.

The reader will note that the book has a greater concentration in the 1930s than in the 1940s, and lightens as it moves forward: fewer films were released in each succeeding decade and also I find those of the 1930s more interesting than those that followed. Style and form were largely set and most of the most essential persons (Fred Astaire, Ginger Rogers, Judy Garland, Eddie Cantor, Alice Faye, Maurice

Chevalier, Jeanette MacDonald) were launched in the 1930s; in fact the five years of sound before the Production Code enforcement of 1934 stand as one of the most exuberant periods in the history of American art. I think the reader will agree, as we traverse the decades, that the period of Al Jolson and Ernst Lubitsch is worth more analysis than that of Betty Grable and Stanley Donen. This is not to belittle the talents of the latter; but they were largely encircled by convention, whereas Jolson, Lubitsch, and their colleagues covered a wide, free territory.

A number of people helped me research this project. First of all, Romano Tozzi, the ranking expert in the field, guided my advance and corrected the numerous misapprehensions I collected early on. George Caudill, Ralph Straughan, Ken Richards, Clint Bocock, and Charles Silver of the Museum of Modern Art generously screened films for me. The photos used here, which originally emanate from the studios involved—Warner Brothers, Metro-Goldwyn-Mayer, Paramount, RKO, United Artists, Twentieth Century-Fox, Columbia, and Universal—came into my hands from a variety of sources, among which should count Jerry Vermilye and Lou Valentino, who advised on procedure, and Ellis Regenbogen, the Columbia lawyer from Columbia Law. Push come to shove, I bought most of them in New York at Jerry Ohlinger's Movie Material Store and Mark Ricci's Memory Shop, pleasantly enough, and a few at Movie Star News, regrettably. Bill Tynes not only screened films on his whiz RCA projector but also helped open my perspective on the awards pages.

The author wishes to acknowledge the support and guidance of Michael Denneny and Paul Dinas and, as always, the wisdom and persistence of his agent Dorothy Pittman. Also, Carol Robinson went over the manuscript with an expert eye and Robert Hoppe painted a stupendous cover. These are all grand collaborators.

The Hollywood Musical

☆ 1 ☆
The Texture of Sound

SILENT FILM enclosed its audience. Live musicians impassioned the adventure; darkness focused it; the absence of color sharpened it. The stories revealed a density of beauty and sensuality that few people could have hoped to encounter in life. The silents served as a consoling dream yet called for great resources of concentration: their "story" was as much expression as action. Miss a single shot and one might miss a major turn in the narrative. The public drew close.

Today's moviegoers cannot get in touch with silent film. It is seldom seen at all, and when it is the film is often projected at the wrong speed in faded prints and with an insufficient musical accompaniment. Worst of all, the extraordinary acting style developed by silent artists comes off as a dead language trying to scream: because it talked in magic. Lacking sound, film could never be natural; and at its best or blandest it seldom tried to be. By 1920, its experimental stage was over; it had largely ceased attempting to duplicate live theatre and was working out its own aesthetic—a fantasy drawing on naturalism. Film looked real, when it wanted to, in ways no stage could, but it behaved overreal, letting the camera's sense of detail, the narrative force of editing, and the intensity of acting define its art. It was a real garden with imaginary toads.

A host of methods for synchronizing sound and film were developed in the early 1900s, but moviemakers were inclined to do without. Reproduction was not faithful, an obtrusive hiss haunted the recording track, and theatres would have to be wired for one of several possible sound processes, not to mention the expense of regearing the industry itself. How would movie personnel function with a microphone hanging over them? Sets were habitually noisy—the camera thrummed, directors coached the team, actors improvised lines, musicians kept them in spirit. Sound would silence the set, make it anxious. But, mainly, there was the artistic problem: where would sound fit into an art already complete without it?

Film was *not* complete. The musical accompaniment was strategic to its suggestive illusion, a kind of middle point that brought the real-life audience together with the romanticized life on the screen. Only urban moviegoers, who had access to the fully coordinated production of lush lobbies, gleaming ushers, auditoriums like pagan cathedrals, and symphony orchestras playing scores especially composed to extrapolate emotionally on each specific film, got as close as film wanted them to get. So sound, as sheer music, would complete film after all—to take that orchestra, tracked in synchronization with the action, to the nation's moviegoers.

Warner Brothers was the studio that initiated the sound era, and in just this way: sound not as dialogue but as music. The four brothers, Harry, Sam, Albert, and Jack, had incorporated in 1923 after a few years of rather informal production and were doing well. Their rise to power coincided exactly with the rise of radio, the all-picture business side by side with the all-sound business. Perhaps the better-established studios were too used to their status quo to note this irony, but with Rin-Tin-Tin the only infallible box-office draw on the Warners roster and without a single foothold in the competition for top-class exhibition halls, the brothers saw a way to better their standing: combine what radio did with what film did.

Radio made music. Radio also talked; but, as Harry Warner observed when brother Sam pointed out that sound film might tackle dialogue, "Who the hell wants to hear actors talk?" Sam secured the exclusive rights to a sound process developed by Bell Telephone, called Vitaphone ("the sound of life"), in which sounds were recorded simultaneously with pictures and played on discs run synchronously with the film. Jack upped the budget on a swords-and-kisses costume piece, *Don Juan*, from $500,000 to $700,000, a desperate act among the stingy Warners. Sam went to New York to hire the New York Philharmonic to play *Don Juan*'s score plus a posh vaudeville to fill out the evening—violinist Mischa Elman, tenor Giovanni Martinelli, sopranos Marion Talley and Anna Case, Efrem Zimbalist and Harold Bauer performing Beethoven's "Kreutzer" violin sonata, and the Metropolitan Opera Chorus. The Warners would almost certainly go bankrupt if their gambit failed, but on paper it was shaping up nicely—*big*, anyway, which it would have to be to go over—and they held an extra ace in the star of *Don Juan*, John Barrymore, almost as imposing an attraction as Rin-Tin-Tin. The double bill of *Don Juan* and "the Vitaphone," as the musical variety show was called, looked like a reasonably sure thing, provided the studio could follow it up with more Vitaphone sound tracks *and* get them out and earning before the Warners silent pictures had closed and the cash flow dried up.

In New York to produce the variety show and *Don Juan*'s soundtrack of William Axt's music and added sound effects, Sam Warner discovered what the entire film business was shortly to discover: sound was mined with traps. Subway rumblings ruined takes, construction blasting vibrated the recording stylus out of its groove, radio waves slipped onto the track out of thick air—the still, dead world was suddenly filled with tunes. Even the arc lights made a contribution on the recording wax in the form of a distinct faint sizzle. Sam worked his way around it all, and on August 6, 1926, at a total cost of $3,000,000 (taking in everything from Mary Astor's incredible "come as thou wert" hairdo in *Don Juan* to the purchase of the Piccadilly Theatre in New York and its refurbishing, as the Warner Theatre, with sound apparatus), sound became current. The double bill was opened by Will H. Hays, who had been President Harding's Postmaster General but resigned to preside over Hollywood's "self"-censorship in 1922 after several murder and drug addiction scandals threatened to destroy the industry with bluenose boycotts. Hays was never implicated in the oil-land swindles of Teapot Dome and Elk Hills, Harding's Watergate, but he looked like a guilty rabbit, and made a drab guide to the new world of sound, speaking of the "speech-film" in his midwestern twang. But once Hays was gone, the Warners brought their project home, in *Don Juan*'s dramatic scoring and, especially, the classical mixed grill. *Don Juan* was the same old love-thriller silent with the novelty of a recorded score in place of a live one, but the Vitaphone had Martinelli singing "Vesti la Giubba" from *Pagliacci* and an all-out effort by the Philharmonic on Wagner's *Tannhäuser* Overture, made vivid by some shy cutting from one section of the orchestra to another. Marion Talley, who sang "Caro Nome" from Verdi's *Rigoletto*, was the project's one fizzle, but then her short career had been entirely created by PR manipulation and was about to end anyway. She was a star rather than a talent; hiring her was a very Hollywood thing to do. Still, whether or not one cared for *Don Juan*, *Pagliacci*, or Talley, the advantage of processing films with their own orchestral accompaniment—thus to make the musical complement to "silence" available to every theatre of any size or budget—was obvious.

Another advantage of the symphonic film score was the arrangers' use of the classics. Many people who had no regular exposure to great music heard it in theatres, Hollywood proudly pointed out—but now that Vitaphone was here, why not expand its territory to include popular music as well? There had been one nonclassical segment in the first Vitaphone, a turn by Roy Smeck on an array of instruments from banjo to harmonica, and the second Vitaphone vaudeville, unveiled on October 5, 1926, in tandem with a comedy starring Charlie Chaplin's brother Sydney, *The Better 'Ole*, stressed popular art. The acts included comedians Willie and Eugene Howard, all-around entertainers Elsie Janis and George Jessel, operatic baritone Reinald Werrenrath (in such selections, however, as "The Long, Long Trail"), and, most significantly, Al Jolson, as big a star as all the others put together. No theatre in the world could have afforded the fees necessary to gather all these performers in one live show; it was like vaudeville with nothing but closing acts. If the camera seldom established any great intimacy with its subjects, preferring a straight-on perspective halfway back into nowhere, still the communication of personality is telling, not least when Jolson turns up in his characteristic blackface makeup in a rural setting to send over "The Red, Red Robin," "April Showers," and "Rockabye Your Baby With a Dixie Melody." Unlike the classical Vitaphone, the pop program incorporated talking as part of the fun—Jessel and the two Howards all worked in verbal comedy. Still, music was the point of the show, music of a universally approachable nature. The appeal—and cultural oneupmanship—of opera and concert material would tempt the film musical throughout its heyday,* from Grace Moore and Johann Strauss to Katharine Hepburn's Clara Schumann (Artur Rubinstein played for her) in *Song of Love.* But as early as the second Vitaphone it was clear that sound's first operation would be the institutionalization of popular music in film.

At least, it was clear to the Warner brothers, who thrust Al Jolson into *The Jazz Singer,* a tale of a Jewish cantor's son whose singing style favors American pop over the pious recitative of his people.

---

*The third Vitaphone program might be said to have inaugurated Hollywood's fetish for getting pop and legit music together, for it featured exemplars of both. The theory behind this coupling might be stated as—to paraphrase Katharine Hepburn's famous analysis of Astaire and Rogers—legit gives pop class and pop gives legit sex.

George Jessel had done the part in Samson Raphaelson's play on Broadway in 1925, and when the Warners bought the screen rights for the usual silent adaptation they wanted Jessel to do it all over on film. But with Vitaphone on hand it seemed wise to stress the character's ambivalent ethnic identity by slipping song sequences into the film, letting music define his Jewish-religious and American-entertainer selves. Jessel, signed to a $2,000-a-week contract, now wanted more—a percentage on any Vitaphone records marketed separately. Negotiations collapsed as the studio considered the other two leading blackface performers of the day, Jolson and Eddie Cantor. Jolson was their man.

The Jazz Singer is mawkish melodrama, the protagonist being disinherited by one culture (in the person of his intolerant father) to fall into the other only after expiating his betrayal by singing the traditional Jewish requiem, the Kol Nidre, at his father's deathbed. Moreover, he bears an insistently Oedipal love for his mother. The Mammy icon, a focus of Jolson's art, is the focus of the character's conflict: she represents the old culture, yet accepts her son's assimiliation into the new. How the Warners could have considered anyone but Jolson for the part is incomprehensible—even Jessel, miffed at having blown the chance to reassert himself in his stage role, admitted that Jolson outdid everyone in that sort of thing.

It was *The Jazz Singer* with Jolson, premiered on October 6, 1927, that inflamed interest in the sound film, though it was a silent with a synchronized score and a few "talking" sequences. These were supposed to have been vocal spots exclusively, carrying a total of five songs, but Jolson never did anything according to the book, and while the mike was on and the cameras turning, he threw in his signature boast, "You ain't heard nothin' yet!" and other rave reviews of his own performance. He also tossed off a paragraph of manic filial gush in a scene with his mother, played by Eugenie Besserer in considerable bewilderment, the usual state for performing with Jolson. Cut off from her for years, her son has risen in show business and now returns to present her with a diamond brooch. "That I should live so long to see my baby again!" Besserer cries, according to the title cards. "Diamonds! . . . You didn't do anything wrong, did you Jakie?" He did: Jakie Rabinowitz has become Jack Robin of Broadway. As the talking segment begins, Jolson stresses the Jack in him with a performance of Irving Berlin's "Blue Skies" on the piano, and then tells his mother that he's going to move her out of the slums into a nice neighborhood: "There's the Ginsburgs, the Guttenbergs, and the Goldbergs. Oh, a lot of Bergs. I dunno them all. And I'm gonna buy you a nice, black silk dress, Mama. You'll see—Mrs. Friedman, the butcher's wife, she'll be jealous of you." Besserer tries to keep up with it all, but she looks edgy and her murmured replies sound like cries for help. "Take me out of this movie!" she seems to plead, but history was manning that mike, and nobody moved. When Jolson gives her his special jazz version of "Blue Skies," with a thumping left hand and plenty of scat improvisation, we understand that Jakie was born to become Jack: his mission in pop music is unstoppable.

That was Jolson off the cuff, and it worked because its casual realism was exactly what film had never had before and was now in the process of acquiring. Till this point, film stars had moved through their remote silence as archetypes of desire and ambition, brutality and self-sacrifice. Even the comics often created an opaquely false world of menace but no real danger, a violence without pain. Jolson's Jack/Jakie came from the real world: with words. He was not only the right man for the part; he was the right man for the whole bloody historical transition from (silent) fantasy into (talking) realism. In 1923, D. W. Griffith had talked Jolson into making a film called *Mammy's Boy*, but Jolson felt like a ghost playing to no audience without his songs and braggart's ad libs, and he quit early in production. But *The Jazz Singer* was the true Jolson. The guy was sound in its essence.

The Jazz* Singer, phenomenon though it was, did not do incredible business, because few theatres were equipped to show it. The more resourceful silent houses screened it without the Vitaphone discs but played Jolson records—not necessarily the appropriate ones—during the vocal sequences. It was the second Warners Jolson vehicle, *The Singing Fool* (1928), that really forced sound on the industry. *The Singing Fool* became the classic of the transition, and was almost always the debut item of houses that had converted to sound.

Like *The Jazz Singer* a "part-talkie"—that is, a silent with occasional scenes synchronized for voice—*The Singing Fool* proposed Jolson as a singing waiter and songwriter who rises in vaudeville, falls in a bad marriage, and rises again with the help of a loving woman. Its most effective element besides Jolson was an intolerably adorable three-and-a-half-year-old, Davey Lee, who played Jolson's son. The child, called

---

*"Jazz" was loosely construed in the 1920s; it covered the whole world of American rhythmic pop music: not only Bessie Smith and Coleman Hawkins, but George Gershwin, Ruth Etting, and "Charleston." In the context of the day, *The Jazz Singer* literally means "The Pop Singer."

"Sonny Boy," inspires the film's theme song, which Jolson, now a doting father rather than *The Jazz Singer*'s doting son, sings on Christmas Eve to the toddler in his lap. Later, Sonny Boy dies, prompting a last reprise of his *Leitmotiv*. It sounds corny, but it stood high in the memory of a generation because Jolson's emotional commitment made it authentic. "B-b-b-boy, I tell you it got to me," he reported shortly after the filming. "I was a wreck . . . If you cried real tears on the stage, you'd panic 'em. But I cry real ones here, and have to keep on cryin' 'em for retakes till I feel like an April shower." Jolson, then, was among the first actors to spot the difference between the artificial arrangement of stage illusion and the imposed naturalism of the talking-singing cinema. The point is not how many times Jolson had to play a scene, but how easily his abundant honesty fitted the new real fantasy of film. Because the old fantasy was doomed.

Even before *The Singing Fool* came out, Warners had produced the first "all-talking" picture, a crime drama called *The Lights of New York* (1928), and the end of the year brought out a third singing silent, *My Man*, with Fanny Brice. The silence was dying away—*Photoplay* magazine dubbed *My Man* "a three-quarters talkie." "From shop girl to show star," the PR phrased it—"a tender, heart-tugging story of a girl who won the hearts of millions after she lost the love of her man." Warners hedged its multimillion-dollar bet on sound in a message at the bottom of the ads: "If there is not a theatre in your community equipped as yet to show *My Man* as a talking picture—be sure to see it as a silent picture." But surely the purpose of seeing Brice was to hear Brice sing "I'd Rather Be Blue Over You," "I'm an Indian," "Second-Hand Rose," and the title song. Similarly, the high spot of Warners' *Weary River* (1929) was the piano-playing and singing of silent hero Richard Barthelmess as (the ads again) "a down-and-outer whose plaintive music reaches through prison's bars to find love and new life a thousand miles away." Warners' PR drooled over the revelation of Barthelmess' musicianship—"a voice so sensationally fine he could have won stardom on it alone . . . now you can HEAR him TALK and play the piano!"

Was sound a passing novelty in film's grammar or its future tense? The Warner boys were doing incredible business, enabling them to buy up theatres and wire them for Vitaphone, and, thus spurred, other studios tried sound. Warner Brothers controlled Vitaphone, but there were other methods of sound recording, the most likely one being sound-on-film (as opposed to Vitaphone's sound-on-separate-discs approach), already adopted by William Fox as Movietone. The continu-

☆ *FROM SILENT FANTASY INTO THE NATURALISM OF SOUND:* above, Don Juan *(Barrymore on balcony);* below, 42nd Street, *"It Must Be June"* number. *Off with the getups and on with the life.*

☆ ONSTAGE AND BACK-
STAGE AT THE BROADWAY
MELODY: *above, King pleads
for Page's love; below, "The Wedding of the Painted Doll."*

ing success of even the dumbest talkies finally convinced Hollywood that sound had come to pass and, as cautious studio heads inquired into patent rights and rental of equipment and learned that everything available had been devoured by more impetuous colleagues, a panic spread through the industry. Not knowing where things were headed, everyone just stood there and screamed, "Move!"

Sorting out the business end of the sound conversion was nothing compared to its technical and artistic problems. These may be divided into two parts: the microphone and the camera. The mike was new to Hollywood, even though Lee De Forest, the unsung "father of sound," had been turning out his talking Phonofilm shorts since 1923. The camera, on the other hand, was the oldest thing in film. But besides the mike's own hazards, it so hampered camera movement that a new filming style for sound had to be evolved in 1928, 1929, and 1930.

Consider the problems of the microphone alone. Some film actors had pleasant or at any rate dramatically useful voices. Some did not; they would have to go. Some were foreign, and spoke English with heavy accents; they would have to go—along with the lucrative foreign market, for what non-English-speaking moviegoer would be able to follow a scenario worked out in English dialogue and lyrics? More problems: some voices turned out to be mysteriously phonogenic, others not; who knew why? Actors without stage experience might not get the hang of delivering dialogue. Film actors were used to blurting out their visuals, so to speak, spontaneously scene by scene; now they would be hamstrung by a text. Most agonizing of all, the mike, which could fail to pick up the strongest voice if an actor happened to turn his head, managed not to miss the slightest rustle of costume, grip's cough, or slip of a prop.

Much of this was recalled with loving fun in *Singin' in the Rain* from the vantage point of several decades of survival. But if one realizes that this meant not the progressive retooling of an industry but the dismantling of an art, the nostalgia becomes more urgent. The camera made noise. The mike picked up that noise. So the camera was placed in a soundproof booth, which severely inhibited its freedom. It stood back, frozen and gaping, then laboriously wheeled in for a close-up and held it, dazed. In the end, an art that had depended heavily on the reportorial mobility of the audience's eye now had to depend on the narrative elaboration of dialogue. By the time the soundless camera was developed, movies had lost much of their kinetics, their plasticity. They had become outdoor plays. "It would have been more logical if silent pictures had grown out of talkies," Mary Pickford told the *New York Times Magazine*, "instead of the other way around."

Sounds like a fanatic, doesn't she? You should have been there then. The uninformed modern thinks of silent film as a romp of vamps, cabaret sheiks, flaming youth running wild, slapstick comedians falling down, and *The Birth of a Nation* and *Intolerance*. In fact, the great last years of the silents brought forth works of profound artistry and thematic depth. Even melodrama, in F. W. Murnau's *Sunrise* (1927) and Victor Sjöstrom's *The Wind* (1928), gained from the imagination stimulated in the moving picture—Murnau's lyrical abandon and Sjöstrom's ghastly Texas sandstorm prove that story in itself was less amazing than how story was told, how it looked. True, irony sometimes needed a title card, as when D. W. Griffith announced "War's peace" in *The Birth of a Nation* and then presented a battlefield strewn with dead men. But what film gained in language it lost ten times over in imagery. One cannot take Pickford's statement lightly, especially as she understood talkies well enough to win her one Oscar as best actress for a sound picture, *Coquette*, in 1929.

By that year, silence was officially over. All Hollywood was geared for sound, and the original plan to make music sound's major element was shelved. Sound pictures were talkies, not primarily musicals, and actors who had assumed they would be spared having to sing found to their sorrow that they couldn't even talk. Could they be dubbed—or, as it was first termed, "doubled"? Few were. Warner Oland, who played Jolson's father in *The Jazz Singer*, was dubbed by cantor Josef Rosenblatt in the musical passages to ensure an authoritative Jewish melisma, and Richard Barthelmess, it finally turned out, had neither sung nor played the piano himself in *Weary River*. But generally actors were expected to cut it or get out. It sounds simple. Those with good microphone voices would be graduated into talkies to do what they did in sound. But it wasn't that simple.

Talkies weren't silents with sound. Aside from the static quality of many early talkies and the primitive literacy of the scripts, the sound films shattered silent fantasy, gave up that remote magic that had poeticized their naturalism. With dialogue, film had to be real—this is where Jolson came in: no one, in any part, was more real than he. But some things the silents did just wouldn't work in the new reality. So it was not just a matter of adjusting film to the technology of sound production, but of adjusting subject matter and approach to a public no longer enclosed by myth.

John Gilbert is generally thought to be the mike's classic victim, the "great lover" of silents whose voice was so high that he was laughed off the screen. Actually, he was a victim of style. He first spoke on film in one of the earliest musicals, *The Hollywood Revue of 1929*, playing Romeo to Norma Shearer's Juliet in the Balcony Scene. In a touch of film-within-film, a voice cries "Cut!" and Lionel Barrymore appears as the scene's director to run it all over in twenties jive at the request of the money bosses in the east, fearful of highbrow art. "Julie, baby," Gilbert obligingly intones, "you're the cream in my mocha and java, the berries in my pie." The choice of role for Gilbert's first venture into sound was apt, as it maintains his silent persona as the ecstatic lover of splendid women. The slang parody, because of its vulgarity, also works—it's so far from the persona that it doesn't challenge it.

However, then came Gilbert's first sound feature in his old style, *His Glorious Night* (1929). Now there was something wrong, but it wasn't Gilbert's voice. Attempting to portray ecstasy in banal dialogue, Gilbert reduced his character from archetype to cartoon. "I love you," he cries, crushing Catharine Dale Owen to him, "I love you, I love you, I love you!" The public giggled and jeered. "It was the problem of an image," director King Vidor noted in a recent interview. "You couldn't put this image into words." Gilbert was not able to reclaim his old identity, or a less florid new one, in succeeding films, though his penultimate movie, *Queen Christina* (1933)—made with his old flame Greta Garbo at her insistence, over the veto of MGM executives—proves that his voice, an okay tenor, was not the problem.

Style was the problem—making it over to suit a chaotically reinvented art. Everything was a wild guess in 1928, in musical formats as well as elsewhere, for while the obvious first move was to imitate *The Singing Fool,* one of the most successful films up to that time, no one was certain how to fill out a silent-with-songs, like Jolson's first two entries, with more sound. More songs? Or dances? More characters who sang? More musical depiction of plot or more songs as part of an entertainment scene, like Jolson's nightclub spots? With all these questions, not to mention the new dull-witted sound cameras and the tricky negotiation of the new film naturalism, it is not surprising that the first film musical to resolve the questions of identity, form, and structure was a cartoon short, *Steamboat Willie* (1928). This was Walt Disney's first experiment in sound, featuring Mickey Mouse as a captain conveying a cargo of animals down a river with Minnie Mouse serving as his crew and Pegleg Pete the villain of the piece. The slim storyline, more a situation than a plot, is not fantastic per se, though the world of cartoon is by nature unreal and of course all the persons in the tale are animals. The only thing distinguishing them from the cargo is that Mickey, Minnie, and Pete wear clothing and own property. What makes *Steamboat Willie* so special is its imaginative score. The animation was laid out to the beat of a metronome and the whole thing sings with rhythm. Disney, besides providing Mickey's voice, worked up a doodle-doo of whistles, cowbells, tin pans, and New Year's Eve noise blowers to guide the sound style, also borrowing folk tunes for the orchestral parts. Obviously, Disney's artists had none of the camera-and-mike trouble that dogged the silent-into-talkie producers of the new tightlocked sound stages, and the characters frolic all over the screen, impetuously musical. Minnie cranks a donkey's tail as if playing a music box and the donkey emits a ditty, while Mickey "plays" a cow's udder and turns the teeth of a bull's huge open mouth into a xylophone. The third of Disney's Mickey Mouse shorts to be made but the first to be released, *Steamboat Willie* was the first fully musicalized talkie. It was a sensation.

But on those sound stages and on location, the makers of the first feature musicals were up to their hairlines in technical experiments of such complexity that they had little time to wonder what their formal aesthetics might be. Furthermore, equipment was in short supply; each studio took every piece it could get and worked it around the clock in the race to get out the first sound films—part-talkies like *The Jazz Singer* or all-talkies like *The Lights of New York*—while sound was hot. Naturally, Warners was far in the lead and—for the first time in its history—solvent beyond most companies' wildest dreams. Universal didn't even have a single sound stage functioning in mid-1928, when it was planning its version of *Show Boat*. Universal's chief Carl Laemmle had bought the screen rights to Edna Ferber's novel when it was published in 1926, and naturally had planned it as a silent. But by 1928 such projects were osmotically turning into talkies. In order to make sound tests for *Show Boat*, Universal borrowed one of Fox's mobile sound trucks, and then—realizing what it had in hand—frantically tossed off one talkie feature and a few sound sequences for already completed silents in what may have been as little as nine days. The talkie, *Melody of Love* (1928), is in a way the first full-length, all-sound musical, though essentially it was a war film strung with a few songs. It was of little consequence, and when word got back to Fox, the truck went steaming back home. But Universal finished and released *Melody of Love* before Fox could release *its* first talkie, *In Old Arizona*.

Show Boat is also one of the first musicals, and its sloppy production typifies the confusion with which Hollywood approached the form. It would have done well as a silent; most of Ferber's books have good film potential, as they deal with grandiose characters caught up in sweeping historical transitions—heroes, fighters, lovers, con men. *Show Boat* contrasts the beautiful patience of the natural world with the restless transformations of humankind in the life of Magnolia Hawks Ravenal, a show-boat captain's daughter who is loved and deserted by a gambler. The story and its various adaptations have become so familiar to Americans that few now recall that when Ferber first wrote her book the show boats of the midwest had become extinct and forgotten. Ferber revived them.

Universal wrapped its silent *Show Boat* just when *The Singing Fool* proved that Vitaphone was no fluke, so it was back to the drawing board to whip up a score and some dialogue sequences. Also, Jerome Kern and Oscar Hammerstein's musical version of the novel had come along at the very end of 1927, and its score, with such resonant numbers as "Ol' Man River," "Why Do I Love You?," "Can't Help Lovin' Dat Man," and "Bill," had made a tremendous popular impression. Universal's *Show Boat* was made from the novel rather than the musical; but wasn't there some way of slipping *Show Boat*'s big tunes into the film to keep up with the public's evolving relationship with the property?

It there was, Universal didn't find it. It came up with a two-hour silent with a synchronized score and dialogue scenes, black spirituals, a few dull new numbers ("The Lonesome Road"), such of the Kern–Hammerstein score as could be accommodated—and a two-reel (about twenty minutes) prologue in which Florenz Ziegfeld, producer of the stage *Show Boat*, introduced some of the Broadway principals to perform a *Show Boat* potpourri. Now, if Universal's *Show Boat* was complete in itself, did it need Broadway spliced in here and there? And if it did need Broadway, how was this self-contained prologue to help, having nothing to do with the story? Worse yet, opening the evening with three performers from the stage musical—Helen Morgan, Jules Bledsoe, and Tess Gardella—put the movie actors—Laura La Plante and Joseph Schildkraut as the lovers, Alma Rubens as the tragic Julie—in a certain perspective. After hearing Morgan deliver Julie's "Bill" and "Can't Help Lovin' Dat Man" in richly forlorn renditions that have since passed into legend, how could Rubens' nonsinging Julie capture attention? After hearing Bledsoe put "Ol' Man River" over in his full basso with the choral backup that the song absolutely needs in its dramatic context, did anyone want to hear La Plante sing it to banjo accompaniment? (No one heard her, anyway: La Plante and her banjo were dubbed by others.)

Furthermore, the sound did not record well and Harry Pollard directed with a heavy hand. Laemmle chose Pollard because he had succeeded with Universal's *Uncle Tom's Cabin* a year before, but Stowe and Ferber have only the southern setting in common. *Uncle Tom's Cabin* is pathetic and ridiculous; the novel *Show Boat* is epic with an edge.* About the only thing the film had in its favor was a genuine-looking show boat, built in Sacramento and filmed floating along the Sacramento River to the thrill and wonder of locals in costume.

No doubt Universal's *Show Boat* would have been better if it had been planned as a musical from the start, but it is notable that as a silent with talkie passages and hodgepodge score it was launched as a special event all the same, with dressy opening nights and inflated prices. Even in its first weeks it did not do anything like the business that *The Singing Fool* had done and was *still* doing, seven months into its run. Everywhere, one heard the same report—*Show Boat* was a well-intentioned, slow-moving dud. The non-Kern songs dissolved as one heard them, and the whole film passed away with scarcely a cheer (though it did make Laemmle some money), for even before it opened it had been superseded on February 1, 1929, by the first of the "all talking—all singing—all dancing" films, the first movie musical, MGM's *The Broadway Melody*.

History is made here. The great discovery of sound was its naturalism, a doom if one attempted to dodge it but a treat for audiences if one met it head on. *The Broadway Melody* meets it. A backstager as zippy as *Show Boat* is weighty, it grins with slang and putdowns, sorrows for the pitfalls in show biz and love, and presents a Broadway where heart and nerve count more than talent. Two sisters, tough little Hank (Bessie Love) and tall blond darling Queenie (Anita Page), come to New York from the midwest at the invitation of Hank's old beau, Eddie (Charles King). Eddie falls for Queenie; she resists him for Hank's sake, and takes up with a playboy to fool them. The story is nothing, but the details are extraordinary. If James Gleason's script overdoes the argot (some of it—"A hotel's for mine," says Hank at

---

*The musical, through which most people know Ferber's tale, sentimentalizes it somewhat by reuniting the heroine and her errant husband at the end; in the novel, he never reappears, and we are left with a picture of the heroine as she ages, weathered and dauntless. Ferber believed in strong women. Universal believed in Happy Endings, and used the musical's resolution.

one point—is way outdated for 1929), the cast plays it and everything else for real. There had been silent backstagers, but not till *The Broadway Melody* could one hear the auditions, the rehearsals, the dress runthrough marred by incidents, and the performance, not to mention King's heavy New York accent. Film historian Alexander Walker has caught exactly the film's sense of creating cliché:

> What was to become convention in every backstage musical is present here in pristine simplicity: the imperious impresario, his cohorts of yes-men, the dilettante backers, the star of the show breaking her leg at rehearsal, her replacement wowing the audience by apparently not even singing a note or swinging a limb or doing anything else except simply stand there, and the big-hearted heroine surrendering her own chance of stardom and happiness for the sake of her kid sister.

One cliché *The Broadway Melody* didn't get to: the urgency of Putting on the Show. Gleason and director Harry Beaumont are less interested in the play-within-the-film, also called *The Broadway Melody*, than they are in Hank, Queenie, and Eddie, and once the show opens, partway through the film, we never hear of it again.

The movie is technically primitive, and some of it is inane. The girls' agent, Uncle Jed (Jed Prouty), is one of those "comic" stutterers who tries, tries, tries, and then suddenly lets out a wholly different phrase. The two girls are terrible singers, and their vaudeville act, "The Harmony Babies of Melody Lane," is a tomato-baiting horror that could hardly have scored the success we're told it has. The title song is plugged unmercifully throughout the picture, and after singing it for the girls in their apartment, King cries out, "Let's pull back the table, kids, and go into our dance!" But only Hank dances, plunking on a ukelele, while the other two make razzle noises. It's a little strange.

Still, these are minor flaws. The overall rightness of the realism—the projection of the contradictions of glamor and drudgery in the idea of Broadway—is very taking. King sings the ballad, "You Were Meant For Me," to the sister he prefers, and, as the tune continues under, he says, "Queenie! I wrote it for you. I wrote it . . . *about* you. It's you. Don't you *know what I mean?*" Just as he is about to kiss her, the door bursts open and Hank blunders in, inches away from them; Queenie, revolted at herself for nearly betraying her sister, pretends to have been arguing with Eddie. It's a banal situation made fresh by its spontaneity. For visual attack, the opening aerial shots of Manhattan followed by a montage of workers in a Tin Pan Alley hive cutting jarringly into each other over Cohan's "Give My Regards to Broadway" and a bit of Victor Herbert's "In Old New York" may be the best of many such sequences that were to open backstagers. And the scene in which the girls audition their act for producer Francis Zanfield suggests *cinema verité* in its seemingly unstructured flow. A nasty chorus girl has sabotaged the piano, and the accompanist stops several times in bewilderment. "Say, are you trying to crab our act?" Hank asks him. The pianist says he's innocent. "Well, will you play it then," she replies, "hot or cold?" The piano's tinny ring, Hank's slang and anger, and Queenie's confusion all create just the off-the-cuff naturalism that sound film had to develop in order to make sound work.

Sound also needed performers with the spunk that Hollywood loves about New York. King has it, and he knows how to project ego without losing our sympathy. Page is the gentle sister who has to appear to go bad before the love plot is straightened out, and she brings off the quandary nicely. Bessie Love, however, steals the picture as Hank, cynical, curious, tense, and then tired until she sees that she is the weak corner of the triangle and sends King into her sister's arms.* Alone in her dressing room, she then goes to pieces, sobbing and laughing; this scene alone was so brilliant that Love was nominated for an Oscar. If she was deficient as a singer and only charmingly odd as a dancer, she was quite an actress, and this was an innovation in the American musical. On Broadway, singing, dancing, and comic play exclusively comprised the musical's expedients. Acting was a sometime thing. But Hollywood, where only acting had been established when the musical was suddenly invented in 1929, could offer thespian commitment that Broadway could not match. Love's subtlety is remarkable in the last shot, inside a cab taking her, her new vaudeville partner, and her agent uncle to the station en route to a tour that will separate her from the two people she loves. The uncle pulls off one last idiot stutter joke, the partner giggles, and Love tries a wan smile. She'll recover, she tells us—but not just yet.

The Broadway Melody was MGM's first sound film, and the aural reproduction is faulty, though Nacio Herb Brown and Arthur Freed's score generally comes through. Everything was recorded on the set

---

*Trivium Footnote no. 1: the Duncan Sisters, Vivian and Rosetta, were originally to have played the parts, but couldn't get out of a vaudeville tour. MGM simply waited until they were free and, some months after *The Broadway Melody*, released a virtual remake, the Duncans in *It's a Great Life*, complete with the stuttering Prouty. Lawrence Gray played the King role.

during filming, orchestra and all, and while this created many head-aches for the techies, it makes each scene very immediate. But when producer Irving Thalberg decided to reshoot the film's big number, a color sequence on "The Wedding of the Painted Doll," it was decided to play back the sound portion of the already shot footage, as the num-ber is a dance and the only singing involves an unseen tenor. Why rehire singer and orchestra when the dancers can simply move to the playback? But then: why not use the playback in general, let-ting the singers prerecord the vocal parts and then mouth the lyrics when the camera rolls? All movie-making is illusion to begin with. MGM tried the procedure on its next musicals, and as it proved vastly more efficient than trying to please the mike on the spot, the practice took hold at all studios on most singing and dancing numbers.

The Broadway Melody was a smash. It cost MGM $280,000 and made $4,000,000; it also copped the Oscar as best film. And it proved that, more than any other kind of movie, musicals exploited sound. But some questions had yet to be answered in terms of what a musical was. How many songs, and for what purposes? What settings, stories, characters work best in music? What actors are right for a musical, aside from who can sing and dance? Theatre stars? Newcomers with stage experience? Or film veterans who can get through a tune or move well? And does every musical have to be a backstager, or will the audience accept characters singing in nonperformance contexts, as they do in theatre?

Hollywood answered these questions haphazardly, and while it was doing so it enjoyed the only artistically ingenuous era in its history. As a novice, the film musical was versatile and open, even radical. As an old campaigner, it sought imitations of past success, ever ready for a remake and treating convention as Scripture. In many ways, we're go-ing to start wild and grow tame as the years go on.

☆ 2 ☆
What's a Musical?

██T WAS A matter of course that Hollywood would draw on Broadway's resources when instituting the film musical, for both creative and performing talent. But there was no certain guide as to what parts of a stage musical would carry over into film, and there were misgivings about how national Broadway was. Jolson was weird and Brice had bombed; what if the rest of Broadway were like them? There was also that touchy naturalism, troubled by plot and character songs that burst out anywhere. On Broadway it was the thing. In film, it was an offense; or so Hollywood thought. So it turned to subjects that would provide a casual background for song and dance. The groundbreaking Jolson and Brice part-talkies presented their stars as entertainers. Entertainers perform. Even in *Show Boat* once the Ziegfeldian prologue was over, the songs came out of situations in which people might reasonably sing—on stage, or to pleasure themselves in a solitary moment. *The Broadway Melody* pointed the straightest way: music is auditions, rehearsals, performance. This rule was continually broken but has held out through the years and may be seen fully operative in such very recent films as *A Star is Born* and *The Rose*, wherein the character songs that tell us who the principals are are filmed exclusively in concert settings.

In the first year of regular sound production, 1929, there were backstagers: *Close Harmony* with Nancy Carroll and Buddy Rogers; *Mother's Boy*, an Irish equivalent of *The Jazz Singer*, with Morton Downey; *Footlights and Fools*, with silent star Colleen Moore in an unusual role as a sweet little girl (typical Moore) who turns into a French sophisticate on stage (unforeseen Moore—but she seems to have brought it off). There were nightclub films: *Honky-Tonk* with Sophie Tucker; *Queen of the Night Clubs* with Texas Guinan; *Syncopation*, also with Downey; and the stage hit *Broadway*, filmed by Paul Fejos on an innovative, noiseless, $75,000 camera crane that shot sixty feet into the air in six seconds flat to look down on a spectacular art deco set that connected this underworld melodrama to the expressionism of the German cinema. There were revues as well. None of these proposed song as a vehicle of narrative motion. In some cases, the narrative was just an excuse to get the entertainers on stage in the first place.

Obviously, Hollywood could not go on indefinitely pumping out musicals about the performer caste on and off stage. It had to coordinate musical and dramatic elements into story forms and expand them cinematically. One musical element had been developed as soon as the soundtrack had come into use in 1927: the theme song. Cut into otherwise nontalkie films, the theme tune might become popular on its own and bounce interest back onto the film retroactively, thus creating new sources of revenue in record and sheet-music sales and "extra" audiences attracted more by the song than by the story or stars. *Seventh Heaven* (1927) had "Diane." *Our Dancing Daughters* (1928), the one in which Joan Crawford fixed an era with her Charleston, had "I Loved You Then as I Love You Now." Eventually, producers realized that a title (or nearly) theme song was the best advertisement; *Ramona* (1928) set the trend with the excessively popular "Ramona." As the theme tune was invariably a love song, this posed problems for the less dovey titles. *Varsity* (1928) came through with "My Varsity Girl, I'll Cling to You," and *The Pagan* made a novelty of convention in "The Pagan Love Song," sung by Ramon Novarro in a loincloth as he lolled on the beach strumming a ukelele. But some attempts to ride a theme song on an immobile title were ludicrous, and the practice fell away in 1931 when the public, glutted with film music, found the pointless singing irritating.

The musical didn't need a theme song, but it couldn't hurt, and *The Broadway Melody* honored the practice with its title tune, whose lyrics encapsulate the film's view of Broadway as Tough-luck City where the show must go on. The theme song, then, would provide a nucleus for the musical film score in such disparate approaches as those tried with "42nd Street" (which is heard at the picture's end and sums up the experience), with *Naughty Marietta*'s "Ah! Sweet Mystery of Life" (which as a longtime pop hit creates suspense for the stars' big duet and raptures on the closing reprise), and with *The Wizard of Oz*'s "Over the Rainbow" (which is heard early in the film and never reprised, but which sets a tone for the entire event). Still, even a slam-bang hit theme tune would not put a full score over—so how many songs did a musical need?

These and other questions Hollywood at times answered by looking east to the stage musical even when it wasn't adapting a stage property. Broadway set a teaching example in the matter of integrating songs into the story, and by the late 1920s had amassed ambitious talents such as George and Ira Gershwin, Richard Rodgers and Lorenz Hart, and Cole Porter, who followed the leadership of Irving Berlin and Jerome Kern in extrapolating American attitudes out of the possibilities in musical comedy.

But think of the traps. Broadway musicals ran two and a half hours, considerably longer than films were willing to run at this time, and had to balance ratios for plot, comedy, song, and dance. Where would the shorter film musical put all the impedimenta of fun? Too, Broadway was still wrestling with comedy as an extrusive component, relying on improvisatory star comedians or extraneous and virtually self-contained sketches. And there was the pitfall of physical shape: theatre musicals were put together with an eye on how the whole stage looked from a point somewhere in the middle of the auditorium, with no consideration of the advantages of film—editing, special effects, spectacle, the pan, or the close-up. Too much Broadway in the recipe—especially given the camera's necessarily static role while recording techniques were being perfected—and the Hollywood musical might end up as an inert duplicate of the stage.

And this is, at first, what happened. The long history of all-talking, -singing, -dancing adaptations of Broadway originals begins with Warners' *The Desert Song* (1929), and the adaptation was faithful. "With all its original stage enchantment," the ads promised, anticipating critics' misgivings that *The Desert Song* had not been sufficiently turned out for film. Adaptor Harvey Gates and director Roy del Ruth aimed a largely unenlightening camera at the original, shearing off some of the book and the Sigmund Romberg–Oscar Hammerstein score. Desert is handy to Los Angeles, so there was real sand at least. There was also a new cast drawn mainly from film people: John Boles as the hero, a dashing sheik who leads an anti-French revolt while masquerading as the milquetoast of the foreign legion post, comics Louise Fazenda and Johnny Arthur, and Myrna Loy as an Arab vamp. Carlotta King was imported from the east to play the heroine, torn between the sheik's Valentino-like allure and the milquetoast's gallantry; neat that she could get both. However, King made no impression in the part. She sings the hell out of "The Sabre Song," but that comes late in the picture, after Fazenda and Loy have erased her from the screen, and King sat out some months of empty waiting for a second role that was never offered before she gave up and returned to the stage. It's too bad, as long as they were hiring theatre talent, that Warners didn't use the excellent Vivienne Segal, who played the part on Broadway. Hollywood could not ignore Segal's sexy voice and dynamite looks, and she did come west early on, but she was trapped in a series of operettas that were far less successful than *The Desert Song*. Going from *Song of the West* into *Bride of the Regiment* and thence into *Golden Dawn* and *Viennese Nights*, all released in 1930, Segal had little chance to convince producers of her worth—they didn't want talent as much as they wanted success. *Viennese Nights*, conceived for the screen by Romberg and Hammerstein, worked out well, but the first three all came from Broadway, and not especially first-rate Broadway at that (though *Song of the West* was derived from *Rainbow*, Hammerstein's experimentally realistic show with a great Vincent Youmans score, hurt by a disastrous production as well as its ambitious nonconformity). With a *Desert Song* to give her career momentum, Segal might have ended up as valuable a commodity as Jeanette MacDonald did. MacDonald's first films argue a strong case in how to launch a career, for among a few flunks and sillies were Ernst Lubitsch's first two musicals, *The Love Parade* and *Monte Carlo*, which not only show MacDonald at her most winning but argue a case in how to sustain a career after death, as they stand among the most frequently revived films today. Segal missed out flat in imperfect adaptations from Broadway, getting no help from directors who didn't know how a musical worked. *The Desert Song* made too stately a movie, true, but the material itself was first-rate and carried it through. Besides, it was the first of the direct-from-Broadway films and the public was curious.

What's a musical? Not everyone who was making them was sure, and those few who lucked into the better ones had the chance to take them wherever they were going while colleagues just as talented fell by the way. MacDonald might have been thinking something along the lines of "There but for Lubitsch go I" about Segal, for when they appeared together in *The Cat and the Fiddle* in 1934, star MacDonald is said to have greeted supporting player Segal with something like, "Enjoy your part, darling; I've had it cut down so badly you'll be lucky to get three words in a row." The tale must be apocryphal—MacDonald wasn't that kind of person. Still, it airs the feeling of competition and insecurity that dogged the musical in those early years when a performer's future depended heavily on the fumbling of technicians.

Another possibility for the musical was the adaptation not from Broadway but from old films: brighten up a script, shift the decor, and slip in four or five songs, ideally into the mouth of someone entertaining at a party but if necessary letting the characters open up and sing out; a musical's a musical. With so many movies being made—335 talkies in 1929, the last year in which silents were still being produced, bringing the total of Hollywood and New York* studios to about 500 films—it was assumed that nobody saw even most of the good ones, and remakes became a regular occurrence. Studios remade their own films, so there was no royalty to pay to Broadway authors, and there were few complaints about Hollywood's repeating itself. On the contrary, moviegoers appeared to like getting the same stories over and over: there are only so many different tales in any mythology. Thus, in 1930, when MGM was building up Robert Montgomery as William Haines' successor in light comedy, it reached back a mere three years to *Spring Fever*, in which Haines played a shipping clerk who bluffed his way into the country club set and romanced Joan Crawford. *Spring Fever* became a musical called *Love in the Rough*. Montgomery and Dorothy Jordan now had the leads; Jimmy McHugh and Dorothy Fields supplied a few songs, pushing hot diggety in "I'm Doin' That Thing," hedging their bets with the old-fashioned "One More Waltz," and peaking in "Go Home and Tell Your Mother (that she certainly did a wonderful job on you)." *Love in the Rough* had less music than *The Desert Song*, but more cinema.

Least cinematic of all, because of its theatrical origin, was the revue. Later, Hollywood would find ways of wrapping its vaudeville in thin storylines, but the earliest revues mirrored the Broadway style, complete with emcees and curtained stages. They did at least strive for special effects impossible in the theatre. Universal's *King of Jazz* (1930) set Paul Whiteman and his band atop an immense piano with keyboard enough for five pianists; *Paramount on Parade* (1930) stuffed Abe Lyman's band into a shoebox and had Nancy Carroll dancing out

---

*In 1928, the coast studios all opened up and expanded supplementary stages on Long Island to exploit the pool of theatre actors for use in talkies; actors busy in a show could face the cameras on their free afternoons. The major film work was accomplished in Hollywood, with its amenable conditions for climate and location shooting, but some Long Island studios remained active through the mid-1930s.

of a shoe; and in MGM's *The Hollywood Revue of 1929*, Bessie Love emerges from emcee Jack Benny's pocket and chats with him from inside his palm. As the all-star Vitaphone revues had done, each studio revue featured a once-in-a-lifetime cast pulled from the contract file. Fox was underpowered. *The Fox Movietone Follies* (1929), dimly unified by a sort of narration, came up with a cast of little reverberation: Lois Moran, Sue Carol, Dorothy Jordan, Dixie Lee, David Percy, and David Rollins. Compare that list to MGM's in *The Hollywood Revue*: John Gilbert, Norma Shearer, Joan Crawford, Marion Davies, Buster Keaton, Marie Dressler, Laurel and Hardy, and William Haines, plus the three principals of *The Broadway Melody* as well as emcees Benny and Conrad Nagel. "More stars," ran MGM's motto, "than there are in heaven."

These all-star revues demonstrated that there was talent available for musicals (though more than a few of their singers and dancers were actors out of their league and some of the chorus lines were embarrassingly sloppy). But there was no organization, no sense of sifting through effective possibilities. Hollywood quickly defined the musical as any film with four or more songs. But it never attempted to define the *elements* of the musical—its shape and point of view, its characters, its use of singing and dancing. Thus, James Cruze's *The Great Gabbo* (1929) has some seven or eight numbers but isn't a musical—it's a drama about a dour ventriloquist (Erich von Stroheim) and the girl (Betty Compson) he abuses, intercut with ludicrous production numbers. What are those numbers doing there? Well, this ventriloquist works in nightclubs, and nightclubs have production numbers, see? At one point, Cruze attempts to fuse music and plot by sending Compson on stage with a nice man (Don Douglas) who wants to save her from von Stroheim, to sing "(When you're caught in) The Web of Love," an apache dance with a spider motif. But neither Compson nor Douglas can hack it, so Cruze films the number with acrobats and splices in close-ups of Compson and Douglas in the acrobats' costumes earnestly mumbling to each other. Okay, this was a primitive era—Von Stroheim's act with his personable but oddly Teutonic dummy Otto is so stupid that even the extras hired to play the audience can't laugh at it, and Cruze didn't bother to reshoot scenes in which von Stroheim flubbed his lines. But was Hollywood learning from such mistakes, or just making them?

One element that seemed a natural for the musical was color. Technicolor had developed a two-color process even before the Vitaphone years, though its fascination with red and green and erratic hold on blue made for an odd look. Musicals were capricious, so the bizarre color scheme only added to their appeal, and many musicals in 1929 and 1930 came out in color or with color sequences stripped in to embolden the production numbers or to close a film on a merry note. However, color was expensive—Technicolor printing costs ran to four times the fee for black-and-white film, and the firm insisted on running its own cameras and sending out its own crew, who would stand around surveying some artist's lovely set and mutter, "You'll never get that yellow into the camera." Worse yet, the thick film tended to buckle in the projector and was easily scratched. Color became so identified with the musical that when the form ran out of juice in 1930–31, color was given up with relief and not used again till later in the decade, after Technicolor had come up with a more lifelike reproduction.

What's a musical? I'm not making it clear in this chapter because it wasn't clear at the time. Certain films seemed to know; others floundered; still others were hopelessly wrong, comedies or melodramas with two or three theme songs too many. Let's examine the full range of musicals produced in the early years before and during the big slump of 1931–32, when few musicals were released and fewer made money, to decide what the film musical happened to be. Happened: virtually by accident.

☆3☆
The Early
Musicals

A<small>N</small> EXTRAORDINARY FILM of 1929, King Vidor's *Hallelujah*, couldn't have been less like a musical, yet showed Hollywood how music may belong to a film so organically that all the worry about how to cue in the songs and dances and what roles should be cast with what types seems trivial and unartistic. *Hallelujah* tells of black life in the south with such zest for the everyday that its melodramatic plot, which takes in several counts of manslaughter and murder, does not detract from the overall honesty. MGM must have thought Vidor out of his mind when he proposed the project, which would almost certainly alienate or altogether fail to reach the entire southern market. A more "appropriate" view of black life would be found in *Hallelujah*'s exact contemporary, Fox's *Hearts in Dixie*: "Hear those hearts beat the cadences of their race," the Fox ads ran, "along the levees and in the cotton fields . . . strummin' banjos . . . chanting [not chantin'?] spirituals . . . All the happy-go-lucky joy of living, laughter, and all-embracing gusto of plantation life"—not to mention the yassuh comedy of Stepin Fetchit. Vidor, one of Hollywood's most socially enlightened directors, would have none of this in *Hallelujah*, and he finally brought MGM around by offering to contribute his fee to the production fund.

Hallelujah really does sound the cadences of a race. Its music is not so much a "score" as it is a momentary substitution for words when the feeling's too strong for speaking, and it chimes in without ado—in a banjo and kazoo duet at a small wedding party, when three little boys dance just for the fun of it; in work songs; in a hussy's dance to a harmonica to lure innocents to a crap game; in a kind of accidental production number in a waterfront dive where the same dancer inspires customers and waiters to strut; in a preacher's trainlike motion as he lectures on evil in a railroad cap and calls repentance "the last station"; in the hussy's attempt to abandon her lover by humming him to sleep so she can sneak out of the house. Most remarkable was Vidor's view of one night and the following morning with the protagonist's family, who sleep in a row of adjacent beds. The mother (Fanny Belle deKnight) starts a lullaby, rocking the youngest children to sleep by turns before they are placed in bed; the next morning, seeing one bed empty, she guesses (correctly) that tragedy has struck and without preamble rouses the household with a wailing prayer. Tucked into this astonishingly casual musicality are two songs by Irving Berlin, the dive number and the folklike, blues-tainted "Waiting at the End of the Road."

Vidor shot the film as a silent. He had to—the company arrived on location in Tennessee to find that the sound trucks had not arrived. This gave Vidor's camera a wonderful freedom but necessitated a post-shooting synchronization procedure that literally gave the sound editor a nervous breakdown. It was easy to overlay a choral track onto a scene of workers coming home from the fields, but difficult to fit spoken words to mouths or find the right "lead" in a crowd scene wherein a number of people are talking at once. *Hallelujah*'s sound quality is poor even for 1929, so poor that the mounting effect of honesty in action and music must make up for the constant drawback of having to strain to hear the dialogue.

The fault is the microphone's, not the actors', for though Vidor's all-black cast had little or no acting experience, they are believable and moving (and distinct when the sound reproduction falls clear every so often), whether as principals in the central story or as extras in the big religious parade, mass baptism, and revival meeting scenes. The main characters are a decent fellow who gets into trouble (Daniel Haynes) and a weak woman (Nina Mae McKinney) who first cheats him in partnership with a crooked gambler and then, when he has become an evangelist, gets religion, falls for him, lives with him, and leaves him for the gambler. Pursuing them, Haynes causes her death and then hunts the man down in a swamp and kills him. This is *Hallelujah*'s most celebrated scene, short but absorbing for its deadpan approach. The camera follows the hunt curiously, wanting to see for itself. It tracks Haynes, tracks his quarry, cuts back to Haynes. The sound almost dies out, except for a few effects—a twig breaks, a bird cries, water slurps—and the melodrama thus comes off more as reportage than as entertainment. Similarly, *Hallelujah*'s last two scenes of Haynes' punishment on the rockpile and his homecoming resist the temptation to suggest an epic. Life, Vidor seems to say, has no perspective in itself; the objective onlooker must supply it. Vidor's uncanny ability to duplicate existence instead of stylizing it makes *Hallelujah* the forerunner of the Italian neo-realist cinema of the 1940s and 1950s. And he has a better sense of tempo than Visconti and better actors than Rossellini.

When *Hallelujah* was released, critics admired it. Even *Photoplay*, the most influential of the fan magazines and somewhat suspicious of art—the best it could say of Vidor's brilliant *The Crowd* was "an interesting experience"—hailed it as an experiment that works, and critics have continued to cite it as a great event in film history. Lately, voguish white guilt has caused some backtracking doublespeak, and a few opportunists have called the film "patronizing." It isn't. The Berlin songs supplement the folk tunes excellently; Berlin was, after all, the father of "jazz" as American pop song, out of ragtime and blues into Gershwin, so culturally he has more than a little black in him. The story is universal in scope and not, as has been suggested, a depiction of black laziness, criminality, and sensuality. Nor does the ecstatic revival scene, with its freakouts being carried out to recover outside the meeting hall, cast any racial slur. Moderns should remember that, in the 1920s, such white-conceived and white-supported concerns as Aimee Semple McPherson's chain of Four-Square Gospel tabernacles equalled any black efforts in that arena. How is *Hallelujah* patronizing? True, it doesn't show us any white oppressors. But you can't have everything.

Vidor, like Ernst Lubitsch and Rouben Mamoulian, was a standout director who instinctively understood what music could do for film. Most of his colleagues learned as they shot—those who learned. A good apprenticeship was the Broadway adaptation, since this was less a matter of creation than of editing: take what you need and leave out the rest. And there was some adding in; because each studio owned a music publishing house (to market all those theme songs; sheet music pulled in a lot of money in the days when everyone played the piano), producers liked to commission new songs for Broadway adaptations. The original score might be superior, but the new numbers would bring in subsidiary profits from the song sheets and recordings. The practice varied considerably. *The Desert Song* was not sullied, but another Romberg operetta-turned-film, *New Moon* (1930), lost more than half its score and suffered a few interpolated indignities. It could go even harder with modern-dress musical comedy, whose scores were considered shallow compared to operetta's more fulfilled rhapsody. *Little Johnny Jones*, George M. Cohan's 1904 show about an American jockey smeared in a bribe scandal in England, seemed a natural for the screen, with its spunky do-right hero and Yankee Doodle score. But First National's screen version (1929), with Eddie Buzzell as Johnny, updated the sound with such new ditties as "She Was Kicked on the Head by a Butterfly" and "Go Find Somebody to Love," which suffer by comparison with "Give My Regards to Broadway" and "Yankee Doodle Boy," retained from the original.

Other Broadway subjects fared less well. *Queen High* (1930), a tremendous stage hit in 1926 for its comic look at two business partners who settle their feud in a poker game, winner take all (including the loser, as his butler), kept little more than its story and star, Charles Ruggles. (Frank Morgan stepped in as the other partner; a sharp team.) Similarly, Bert Lahr and the plot were about all that remained of *Flying High* (1931), though the film did give Charlotte Greenwood a fine opportunity to test her dryly agile style against Lahr's moist burlesque. They made a great pair, which is more than was said for Grace Moore and Lawrence Tibbett in *New Moon*. "She drew him quietly into her boudoir," the ads moaned. "Tonight she was his, but tomorrow she was to be the wife of another!" Actually, Moore looked as if she would like to draw Tibbett a map back to the Met, whence they both issued. It appears that Moore hadn't yet figured out how to apply her abundant oomph to the screen. Tibbett alone had been a sensation in *The Rogue Song* earlier that year, but Moore and *New Moon* almost finished him in Hollywood.

Audiences took casting more seriously than producers, who were concerned with finding work for stars already on salary rather than with finding the most suitable possibilities for set roles. Producers trusted fame—or tried to create it—more than they trusted the material itself. Sometimes even good casting didn't work; maybe that made them cynical. Jeanette MacDonald and Dennis King made an odd couple in *The Vagabond King* (1930), the Rudolf Friml piece about François Villon and a screen favorite in several versions with and without music, from a one-reel silent (drawn from Justin Huntley McCarthy's E. H. Sothern warhorse, *If I Were King*) to a remake of the operetta in 1956. Paramount did a real job on Friml's version, keeping most of the score and filming it in two-strip Technicolor. Carrying over King's Broadway Villon seemed as wise as following up on Mac-Donald's smashing debut in *The Love Parade* the year before: she makes a svelte heroine, and King is surprisingly sinewy for an operetta baritone, with the pale, flawless face that the silent camera would have made love to. But his hammy stage style took the sound camera by too much force. He was a John Gilbert of operetta, overlover, and MacDonald, possibly bored in a dull part, didn't extend herself. It can't have been fun to play opposite a terminal matinée idol, either. It was director Ludwig Berger who really ruined the film. In the duet "Only a Rose" Berger decorates his close-up of MacDonald with bits of King's profile—*while* MacDonald is singing. She later dubbed the business "Only a Nose."

Rarely, a film version of a Broadway show focused a scattershot original; *Good News* (1930) is an example. The college musical is one thing Hollywood got down fast for its youthful zip, hedonism, and chaste romance. Such entries as Universal's *College Love* (1929), Paramount's *Sweetie* (1929), and First National's *The Forward Pass* (1929) set the style—*College Love* with its Greek parties and dances; *Sweetie* with its definitive *dramatis personae* of sweet coed Nancy Carroll, football hero Stanley Smith, wacky-cute comedienne Helen Kane, and wacky-ridiculous comedian Jack Oakie; and *The Forward Pass* with its culminating Big Game footage. When MGM tackled *Good News*, a 1927 Broadway hit, tradition advised the adaptors to keep the love plot (coed and football hero), the wisecracking secondary couple, the best of the songs ("Lucky in Love," "The Varsity Drag," "The Best Things in Life Are Free"), and to dump just about everything else. It was a good trade. Much of what is lost was fill; the new stuff is the real collegiate hot-cha, from the use of John Held, Jr., sheik and sheba caricatures—the emblem of the age—on the posters to the inclusion of Cliff Edwards (known as "Ukelele Ike") for strumming *ton*. As usual, MGM had some new songs run up by house writers, and they go well with the B. G. DeSylva–Lew Brown–Ray Henderson originals. "Gee, But I'd Like to Make You Happy" has tender bounce, "I Feel Pessimistic" spry introspection, and Nacio Herb Brown and Arthur Freed donated two samples of their art of making the inconsequential sound totally committed: "If You're Not Kissing Me" and "Football." Casting was right, too. Broadway's heroine, Mary Lawlor, and chief comic, Gus Shy, were brought in to do what they did; Shy was paired with Bessie Love, utterly in her element as a clown after her dire Hank in *The Broadway Melody*. Even the chorus was ace. However, the college genre turned out to have no potential for expansion. If *Good News* was the best, it was already rich in cliché, though the form (discounting the college silents) was scarcely a year old.

One of the best of the Broadway adaptations, oddly, was the most faithful to the original, RKO's *Rio Rita* (1929): full score (additions by the original authors), static camera, mixed cast of screen and stage veterans, last third in color. It's horribly primitive—sound troubles on the set were almost insuperable. Bebe Daniels' fan sounded like the crackle of fifty crackers until specially treated, and though in a garden scene every other potted plant seemed to hide a mike, each turn of Daniels' hand meant a gap in her dialogue. Moreover, as *Rio Rita* is a modern western, outdoor shots of mounted rangers were unavoidable, though this meant filming silent and then adding the sound, *Hallelujah*-style. The whole thing was shot in twenty-four days, and while Daniels for one found it impossible to post-dub her part and had to get it down during filming or not at all, the choral singing clearly doesn't match the lip movements and must have been recorded separately. The technique of mating sound arbitrarily to moving mouths was called "wild track" dubbing; a number of these early musicals resorted to it. But when John Boles and his fellow Texas Rangers team up for "The Rangers' Song" and we notice that they don't seem to be singing what we're hearing—not at the second we're hearing it, anyway—we stop enjoying the show and begin to concentrate on technique. Underscoring obscures the dialogue, balance in duets is a problem (especially in regard to Daniels' and Boles' relatively high voices), and at each new sound series the track cuts in with a little explosion. The camera, locked into its soundproof booth, also adds to the rough quality of the film; at one point late in the action, Boles is in hiding around a corner and Daniels leans around to speak to him. As they confer, the camera just sits there, showing us . . . nothing.

Yet the film is a great pleasure even so, and earned a huge success. A shoot-'em-up complete with villain who almost takes Daniels from Boles, *Rio Rita* was originally a Ziegfeld show poised halfway between flowery operetta (sample love song: "If You're In Love, You'll Waltz") and wiggy musical comedy (a comic duo wanders in and out with little or no reference to the action). Ziegfeld staged it sumptuously, and RKO attempted to follow suit, though the color sequence had to be shot at night because the studio's one Technicolor camera was tied up on another film in the daytime. The Harry Tierney–Joseph McCarthy score is cute, and by drafting the stage original's two comedians, Bert Wheeler and Robert Woolsey, RKO filled its two-and-a-half-hour special* with all the intent charm that Broadway musicals have. It has been called stagey, especially for the straight-on angle used in the dance numbers, but Daniels and Boles valiantly sustain a sense of movement in their garden scene, to hell with the microphones, and Wheeler and Woolsey really keep the film hopping. Baby-faced Wheeler is the stooge of the pair, Woolsey the hustler. Their friendship is amorphously friendly-hostile, like those of some silent comic pairs: Woolsey is nominally Wheeler's lawyer yet continually gets him into trouble. Near the end, when Woolsey takes Wheeler's first wife off his hands so he can gambol with Dorothy Lee, the two couples sit on the rail of a ship, the girls on the outside and the men between them. The girls launch a reprise of the song, "Sweetheart, We Need Each Other"—pointlessly, and they seem to know it; they keep looking away at nothing or smiling to themselves—while the men play Laurel-and-Hardy-like "hits" on each other. At length they embrace and fall backwards into the water. The girls do, too. The whole thing is wonderfully stupid, recalling the rhythms of silent comedy (officially dead that same year) when structural symmetry mattered more than sanity.

If the Broadway adaptations pointed to nothing peculiarly cinematic, they gave inexperienced filmmakers a chance to learn their craft while dealing with material of a strong narrative drive. Perhaps this was why the revues seemed so lifeless: they reflected Hollywood's uncertainty about story, vocal range, and character, its fear of flying. A revue was a cinch, Hollywood thought: anything goes. It was hard to miss them—MGM advertised *The Hollywood Revue of 1929* with two billboards of living showgirls, one each in Los Angeles and New York—and revues did boast an eye-catching collage of celebrities. But movies were supposedly killing vaudeville, not adopting it. How hard they worked to make you like them. *The Hollywood Revue* had Marion Davies tap dancing (well, by the way) on a drum, Joan Crawford singing "Gotta Feelin' For You" and kicking into her famous charleston, Laurel and Hardy messing up their magic act (Hardy slips on a banana peel, crashes into a huge cake, and primly observes, "I faw down and go pwop"), and then everybody troops on in slickers at the end in a big production number based on "Singin' in the Rain" (another two-

---

*This timing refers to the original roadshow release, two screenings a day at top prices. Neighborhood houses got a shortened *Rio Rita* and surviving prints run even shorter, with whole numbers missing.

color reel, wisely set in an orange grove so the green looks almost reasonable). Big.

John Murray Anderson's superb revue *King of Jazz* was even bigger, opening with a cartoon on Paul Whiteman among the jungle animals, where jazz is born, going on to "The Song of the Dawn," led by John Boles and featuring some five hundred cowboys galloping out of the ocean onto a beach and into the sky, and perching one number on a gigantic staircase with sixteen bridesmaids supporting the biggest bridal gown in history. The aim was to out-Broadway Broadway, and *King of Jazz* did. But this was the wrong aim: film must out-film *silence,* not imitate another medium.

Paramount on Parade (1930), one of the better revues, was comfortably cinematic, neither stage-bound nor crazed for spectacle. Elsie Janis, a veteran Broadway revuer, supervised the program, but nearly a dozen directors (including Lubitsch) kept it three-dimensional, and an imposing array of stars gave it personality. Its comedy is shaky, but the musical segments are quite good, especially the finale, "Sweeping the Clouds Away," in which Maurice Chevalier and chorus girls dressed in rainbow colors dance up and down peaked roofs and are last viewed high up in the heavens. Everyone gets to do what he or she does best, except Ruth Chatterton (famed in the first sound films for her lustrous speaking voice), who is made to sing as a lonely Parisian tart, and Clara Bow, who sings "I'm True to the Navy Now," walking here and there on a battleship while a squad of sailors works hard to make us think she's dancing with them.

I said enough in the last chapter on the defects of the revue as a form, but let's look at one in detail, Warner Brothers' *The Show of Shows* (1929). This was the most stage-bound of them all, literally performed on one, curtain and all. It's worth investigating because it illuminates Hollywood and would-be Hollywood talent in what the Chinese call interesting times: when the studios were trying to decide who and what was musical material. For some of the cast, *The Show of Shows* was not unlike an audition.

The potpourri opens with a drastic and irrelevant scene at the French guillotine. An aristocrat is beheaded, a revolutionary proclaims "The Show of Shows!" and we are whirled into too much footage of a military march routine in geometric groupings. At length, emcee Frank Fay introduces a double sextet, "What's Become of the Six Original *Florodora* Boys?" sung by the Girls and succeeded by six comedians (including cross-eyed Ben Turpin) who show by their waiter's, iceman's, and other such uniforms that the Boys have fallen on rough days. The staging is awkward, the camera following the dancing as best it can. Fay returns to attempt "She's Only a Bird in a Gilded Cage" but is interrupted, and a big Pirate Number is unveiled, featuring Ted Lewis and his band (in tuxedos) trapped on a pirate ship, where Lewis trucks and warbles, calling himself a "pirate of jazz." Everyone trucks off stage left, including the pirates, who truck clumsily, which is supposed to be funny.

Next—stay with me; I'm driving at something—a top-hat-and-tails man leads the girls in a dull tap routine; all strip to gym togs and do dull exercises. Fay attempts another number, but is interrupted by the next performer, Winnie Lightner, who delivers the ebullient "Pingo Pongo." Lightner is full of pep and the song is strange and fun, the first item so far that works. Fay now attempts to interrupt singer Nick Lucas, fails, and eventually joins Lloyd Hamilton, Beatrice Lillie, and Louise Fazenda in a tedious blending of four "art" poems in quartet style, ending with chic nonsense verse on "Your Mother and Mine," one of those "M is for . . ." numbers but with a wrong letter correspondence and no mention of mother.

At least Fay is gone; his pushy self-belief has been a little wearing. Richard Barthelmess introduces a huge number made up of six (real-life) sister acts, each with an ethnic ditty, twin costumes, and a change of backdrop. The dancing again follows stage patterns, letting the camera serve as a remote eye instead of a frame for composition. Winnie Lightner returns and *The Show of Shows* comes to life again. Her number, set in a bathroom, is "Singin' in the Bathtub," and the hulking, slosh-mouthed Bull Montana joins her at the end for a put-on of *The Broadway Melody*'s "You Were Meant For Me."

Comes next Irene Bordoni, French, suave, and lovely, to sing, to piano accompaniment, in a surprisingly sexy style—surprising not for Bordoni's Broadway but for Hollywood. Now Warners pulls out its biggest star, Rin-Tin-Tin, who introduces (by pulling off the cover of a vaudeville signboard with his teeth) an inscrutably hebetudinous Chinese Number led by Nick Lucas and Myrna Loy. Their song, "Li-Po-Li," deals with some sort of tai-pan who does fearful things. He will, one couplet asserts, "take away all your rice-cakes" and, rather inevitably for this level of songwriting, "take away all your spice cakes." This leads to chorus girls climbing up and down ladders while the orchestra plays the tune over and over. The whole act, in song, dance, and decor, is of a monumentally failed ineffability.

Worse yet, Fay is back, harried by comedian Sid Silvers, who does a comically poor Jolson imitation. At Silvers' second overgone

"Nyaah," Fay says, "What is that, asthma?"—his first (and only) good line of the evening. A Bicycle Number follows, stationary cycles pumped against a moving background. Fay and Silvers return for a round of halitosis jokes—really—capped by "If Your Best Friend Won't Tell You, Why Should I?" Now for a bit of Pirandello: the Black and White Girls dance on a tremendous stairway in dresses half black and half white. Partway through they give up and call Fay onstage to complain about the length of their dresses.

Fay now takes his big solo spot, the apex of dreary. John Barrymore does a scene from *Richard III*, the comics play a firing squad sketch, and we have reached a grandiose finale based on the song "Lady Luck." The singer, Alexander Gray, is post-dubbed very poorly, his rich baritone coming out constricted and out of sync, and the dancing goes on forever—acrobatics, shimmy, tap, black minstrels, the show-to-end-the-show-of-shows works. At last, the stars (including Rin-Tin-Tin) reprise "Lady Luck," their heads poked through holes cut in canvas, the cheap effect refreshing after so much forced splendor. One hundred thirty minutes of two-strip Technicolor are over.

And what have we? The least pretentious numbers are the best—Bordoni does more with one piano than the feet of the entire Warners backlot can in "Lady Luck," Barthelmess' amused dignity goes down more affably than Fay's practiced shtick, and Lightner's socko fun provides a more natural comedy than the contrived sketches. And note the wide range of possibilities here—Bordoni's sensuality, Barthelmess' self-possession, and Lightner's lampoon dovetail nicely, because they seem really to be what they seem. Most of the theatre people are gaming with what they are, even as they seem to be something else. That's one paradox too many for film to encompass.

Warners disclosed no new useful talent with *The Show of Shows*. Barthelmess, Barrymore, and Rin-Tin-Tin went back to their habitual roles, and Bea Lillie, Ted Lewis, and Frank Fay (the last after several further attempts to found a film career) went back to the stage. Bordoni, in Hollywood to film her stage hit *Paris* (1929), was for all her appeal too special for Hollywood. Lightner, too, though she figured prominently in a number of films in these early years, made no place for herself and ended up in featured bits. She was a little overweight and underpretty for the styles of the age, even for sidekick parts, and her high spirits had an earthy base to them that the musical wasn't ready to utilize.

Warners' choreographers Larry Ceballos and Jack Haskell had not developed anything even vaguely suitable for cinema, and, given *The*

Show of Shows' explicitly theatrical concept, director John Adolfi had no chance to conceptualize a film revue. But what is most wrong about the piece is the material, with its wild gallimaufry of tones—its sophisticated literate comedy side by side with slapstick and vaudeville standup patter; its screwy Lightner spots (which still give pleasure) next to the misfired romance of the Chinese number (instant camp); its creaky exhibition marches and exercises leading up to the final greedy collage of dances traditional and contemporary. *The Show of Shows* is not only a mess; it lacks character. That was true of many of the early musicals. They maintained silent film's narrative tropes but couldn't use the nimble silent camera. They borrowed Broadway's output but marketed it for a public not entirely used to Broadway ware. They hired film actors and Broadway actors arbitrarily, failing to make use of talent at hand and misusing new talent. The studio chiefs, producers, and directors simply did not understand the musical form, either historically (in its stage evolutions) or imaginatively (in what film could do with it). Certain moments in *The Show of Shows* reveal a savvy innocence—an informality cynical about life but romantic about film's role in the culture—that was to survive these difficult early years to guide the musical film in its greatest days.

It happens that some of the least durable first musicals got this informal tone down without much trouble. Conceived for the screen and relatively well written and cast, they weren't filmed well and now seem horribly leaden. DeSylva, Brown, and Henderson brought their distinctive vernacular touch—lowdown in rhythm, piquant in love—to Fox' *Sunny Side Up* (1929), the tale of a Manhattan waif who loves and finally wins a Prince Charming of Southampton. As authors of smash hit Broadway scores (*Flying High* and *Good News* among them) they held a close collaboration, and wrote all of *Sunny Side Up*, screenplay as well as score, pinning its appeal on Janet Gaynor's charm as the heroine. The star of such great silents as *Sunrise* and *Seventh Heaven*, Gaynor revealed a bearable singing voice, and if her constant screen lover Charles Farrell didn't, that did not militate against his taking the indicated part in *Sunny Side Up*. Gaynor carried the show, singing the title song, a champion cheer-up rouser, and what in part-talkie days would have been the film's theme song, "(I'm a dreamer) Aren't We All?" Many would call it the theme song of all Hollywood musicals, but this is to discount the earthy sarcasm that complements the wishfulness. *Sunny Side Up*'s six songs feature with-it complacence more than optimism, for the authors were adept at capturing the slangy, self-boosting world of the lower-middle-class drifter who emphasizes fun over ambition. "If I Had a Talking Picture of You," "You've Got Me Pickin' Petals Off of Daisies," and "You Find the Time, I'll Find the Place" may sound like love ditties, but in tone they slyly mock the sentimentality of "Aren't We All?," and for all their naiveté they are more about making love than being in it.

Gaynor and Farrell still had magic for many moviegoers, and the film did so well that Fox more or less remade it a year later with Gaynor as the heiress and Farrell as the waif in *High Society Blues.* But both these films and DeSylva, Brown, and Henderson's second original, *Just Imagine* (1930), were handed over to a director, David Butler, who had no sense of pace. He can't connect one line to another, lingers over the insufferable contortions of comedian El Brendel, and renders *Sunny Side Up*'s production number, "Turn on the Heat," almost motionless.

At least *Sunny Side Up* had a good score and Gaynor. *Just Imagine,* a look fifty years into the future, has nothing. Suddenly, DeSylva, Brown, and Henderson—or Fox?—got nervous about letting characters express themselves as the musical spirit moved them, so every number has an "excuse"—party entertainment, a club drinking song, even a dream vision. However, the film's structure is like that of the authors' stage musicals, with its two couples, one romantic (John Garrick and Maureen O'Sullivan) and one dizzy (Frank Albertson and Marjorie White), a lead comic (Brendel again), forced gag finishes to each scene, and an "umbrella" for jokes (like *Flying High*'s aviation or *Good News*' anti-intellectual undergraduate life): the future. The opening shot of New York in 1980, with low-flying aircars humming past art deco skyscrapers, is intriguing, but after that the movie looks as if it cost fifty cents. One can't blame *Just Imagine* because many of its pushbutton luxuries, viewed as wild in 1930, are old hat today. But the combination of Brendel as an inhabitant of the past brought back to life and Butler's sleepy camera makes this one of the worst musicals ever made. Brendel had a light Swedish accent, a clown's face, and no sense of humor whatsoever. He joins the two male leads on a trip to Mars, saves them from a hostile Martian, and brings the latter back to earth—which, for reasons not worth going into, resolves the love plot. Let's try a sample of Brendel's art just for the record:

BRENDEL: So this is Mars? We got a place just like this three miles from my hometown.
ALBERTSON: You should be on it.
BRENDEL: [With neither timing nor inflection] You're telling me!

☆ *MASTER DIRECTORS: above, Josef von Sternberg's* Morocco *(Dietrich and Cooper in the "What Am I Bid for My Apples?" number); below, Ernst Lubitsch's* The Merry Widow *(MacDonald in window).*

Other than *Hallelujah*, we have not seen much to build an aesthetic on, but there were works of astonishing quality in this time, all of them from Paramount and some of them as good as anything that followed. They were the work of directors Ernst Lubitsch and Rouben Mamoulian, and suddenly we find no stymied camera, no confusion about format, no fumbling for character. Lubitsch, with his famous "touch" of arch eroticism, and Mamoulian, with his kaleidoscope of images and sounds turned simultaneously, found the personality for a musical cinema.

Influential as they were, their styles flourished only from 1929 to 1932, when Lubitsch produced his first four and Mamoulian his first two musicals. They were too special to create a trend; moreover, the institution of the Legion of Decency by the Catholic Church in late 1933 promised an end to the subjects and characters that Lubitsch especially dealt with. Coming at a time when movie attendance figures had hit a disastrous low, the Legion of Decency's threatened boycott forced Hollywood to revise the Hays Production Code of 1930—more precisely, to enforce it. This didn't stop Lubitsch from completing his series of salacious operettas with *The Merry Widow* in 1934; still, it sounded as if in a vacuum.

Lubitsch's first musical, *The Love Parade* (1929), brought Jeanette MacDonald and Maurice Chevalier together as the queen of Sylvania and her prince consort, who is treated as Sylvania's royal lapdog until he compels his wife to turn over the power to him. In a medium that couldn't decide what sort of stories to tell, much less how to tell them, Lubitsch's exposition plays like lightning: in Paris, Chevalier and a woman are caught in adulterous tryst; Chevalier just has time to fill the audience in on the facts. "She's very jealous," he explains of the woman, and, when a man enters, "Her husband." She shoots herself. The husband takes the gun and shoots Chevalier in the chest at point-blank range. Chevalier feels for the wound. Nothing. A little embarrassed, he shows the husband that he's unhurt. They turn to the woman; she's unhurt. The gun was loaded with blanks. Chevalier drops the gun into a drawer—filled with guns. About to leave, the husband tries to draw his wife's zipper. He fumbles. She impatiently goes to Chevalier, who suavely pulls it to. "Voilà."

The whole film is like that, reducing every event to its center, dressy, unblushing, velvet with bite. Everything in *The Love Parade* is different from everything else so far, and it seems impossible that it inaugurated rather than capped a tradition. Not only Lubitsch's direction, but Ernest Vajda and Guy Bolton's screenplay (from a French piece), Victor Schertzinger and Clifford Grey's score, and the cast are all unexpectedly confident. Chevalier and MacDonald especially were made for sound. His "Paris, Stay the Same," sung when he is recalled to Sylvania because of his wicked life, and "Nobody's Using It Now," when neglected by the queen-oriented court, sound a note of jauntiness and manly grace beyond matters of portrayal: Chevalier *is* a prince; he must dominate; MacDonald will succumb. Her "Dream Lover" promises it, though her "March of the Grenadiers," delivered in full uniform to (and with) troops on parade, suggests a stalwart woman. And she does have the power. But he's the man.

Like *Just Imagine, The Love Parade* has a secondary comic couple, his valet (Lupino Lane) and her maid (Lillian Roth), but the comedy is built into the story, not painted onto it. And, as opposed to *Just Imagine*'s cardboard fantasy, *The Love Parade* doesn't only refer to castles, it inhabits them. Lubitsch rides his camera up and down halls, out onto terraces, into the opera house, showing only essentials. MacDonald first meets Chevalier in her office, where she reads a report of his escapades. Nothing need be said—Lubitsch has the orchestra quote a theme heard in the first scene to recall Chavalier at his sport. They love each other from the start, of course, and have dinner while her Cabinet, the servants, and the populace in general watch anxiously outside. At last their queen will marry! We see the new couple through outsiders' eyes, through the window. The pair enter her boudoir and, later, MacDonald sits at a piano to sing a reprise of "Dream Lover." But we only hear her do it: Lubitsch focuses on a group of couples on a patio—each a mirror of Chevalier and MacDonald—on the Cabinet, and on Lane and Roth listening blissfully. The new naturalism of sound can absorb fantasy as long as we in the audience can enter the story ourselves, eavesdropping and peeking.

Lubitsch had less to work with in *Monte Carlo* (1930), though the quality of sound had improved. (Every other line in *The Love Parade* seems pitched at a different volume, and the orchestra and voices, shoved together into one track, dissolve into mush at times.) MacDonald is back but Jack Buchanan's got her, as a count masquerading as a hairdresser. The Richard Whiting–W. Franke Harling–Leo Robin score contains "Beyond the Blue Horizon" but the script is dull and Buchanan, a smarmy British wimp who played opposite Irene Bordoni in her *Paris* film, has a voice like tapioca pudding on a high speed and the most irritating laugh a leading man ever tried to get away with. One scene has made *Monte Carlo* famous, that of MacDonald's flight from an arranged marriage with a pompous old prince. The film opens with the wedding, lingers just long enough to establish that MacDonald isn't going to show up, then cuts to a train standing in a station. A woman gets on—MacDonald, it seems—and from this standing start Lubitsch turns her trip into an experience of space and bulk and motion—the straining on the tracks, the pulse of the iron ride, the adventure hissing and steaming as much in music as in cinema. The chugging and whistling turn into the accompaniment to MacDonald's song as she settles by the window seat of her compartment. The opening wedding had been shot in the rain, but now the sun beams on the heroine: the rules of romance favor beauty. The ostinato of train noises thickens as the voyage roars on and, her scarf flying in the breeze and peasants in the passing fields waving to her, MacDonald soars through "Beyond the Blue Horizon," voice, music and lyrics, and visual expression all expanding in one moment of exhilaration.

Chevalier, a bigger star than MacDonald, drew better projects without her than she did without him, as in Lubitsch's *The Smiling Lieutenant* (1931), based on Oscar Straus' operetta *A Waltz Dream*. Chevalier played "between" Claudette Colbert and Miriam Hopkins, and his endless charm even brings off Clifford Grey's extreme lyric to "Breakfast Table Love" (such as "With every bit of liver I start to quiver"). But Lubitsch reunited the ultimate operetta twosome in *One Hour With You* (1932), a very up-to-date piece about a doctor (Chevalier) madly in love with his wife (MacDonald) but trapped into infidelity with her best friend (Genevieve Tobin). *One Hour With You*, a boudoir comedy that gets around, is less musical than Lubitsch's earlier trio, tossing off some of its lyrics in lightly accented speech, avoiding the heavy character songs that enriched *The Love Parade,* and doing a full-out number only in the title song, performed at a dinner party by dancing couples who glide in and out of each other's arms trying to arrange assignations.

At first, Lubitsch was to produce the film and George Cukor was to direct it. But midway through shooting Lubitsch began to horn in with advice and Cukor departed. It's impossible to tell Lubitsch from Cukor in the finished product; examples of the Touch abound everywhere, as when Charles Ruggles, dressed as Romeo for what he believes to be a costume party, learns that it's a simple black-tie affair. It's the butler's fault—why did he tell Ruggles to don a getup? "Oh, sir," says the butler with a shameless grin, "I did so want to see you in tights."

Lubitsch was already a Hollywood pro when sound came in (*One Hour With You* was a remake of his 1924 comedy, *The Marriage Cir-*

cle). Rouben Mamoulian came in for sound from Broadway, where he had led the so-called art movement into the highly collaborative production that blended acting, motion, sound effects, decor, and lighting as one conceptual organism. Movie historians regularly cite his dynamic orchestration of noises in the opening scene of DuBose and Dorothy Heyward's play *Porgy* (based on Heyward's novel and the source of Gershwin's opera *Porgy and Bess*), a jazz of street workers, snores, brooms, rug beatings, knife sharpenings, and so on in harmonious and competing rhythms as dawn comes up and the black ghetto comes to life. "Inside his brain," wrote critic Tom Milne, "there must be an invisible metronome . . . One is almost tempted to say that every Mamoulian film is a musical." In *Hallelujah*, King Vidor washes his action in an overlay of emotionalism. Mamoulian pumps a heartbeat into his.

Mamoulian learned film at Paramount's Astoria studios watching Herbert Brenon direct Jeanne Eagels in *Jealousy*. He was signed to slide into the business as a "dialogue director," meaning a coach for witless actors. But he picked everything up so fast that in little over a month he was directing *Applause* (1929), a sordid look into the life of a fading burlesque dancer. *The Dance of Life* (1929) upped burlesque's tempo with high-stepping numbers; *Applause* is as shabby onstage as it is off. The famous opening sequence proves Mamoulian's genius for film in its cascade of messages cued into the cheesy street parade of Kitty Darling and her Gaiety Girls. A poster fluttering in the wind announces the procession, a mutt tears at it, a little girl picks him up and more children race up the lane to see the fun. Some fun: as the parade passes, the band music dissolves into a cheap music-hall tune and the camera steals into a burlesque theatre to spot the heavy legs and exhausted gaudy of the Gaiety Girls.

The role of Kitty Darling gave Helen Morgan the challenge of her career. Exploited by her lover and an embarrassment to her convent-reared daughter, Kitty slides from despair to despair, but Mamoulian cuts the tale's potential for easy pathos with his constantly essentializing images, forcing the spectator to apply the same alert eye that the silents required. When Garrett Fort's script brings in a sailor to spark some palliative love interest with Morgan's daughter, Mamoulian hammers sorrow home by cutting from a shot of the daughter drinking a glass of water to one of Morgan drinking poison.

Morgan's two onstage numbers and some incidental use of folk and old pop tunes give Mamoulian's sharp musical steerage few opportunities for song-and-dance narrative, but he has his moments. He entered the annals of technical reform in a scene in which Morgan sings a lullaby and her daughter whispers a prayer, simultaneously. The sound and camera men insisted it couldn't be done on one mike, with one-channel recording. "Why not use two mikes and two channels," Mamoulian recalls asking, "and combine the two tracks in printing?" Unheard of. But Mamoulian was nothing without his sound sense, and he was something. "I threw down my megaphone . . . and ran up to [Adolph] Zukor's office . . . 'Look,' I said, 'Nobody does what I ask' . . . So Zukor came down and told them to do it my way, and by 5:30 we had two takes in the can." Mamoulian knew he had brought it off for sure when he got an effusive welcome from the studio doorman the next morning.

Mamoulian's second musical (if we count *Applause* as his first; many don't) ranks with Lubitsch's *The Love Parade* as one of the two masterpieces of the era. Like the Lubitsch film, *Love Me Tonight* (1932) is a continental fairy tale without sorcery. Its magic charms comprise a superb score and cast and a sense of motion so palpable that one rides right into it on a dream cloud without having to pay the price in prefabricated sentimentality that too many operettas were charging. It's more beautiful than life, yet its appetites are realistic. "Love, Your Spell Is Everywhere," sang Gloria Swanson in her first talkie, *The Trespasser* (1929); that might well be the theme of *Love Me Tonight*. Consider its opening sequences, three songs and some dialogue scenes unfurled in a medley and presenting two different worlds, that of vital Paris and that of a sleepy country chateau where ancient nobles play eons of bridge and an anemic princess waits for a man to kiss her awake. Mamoulian opens in Paris as the day begins, with his hero, a tailor named Maurice, cataloguing the noises of the day in "That's the Song of Paree." En route to his shop, he greets tradesmen and girl friends in the immediately succeeding "How Are You?", the various characters jumping fluently from song to speech though every line is in fact a lyric. In his shop, Maurice finds music latent even in tailoring, and a conversation with a customer grows into another song, "Isn't It Romantic?", which now leaves Maurice to follow different people around the town—the customer reviews the tune, passes it to a taxi driver, who passes it in turn to a musician, who gets off at a train station. Chugging wheels urge the tune on; traveling soldiers toss it to marching troops, who give it to a passing gypsy violinist, who brings out its sensuality at his camp in the forest. We have reached open country, and Mamoulian takes us to the song's last beneficiary, Princess Jeanette, who sings it full out with a new set of lyrics. "Isn't it

romantic?" she asks. "Music in the night, a dream that can be heard."
We have spent a whole day in minutes, with all its persons and events,
and have met our hero and heroine in their respective settings: the artful tailor, engaged by the adventure of living, the languishing princess
in her bloodless storybook castle, and love's spell heading her way on
the energy of song.

Jeanette and Maurice are, of course, MacDonald and Chevalier,
contributing to, yet undercutting, the fantasy by using their real-life
first names. They are splendid, and the score, by Richard Rodgers and
Lorenz Hart, exactly amalgamates their separate qualities of (his)
brisk urbanity and (her) romantic vulnerability. His "Mimi," sung
when they meet, is raffish, but it gives away a secret: he loves her. Her
"Lover," sung just before they meet while she is out riding, is elegant
but comically interrupted by commands to her horse.* One duet, "The
Man for Me," written for the film but cut before release, stresses comedy. She is writing to a friend and he dictates some ideas, flattering to
himself; she takes the second chorus, deflating his vanity. Their other
duet, the title song, stresses romance. Mamoulian splits the screen,
and the two separately affirm the inevitable romance in wonderfully
wide-spanned tune, insistent in off-the-beat accents.

Chevalier has come to the chateau to collect on debts owed by Jeanette's cousin Charles Ruggles. He impersonates a noble, is unmasked
to general horror, yet wins Jeanette anyway. Actually, she has to win
him, by riding after his train to halt it by planting herself on the
tracks. The chateau scenes provide the bulk of the ninety-minute running time and give Mamoulian plenty of chances to cast his signature
shadows and shoot huffy servants from below. This gloomy manse
even has three witches in residence in the persons of Jeanette's aunts;
it also has early Myrna Loy in one of her best roles, as a man-chasing
cousin. When Jeanette faints, Ruggles asks Loy, "Can you go for a
doctor?" and she replies, "Certainly, bring him right in."

What did these six films have that their contemporaries did not?
Style, sophistication, sex—a continental personality, richer than the
all-American product. They also had technique, obviously, with
scripts, scores, and visual planning by masters. More than anything,

---

*Trivium footnote no. 2: "Lover," one of Rodgers' loveliest waltzes, has be-
come a standard, but in the film its lyrics are so wedded to the situation that Paramount's publishing house despaired of selling it and didn't bring it out till 1933, with a
plain cover and all-purpose "love song" lyrics.

they had a sure sense of themselves, which leads them from a smart premise through congenial development to the right resolution. What did they lack? Dance. Not till Astaire and Rogers would choreography be integrated into narrative, and Lubitsch and Mamoulian preferred doing without to underdoing.*

However, even these films suffered from the general distaste for singing cinema that rose up in 1930. Hollywood had churned out too many shapeless musicals without tempo or grace; the public began to balk, and Hollywood cut back. Warners, the studio that virtually invented the film musical, pulled all the songs out of *Fifty Million Frenchmen* (1931), from a Cole Porter stage hit; Fox's *Oh, For a Man* (1930), a Jeanette MacDonald–Reginald Denny comedy about an opera diva in love with a singing burglar, lost most of the numbers that told who these people were; and Universal's *Reaching for the Moon* (1931), a Douglas Fairbanks vehicle with Bebe Daniels, Bing Crosby, and an Irving Berlin score, lost all but a song or two. (Even the title tune, the theme song so endemic to filmmaking but two years earlier, was thrown out except in underscoring.) Nineteen twenty-eight had produced some sixty musicals, and 1930 more than seventy, but less than fifteen were released in 1932 and only two of them—*One Hour With You* and an Eddie Cantor romp, *The Kid From Spain*—made much of a profit.

Darryl F. Zanuck, Warners' head of production, broke the bottleneck on a hunch. Something had to work—maybe something with a more everyday flavor than the musical had yet tasted. Zanuck decided to pull off another backstager, this one with a New York pulse to it, greasy with sweat and paint—something to do for show biz what *The Love Parade* and *Love Me Tonight* had done for romance, something to fall into its subject and be, rather than indicate, it. This is something special: a $400,000 musical at a time when even cheap ones were a poor gamble, filled with the slick Broadway types that most Americans dislike, and created entirely by Hollywood, not New York, tal-

---

*This is not to count the occcasional waltzing, a ground-zero minimum in operetta. By dancing, I mean out-and-out character choreography. Lupino Lane and Lillian Roth dance in *The Love Parade*, showing some relation to Broadway, where secondary comic couples often broke into relatively meaningless "eccentrics" to put a song over. Still, Lubitsch has them more sparring than dancing, making Roth seem tougher than she is. She climaxes their "Let's Be Common" by throwing Lane out of a second-floor window, right through the glass.

ents. The structure is familiar. A number of people with diverse stories work together to put on a show; at the last minute, the star is knocked *hors de combat* and an unknown goes on for her with terrific success. Zanuck had to keep the project as secret as possible, for in those days a movie could be written, shot, edited, and released in a few months, and trend starters could find themselves scooped by their competitors if they dallied.* On the quiet, he got a screenplay from Rian James and James Seymour, based on a novel by Bradford Ropes; it's hard to imagine the kind of novel that would translate into this particular movie, flimsy in plot and character but rich in atmosphere. The cast is a big one, and Zanuck filled it more with actors than with singers: Warner Baxter as the director, Bebe Daniels as the star, George Brent as her lover, Guy Kibbee as her elderly protector, Ned Sparks as a producer, Dick Powell as a juvenile, Ginger Rogers and Una Merkel as chorus girls, and Ruby Keeler in her film debut as the novice who goes on for Daniels. Lloyd Bacon directed and Busby Berkeley, a three-year veteran of film musicals, choreographed, taking over the camera himself for the musical sequences. All these people somehow caught the alienation and community and enchantment and exhaustion of the New York theatre world. For the first time, a mass-appeal film musical got so close to its subject that it made audiences understand why sound had to happen, how the artful naturalism of cinema worked, after all. This film has the pace and the vernacular. It introduced an aesthetic of dance conceived for the camera. It saved the musical from extinction by setting a new style for it. Right from the start, so you'll know where you stand—even before you see the street signs and hear extras shout "Jones and Barry are doing a show!" and note Bebe Daniels reading a *New Yorker* with Eustace Tilley on its cover— the film tells you it's hot-shot, ace-high, lowdown, dirty, crazy New York show biz by its very title: *42nd Street.*

Nothing like it preceded it. It's tough—not lovable tough, either. Rogers is known as Anytime Annie; she walks into Baxter's auditions faking an English accent, carrying a pug dog, and sporting a monocle. But she's recognized, and Baxter's choreographer calls her out to her face: they dubbed her Anytime, he tells us, because "She only said no

---

*Today it takes four or five years to get a trend going. Except for quickie exploitation films, the average American movie counts some fifteen months from planning to public viewing, and such recent movements as extrasensory horror and the revival of space fiction took half a decade to implant themselves. In the 1930s, one could pull off such a development inside of a year. When six imitative films from as many studios might hit the screens within five months of their mutual predecessor, innovators have to work fast to assert a cultural copyright.

once—and then she didn't hear the question."* A few other chorines razz her, and Rogers hits one of them and says, "It must have been hard on your mother not having any children," as she stalks off. The sass has grit. True, much of it is simply funny, as when the choreographer nudges Baxter, indicating Rogers, Keeler, and Merkel. "How about keeping the three on the left?" he asks. Baxter is wise: "I suppose if I don't, you'll have to." Still, the atmosphere of nonstop putdown is heavy.

As in the real-life theatre, much of this is because the people involved are insecure and so anxious for recognition. The desperation to succeed spills over into their love lives—there are almost as many liaisons as there are principals—and their professional day-to-day life, so everyone snaps at everyone else. Yet the characters are so fully drawn that the authors can express the fellowship of Broadway, the sense of sharing that hides in the snapping, without straining credibility. Bebe Daniels is at her considerable best as the star of *Pretty Lady*, running through a song with aplomb at the piano, alternately trusting and doubting her lover, drunkenly repudiating her sugar daddy, and, at last, after a broken ankle throws her out of the show, confronting Keeler on crutches. Direly, she eyes her replacement. "So you're going to take my place!" Keeler is sympathetic: "I—I'm sorry, Miss Brock." But Daniels isn't there for Keeler's apology:

> You're nervous, aren't you? [A pause while we wait to learn what her mood is.] Well, don't be. The customers out there want to like you. Always remember that, kid. I've learned it from experience. And you've got so much to give them—youth, beauty, freshness. Do you know your lines? And your songs? And your dance routine? Well! You're a cinch!

The toughness and the fellowship combine in the urgency of getting it on, an urgency felt right from the start, when we learn that Baxter is ailing and wants to cap his career with a tremendous hit. *Pretty Lady* must be perfect, as Baxter angrily points out after witnessing a runthrough of a terrible production number built around a tedious ditty and couples waving garlands. "Don't you like this number?" he is asked. "Sure, I like it," Baxter replies. "I liked it in 1905. What do you think we're putting on, a revival?" This is exactly what *42nd Street* is

---

*Historians joyfully lore over this line, but it's a bloody rude thing to say to someone, and if you watch Rogers carefully while he says it, you'll see a nice woman refusing to show it but feeling terribly hurt. (I mean, of course, Rogers as Annie, not Rogers herself. Let's not confuse actor and character yet; we'll get to Judy Garland in good time.) It only lasts a second, but for my money this is one of the most uncomfortable moments in film.

not. Its proletarian outlook, characteristic of the Warners studio, changes its familiar elements. The things people say, who they are in the first place, what they need, and even the subjects of the songs—the familiar has been rendered so real it's strange. *42nd Street* spawned a series of backstage musicals allied with Depression attitudes to the extent that a successful opening night is no longer an event of gathered glamor but of mass employment. "Two hundred people!" Baxter cries, rallying Keeler just before she goes on. "Two hundred jobs!" And he hands down the famous command, half shopgirl's dream and half egalitarian imperative: "You're going out there a youngster, but you've *got* to come back a star!"

Keeler does, which might seem to throw *42nd Street* off its realistic axis. She's certainly pretty, and if her true-life identity as Al Jolson's new bride carried an interest to *42nd Street*'s first audiences not shared by *Pretty Lady*'s, still she does have that freshness Daniels mentions. Her singing, however, is less than passable and her dancing, though excellent in its speed and power, is sometimes ungainly. Worst of all, she appears to have no conception of language. When she has to deliver two sentences in a row, she sometimes glides right over the break between them as if the words were an incantation in an occult tongue. But in the end the uniquely charming Keeler's replacing the meticulously expert Daniels is not a mistake, because the Warners backstagers see Broadway not so much as the pinnacle of show biz as its foundation. Broadway is where you start—Hollywood is where you finish, though this is never mentioned, to avoid wrecking the illusion of the Broadway success as the happy ending. If we were to root for the most *talented* character, then *42nd Street* is a tragedy: Daniels doesn't go on, even if she does apparently end up with lover Brent, which is fine with her. We root, rather, for the most pleasant character, the one with the open, determined rightness. Admittedly, Keeler can't portray this for us. But she doesn't need to: she has it naturally.

So it is the personality, the racy efficiency, of *42nd Street* that makes it different. But more: its musical numbers accord with the overall tone, besides setting up Berkeley's geometric spectacles of a theme multiplied into countless interchangeable variations. He gets four numbers to stage, not counting the garland thing which presumably is dropped in rehearsal, and the quartet builds gradually in size and impact, stopping just this side of epic—that would come a few months later in *Gold Diggers of 1933.* The first of the four, "You're Getting to Be a Habit With Me," staged midway through the film during a dress rehearsal, is simple: Daniels, a bench, four men in sweaters, and a Father Time figure who comes out to sing the final line and truck off with Daniels. Later, the last three numbers come all together on opening night. "Shuffle Off to Buffalo" is presented as it might look on a real stage, featuring one special effect when the end of a train jackknifes open to show a sleeping car in cross-section. The lyric expresses banal honeymooners' plans, but composer Harry Warren and lyricist Al Dubin fell right in with the general air of naiveté mixed with cynicism, so Merkel and Rogers, chomping on fruit in an upper berth, offer a burlesque second chorus of the song, involving the "well-known traveling man," the farmer's daughter, their shotgun wedding, and a Reno divorce; at one point, Rogers charges into the word "belly" only to change it to "tummy." The vulgarity is so correct for the film that it defines the number better than the prancing of the honeymoon couple (Keeler and Clarence Nordstrum) or the pantomime of a porter falling asleep as he shines shoes.

Berkeley is known not only for his imaginative layouts, but for how his camera picked them up, and the third number, "Young and Healthy," plays around with odd angles, both from overhead and underfoot—literally so at the end, when Berkeley pans around the lip of his three-tiered revolve beneath the girls' legs for a close-up of Powell and a blonde resting supine. Berkeley's great invention was filming dance from a dancing camera, taking part in his own action. "Young and Healthy" is staged as it might be in a theatre, only we see it more variously than a theatre audience could. In the finale, "42nd Street," however, Berkeley steps out of the theatre somewhat. Here again, Warren and Dubin come up with a song as hard-hearted as it is fun-loving, pitched in a minor key to suggest the sinister Tenderloin, "where the underworld can meet the elite." As Berkeley stages it, New York is a ceaseless dance whose drive impels crimes of passion and contemplation, numbers runners and players, shoeshine boys and "little nifties from the Fifties," secrets and headlines. Keeler launches it, tapping on what is revealed to be a limousine taxicab; the dancers take over as the set expands to beyond theatre proportions, and Powell surveys the scene from a second-floor window, bootleg hooch in hand. Now occurs the strongest indication so far of what was to come from Berkeley, as files of dancers line up on a broad stairway carrying dark patterns. When they fill the view, they turn—and vanish behind the patterns, cardboard cutouts of the New York skyline. A center aisle between them dissolves into the projection of a skyscraper, and Berkeley flies up to its summit, where Powell and Keeler grin delightedly. It makes a good finish—but Bacon has one last picture in mind, that of

Baxter watching wearily as ritzy first-nighters leave the theatre. It's strangely downbeat, but then the crescendo of noise and motion in the three closing numbers has given us too much of a lift, perhaps, floated us high on the electricity of entertainment. "The big parade goes on for years," Powell has sung from his eyrie over the town. "It's the rhapsody of laughter and tears." Accordingly, Bacon wraps the film with his director, physically and artistically spent. After the enchantment, exhaustion.

42nd Street is often said to be a remake of an earlier Warners backstager, *On With the Show!* (1929). This could only be said by someone who has not seen them both. *42nd Street* follows *Pretty Lady* from auditions through rehearsals to opening night of the Philadelphia tryout, showing little of the show itself until the final reels, to concentrate on how its characters live outside the theatre. *On With the Show!* (which derives from a different source in the first place) happens entirely in the theatre in which *The Phantom Sweetheart* is playing, on a Broadway-or-bust Saturday night in an unnamed city, and has no equivalent for any of *42nd Street*'s characters. *Pretty Lady* is a weird piece, fun with a bite; *The Phantom Sweetheart* on the other hand is utterly conventional, one of Hollywood's few attempts to duplicate the Broadway style. An updated "plantation show," the tale of a young man who falls in love with a veiled goddess on the eve of his wedding to another, it has the hurdy-gurdy opening chorus, the pointless dance specialties, and the idiotic storyline that American musical comedy was in the process of retiring, while *Pretty Lady*'s numbers are one-of-a-kind oddities. Larry Ceballos' *On With the Show!* choreography is amusing but stupid, and Harry Akst and Grant Clarke's score is too willing to engage the available Broadway clichés (as in "Lift the Juleps to Your Two Lips") whereas *42nd Street*'s Busby Berkeley and Warren–Dubin team distills the sense of Broadway through cinematic conceptions. Furthermore, Robert Lord's *On With the Show!* script is quaint even for 1929, whereas *42nd Street* has dated only in its slang.

Even the two casts, separated by a mere four years, tell how different the two works are: *42nd Street*'s mix of old hands (Baxter, Daniels, Brent) and newcomers (Keeler, Powell, Rogers) shows prudent observation of film's ability to "sell" certain personalities. *Everyone* in this cast plays successfully not just as an actor but as a person. Baxter has the command and the desperation of a famous showman who may be terminally ill. Daniels truly seems the talented star who's tiring of the stage. Brent is the perfect third-rater, Keeler *the* youngster, and so on. Next to them, *On With the Show!*'s gang is a lot of bad news from the west. Only Ethel Waters comes through—and she plays herself, singing two songs, "Am I Blue?" and "Birmingham Bertha," on the fringe of the stage while the stagehands ready the next big set behind her. Arthur Lake, *The Phantom Sweetheart*'s juvenile, can do nothing right but whine. Joe E. Brown, *The Phantom Sweetheart*'s comedian, isn't, not this time out. Star Betty Compson, dubbed behind her veil, producer Sam Hardy, hat-check girl Sally O'Neil, usher William Bakewell, and gold digger Louise Fazenda are hampered by a weak script and Alan Crosland's weak direction, which says everything twice in slow motion. O'Neil provides *On With the Show!*'s one discernible link with *42nd Street* in that she goes on in the veil when Compson refuses to play her last scenes, but the little bit we see O'Neil do is enough to conclude a performance, not make her a star.

This comparison between 1929 and 1933 shows how far the film musical had come. Technical defects in sound reproduction and camera movement cut *On With the Show!* into two parts, picturefilm and soundtrack; we can't make out the words when the chorus sings, and when Waters finishes "Birmingham Bertha" she ad libs a parting shot at the audience that doesn't turn up on the audio portion, leaving a foolish pantomime. *42nd Street* has no such problems. *On With the Show!* also comes from the two-strip Technicolor days—it was the first all-color sound feature—and has the patronizing insecurity of that time when musicals were being milled like product, without imagination. *42nd Street* belongs to a more structured time. It, too, was product, but one manufactured by specialists. *On With the Show!* can't figure out how to make music without taking it from Broadway; *42nd Street* loves New York but doesn't trust it, and hears its own sweeter melodies. In 1929, the musical film is shouting blind. Four years later, it has been tamed and taught where to look.

Another point: *42nd Street* located the naturalistic style that the musical needed to complement the airier art of operetta. The latter, whether Lubitschian satire or the-student-prince-meets-the-goosegirl, plumes itself on extramusical values and escapism. Modern-dress musical comedy prefers less definitively musical pop tunes and an everyday directness. Operetta will survive into the 1950s (and occasionally thereafter, in such instances as *The Slipper and the Rose* and *A Little Night Music*), but the *42nd Street* model will predominate. The model is flexible. It leans to vernacular guts in the 1930s and to patriotic nostalgia during World War II, and seeks out an odd hybrid realism in period costume in the late 1940s. With its contradictory elements of zip and tension, *42nd Street* has created a rich and influential form.

☆ 4 ☆
The First Stars

IF THE MUSICAL as form at first baffled the studios, marketing techniques did not. Eager to amass a pool of talent who through PR manipulation would consolidate an audience for their work on an indefinitely self-renewing schedule, producers cast their first musicals in a kind of flash-forward in time. They knew where they wanted to end up but not where to start.

Counting the part-talkie *The Jazz Singer* as the start, they lucked into something exactly right, for the time being. Al Jolson was the essential stage entertainer, helpless without his spontaneity and inter-communication with a responding public; but this very life force made Jolson's screen debut and the debut of story sound a sensation. Sound exacted its condition of film—fantasy is dead—and Jolson, with his ad libs and lack of polish, was as real as they come. He called himself "the world's greatest entertainer," got his friends to publicize the notion, and it caught on. He wasn't the world's greatest anything, but he fascinated because his image—he was nothing but an image, playing it in every role—was so ambiguous. He is hardly good-looking, yet he does well with women. He prances and minces in an uptempo number, yet he is all man, very believable in his hunger for sex, gambling, and booze. He is irreverent, yet ballads bring out a flood of bathos. Nothing in his parts suggests anything ethnic, yet he continually inserts Jewish jokes and occasionally even an obscure phrase in Yiddish. In a business where almost everyone was a type, Jolson was a riddle.

Everything he does is so unforced, however, that one suffers no frustrating mystery watching his films. Jolson is, typically, a man in one of the "unsettled" professions (a singer, a nightclub owner, a jockey) mixed up in some shady business (murder enters into at least four of his films), who loves either his mother or his little son with a gargantuan trembling heart, and who best expresses himself in singing, especially in blackface. The clichés work because Jolson obviously lays so much importance on them. No one else would have wanted to come out in the overstated black makeup and costume to clutch a straw hat and put so much into "Let Me Sing and I'm Happy" (which cites as utopian lyrical references "Dixie's charms," "mountain fields" and "Mammy's arms") and follow this minutes later with "(I'm everything to my) Mammy," as Jolson did in *Mammy* (1930). He sang in the old vaudeville "sell it!" style that had already fallen out of fashion, replaced by a more evenly leveled belt or the radio croon, and he adds words, scants notes, and sometimes rewrites whole melodies. But he adds to a song's spirit—no, to *his* spirit. All Jolson material was by process of performance transformed into a component of Jolson.

Which returns us to who he was. His incessant blackface routines suggest an ambivalent sense of identity as much as his nervous laughter and momentary escapes into arcane Jewish references. In *Say It With Songs* (1929), Jolson is a radio singer approached by distributors of the Excelsior automobile, who want something special for their radio show. Jolson mockingly suggests a theme song, "Excelsior, I Love You." The businessmen have something else in mind, along the lines of "I'm Going to Smother My Mother With Kisses When I Get Back to My Home in Tennessee." "Let's see," says Jolson. "How would it be if he said, 'I'll Smother My Father in Gedaemfte Rinderbrust* When I Get Back to Odessa'?" *Say It With Songs* finds Jolson in prison, cutting into his time for donning the black, but he played all of *Bigboy* (1930) as a Negro, and made this transracial turn the big moment in his films wherever possible. Why? The blackface tradition, like Jolson's overacted vocals, was outdated by 1930. It grew out of the segregated acting troupes of the 1800s (when whites went on in the outlandish makeup or couldn't have played a decent *Uncle Tom's Cabin*), and fell out of use when black performers such as Bert Williams

---

*Pot Roast. *Say It With Songs*, looking back at *The Singing Fool*'s phenomenal profits, brought little Davey Lee back to life as Jolson's kid, called Little Pal—so was the movie, until just before release. For all Jolson's spoof of the theme song craze, he plugs *Say it With Songs*' theme, "Little Pal," with fanatic abandon. "Doesn't my Daddy thing thway-yull?" lisps little Davey, an ear on the radio and an eye on the invisible millions in the theatres. I'll say: a recording of "Little Pal"—and a double-exposed vision of Daddy Jolson—brings back the child's voice, lost traumatically in an auto accident.

and Ethel Waters broke the color bar on Broadway's main stages. It can't be a coincidence that the best-known of the last bigtime blackface performers were largely Jewish; possibly they were having a joke at the expense of white Christian audiences, doubling their own outcast status in contempt for bigotry mingled with self-abnegation. Nowhere is this double identity more acute than in Jolson. His cantor's son in *The Jazz Singer,* culturally assimilated yet possessive of old-world ties, was an odd character to preside over the launching of a new phase of American film. But possibly the Warner brothers, also Jewish, suffered the same problems of identity. Is Jolson Jakie Rabinowitz or Jack Robin? Throughout his career, he kept the question open, and thus maintained a now vigorous, now tenuous hold on the public: they thought him exciting, yet tired of him at intervals.

When Jolson was at his peak of popularity in Hollywood, in 1928, Warners attempted to follow him up with a chip of what they presumed was the same block, specifically the Lower East Side comic-singing establishment. But Fanny Brice was different from Jolson in style, more continually Jewish in inflection, and less outgoing, though no less giving, in song. Not remotely good-looking, Brice made an unlikely romantic heroine, but in the aforementioned *My Man* she won, lost, and won him (Guinn Williams) back, and in her first all-sound musical *Be Yourself* (1930) she did it again as a nightclub singer who manages a boxer (Robert Armstrong). Boxer strays, Brice sets him up to lose a championship fight (by coaching his opponent to smash Armstrong's proud new nose job), boxer comes back chastened. It was too much like *My Man*, though it did give Brice her first chance to play a character whole, through serious and comic dialogue as well as through her amazing versatility in serious and comic songs. In her opening spot, "When a Woman Loves a Man," she is still in the flirting stage with Armstrong, and plays her number to him from the nightclub floor. In "Cooking Breakfast for the One I Love" she does just that while he reads the paper and she examines the bacon with her google-eyed grin. In her last number, "When a Gal Cares for a Man," a torch-carrying complement to "When a Woman Loves a Man," she gives it all she's got yet underplays, so that we lean into the song rather than have it mashed into us, Jolson-style.

Brice was too special. *Be Yourself* is an apt title, for as Fannie Field, Brice is herself in all but the final "y" in her first name. She was a lot for Hollywood to take, aggressive and only reluctantly vulnerable. She couldn't faint or twinkle like her woman colleagues, and in a business run by men she must have seemed natural in a troublesome way: subversive. "Just another movie," *Photoplay* called it. Anything but. Just another movie in which a heroine of unconventional appeal creates a formidable character—likeable but not to be challenged—who attracts us despite the pedestrian script and supporting cast. *Be Yourself*'s failure, however, is ultimately not one of material. Nor can one blame the director, Thornton Freeland. A capable storyteller, he cuts from a shot of Brice and Armstrong lazing around to the same shot—with Brice replaced by her successor in Armstrong's love life. And he shoots part of Brice's big torch song from Armstrong's table, letting Armstrong and his new girl, cooing at each other, frame Brice, a dim figure in the distance. *Be Yourself*'s obstacle, unfortunately, was Brice. No, the obstacle is Hollywood's narrow world view. How can it make use of the most gifted performers when their very gifts render them too eccentric to adhere to the set, or still setting, code?

Absorbing eastern stage talent was a tricky business; better to ride on already flowing tides of cinema personality, if possible. But such was the level of panic when sound was thrown into production that not all possibilities were scouted. Through wasteful pep, studios tested some stars for sound and singing but not others. Or they successfully piloted a silent star through debuts in first a talkie and then a musical—and suddenly, mysteriously, dropped the whole thing. Ironically, the most successful talkie-singie debut belonged to Bebe Daniels, whose studio, Paramount, had written her off without a test when sound came in. Daniels sold the remainder of her contract to RKO, suggested herself for the title role in *Rio Rita*, and walked off with one of the big critical and popular successes of the year. Daniels' singing voice was not all that superior to those of her colleagues, but it had a wide range that enabled her to switch from high soprano to Broadway belt. She had trained well, somehow getting down not only the rudiments of vocal projection but a detailed understanding of musical theatre styles as well. In *Rio Rita* she is all passion and high notes, as befits the character; in *42nd Street,* she is down to earth, the New York pro at ease on her turf. Janet Gaynor could have sung "You're Getting to Be a Habit With Me," but not with Daniels' confidence, nor could she have brought it off "on stage" dancing and clowning the way Daniels does.

As with Daniels, John Boles' and Walter Pidgeon's careers received adrenalin shots when they revealed viable singing voices. (Boles revealed several—a light baritone, he could sound higher or deeper than himself depending on what sound expert manned which mike.) Daniels' husband, Ben Lyon, also fitted nicely into musicals, though his singing was more game than accurate. There was Something in one's look, in the way one moved, in the way one dealt with comedy or pathos, that added up to a characterological dossier for musicals. Aside from the voice and, sometimes, an ability to pass in dance, actors needed that Something, and if producers didn't know what to call it, they thought they knew what it was. Neglecting to strive for pace, art direction, musical editing, or any of the many factors that film depends on, producers put everything into casting, looking for Something to build a genre on.

Before *42nd Street* articulated the musical's latent qualities of cynicism, human inconsistency, self-belief, and ribald facetiae, the ideal Something ran to a pliant virility in men and a crumply cuteness in women. This is why *The Show of Shows* seems so wrong, with its Frank Fay and Irene Bordoni, and why *Paramount on Parade* seems so right, with its Chevalier and Nancy Carroll. It was not a question of talent. Fay, in the right role, carried whole plays and films on sheer personality, and, in the realm of womanly give, Bordoni was the goods. It was a question of what most Americans wanted to see and also of what producers thought they wanted—not necessarily the same thing. Especially after 1934, when the Joseph Breen office put the Production Code into effect, a lot of the rich character of humankind—the real-life Something—was outlawed on the screen. This meant a smoothing down of some people's interesting edges and an implementation of supposed universal American attitudes that turned people into genres—good-hearted loose women, strong-hearted men, tolerant, passively long-suffering good women, strong but selfish men who go bad; one collection for crime drama, one for backstagers, one for society comedy, and so on.

Even before 1934, however, producers sought a code for painting personality in a limited number of colors—the code was the Something. The status quo for the American male was set by Buddy (nominally Charles) Rogers in his medium-dark, unthreatening handsomeness, easy singing style, and walkaround nonchalance. Rogers was the sort of man who looks comfortable in a bowtie and doesn't take art so seriously that drama utterly subsumes him. Women thought him cute and men liked him. Hollywood tried to coach several would-be Buddy Rogerses, but the model could not be readily copied.

Then try other models; find Something. Hollywood imported eastern talents by the trainload, but the studios weren't always able to fit these diverse people into workable forms. As a musical hero, for instance, Lawrence Tibbett was wonderfully powerful but right only in extravaganza roles; his operatic *confrère* Everett Marshall was a dud in anything, but especially in *Dixiana* (1930) with Bebe Daniels; Stanley Smith looked pallid even in college musicals; Rudy Vallee, hauled in from radio for *The Vagabond Lover* (1929), seemed completely out of his depth; Harry Richman in *Puttin' on the Ritz* (1930) revealed too much of the New York slick; Lawrence Gray had a toneless singing voice and the same last name as Alexander Gray, a grand singer a little short on acting charm. Both Grays turned up in *Spring Is Here* (1930), an adaptation of a Rodgers and Hart show (with all but two of the original songs dropped) that could stand as a textbook case in the pre-*42nd Street* musical: silly, simple middle-class plot, breezy girl– and boyfriends, and dignified theme song (by Harry Warren, Sam Lewis, and Joe Young), "Have a Little Faith in Me." *42nd Street*'s city hustle swept this all away, but until it did, searches for Something led up some odd alleys while refusing to take some highly promising roads. Ethel Merman should have been just what Hollywood needed, and she came along at the right time, turning instant Broadway star in the Gershwins' *Girl Crazy* in 1930 for her *con blasto* vocals, no-fault diction, and all-around gutsy allure. But Merman's early film roles were all supporting parts as scheming molls or screwball friends, and failed to exploit her remarkable instrument. She got onscreen as early as 1930, in the Ed Wynn vehicle *Follow the Leader*, and made a cute short called *Roaming* (1931) as a romantic waif in a medicine show, singing "Shake Well Before Using" and "Hello, My Lover, Goodbye." But Hollywood had no place for a waif with a voice as big as a small country. Merman's stage roles defined her as a brassy dame who cried for men but didn't turn gooey at the sight of them, and her great parts had to be toned down for film to such an extent that Merman was no longer right for them. Except for her Reno Sweeney in *Anything Goes* and her Sally Adams in *Call Me Madam*, all Merman's parts went to others in the film versions—Ann Sothern got *Panama Hattie*, Lucille Ball *DuBarry Was a Lady*, Betty Hutton (replacing Judy Garland) *Annie Get Your Gun*, Rosalind Russell Mama Rose in *Gypsy*. They never gave Merman a chance; as early as 1932, when *Girl Crazy* was filmed, Kitty Kelly was playing what was left of Merman's part, even singing Merman's big tune, "I Got Rhythm."

On the other hand, Paramount tried to mold Lillian Roth, a singer not unlike Merman, into a heroine with suitable Something. It never panned out. In her extremely short French maid's skirt in *The Love Parade*, Roth wears a simper when looking on MacDonald and Chevalier's romance and an assortment of leers when pushing fellow servant

Lupino Lane around—she seems to be two different people. In *Paramount on Parade*, she delivers "Any Time's the Time to Fall in Love" with Buddy Rogers and a chorus, and does achieve an ingenue's melting agreeability, except when the choreography has her (and the girls) bullying Rogers (and the boys). She also sings in a pleasant high register Broadway belters don't normally have access to. So far, Roth is potential. But in *Honey* (1930), as a fun-loving heiress, Roth must look conventionally fetching, which she doesn't, and in *The Vagabond King* she looks rather lost as Huguette, a fun-loving prostitute whose numbers call for a fuller sound than Roth's. Where Merman was left out of the right roles, Roth was cast in the wrong ones.

Marilyn Miller, the epitome of Broadway's idea of ingenue Something, had no casting problems—two of her three film roles were hers from Broadway originals, and the third was more or less suitable. But her famous elfin charm, so lovely from the fifth row across an orchestra pit, dwindled on screen into a crazy grin and, for a dancer, some bizarre ideas on posture. First National's accountants, surveying the take on Miller's three films, must have thought Broadway mad—what was it that Miller was supposed to have? But this trio was hardly the stuff on which a career is built. *Sally* (1929) is a reckless spectacle, *Sunny* (1930) a small musical with almost no music, and *Her Majesty Love* (1931) confusedly European in feeling.

In *Her Majesty Love* Miller plays a waitress at the Berlin Cabaret, courted by playboy heir Ben Lyon. His snobbish relations come between them and Miller has to marry titled roué Leon Erroll before Lyon can win her back—before her wedding night, of course. (A twist ending: his family had made him sign an agreement not to wed Lia Toerreck—Miller—but made no mention of the Baroness von Schwarzdorf, which she has just become.) Director William Dieterle does some nice things pictorially, as when Lyon decides to forget his troubles in Venice and the office papers he scatters in the air turn into the pigeons of St. Mark's Square. But an insistently continental gleam in the proceedings leads one to expect the imminent entrance of Lya de Putti or a consort of *Ländler* dancers. Even W. C. Fields, playing Miller's father, has been affected, almost transformed. In a moustache and attempting a German accent (luckily only in his first few lines), Fields does what he can to lift the tempo, horrifying Lyon's relations by juggling their plates at a fancy dinner and repeatedly referring to Miller's obsequious husband as "Bar*on*" in his characteristic vacant growl. And Miller does have one good moment when she shows up at a banquet of the Lyon clan, tells them off, and overturns their laden table. The lesson is one of Hollywood's favorites: the working class has vitality and only democratically minded plutocrats (like Lyon) are interesting. But the one thing that Miller certainly could do—dance— she never does once in the whole film, except for a routine, nonexhibition tango with Lyon.

Something was elusive, yet some had it to spare. Among the men, Maurice Chevalier easily led the ranks in the romantic class, his Gallic flavor coming across in the midst of the typical American strong, shy silence as a natural hot, emphasized in the roles and songs written for him. He seemed to toss off his love plots to conserve energy for singing: head lolling, lips swimming, arms beating out the rhythm. John Gilbert was not so much hot as flaming; Chevalier brought the great lover syndrome into the perspective of sound, setting his own terms for type and defeating the character code Hollywood was trying to institute. If he hadn't been unique, the studios might have pinned their code on him, for his films were immensely successful, even in the post-1929 musical slump. But he was unique, and after he departed the scene in the mid-1930s, the studios got deeply into genre; one can speak of an Alice Faye musical, a Shirley Temple musical, a Danny Kaye musical, or a Doris Day musical and be reasonably clear on a host of set variables from costuming and costars to quality of score and direction. But the musical's first years, predating the studio codes, offer a welcome diversity in their floundering.

Chevalier, in a way, inspired his own genre at Paramount: risqué romantic comedies with strong scores and delectable leading women. He had first tested for MGM, in Paris, when Irving Thalberg and Norma Shearer caught his act at the Casino de Paris, where he sang some of his numbers in a heavily accented but comprehensible English. Negotiations collapsed, but a few weeks later Paramount chief Jesse Lasky screened the test and closed a deal. Chevalier's debut as a singing junkman in *Innocents of Paris* (1929) put him over in second-rate material, and the much better succeeding films placed him to general satisfaction. The protruding lower lip, the commentative eyes and nose, the explosive consonants, the poise under fire, and the dash in courtship were not only different from what all other screen heroes had, but were more correct, artistically, for what the musical—Paramount's musicals, anyway—could use. Lawrence Tibbett invaded a song, John Boles comforted it. Chevalier attended it as if it were a party in his honor. His "That's the Song of Paree" that opens *Love Me Tonight* captures a wonderful bemusement containing both affection and irritation; his "Mimi" is nothing less than a seduction on promise, and it

☆ *STAGE STARS IN HOLLYWOOD: clockwise from above left: the one true Jolson as* The Jazz Singer; *Guinn Williams confronts the perhaps even truer Fanny Brice in* My Man; *Joe E. Brown at the fights (with Winnie Lightner) in* Hold Everything; *Marilyn Miller (with Lawrence Gray) in* Sunny. *Miller alone repeats a stage role she created.*

won't take long; his "The Poor Apache" spoofs the brutal lover yet respects the need his brutality fulfills; his share in "Love Me Tonight," even after he knows he has won MacDonald, is earnestly playful, almost two different versions of the song in one chorus. So what if he often fell flat of a note or revised a high-running melody to fit his limited range? No one else sang half as well or had as much fun in his parts. In *Paramount on Parade* he crashes into the second verse of "All I Want Is Just One Girl" a whole beat behind the orchestra, but his joy is so telling that one must forgive him. Chevalier is so into it that even when he looks right into the camera and addresses the audience—which he does in several pictures—he retains his character.

He had good luck in his directors, writers, and costars, not least in Jeanette MacDonald, in what might be termed her negligée phase because of the views of her getting into and out of bed that thronged her early operettas. A Broadway veteran but not yet a star, MacDonald got only featured billing with Chevalier, but without him, more prominently billed, she found herself in lackluster events such as the shipwreck farce *Let's Go Native* (1930) or Rudolf Friml's operetta *The Lottery Bride* (1930), with characters named Jilda, Nels, Olaf, and Boris, and MacDonald in blond pigtails. Some of her early films had few or no songs at all and drew only on her comic talents—good enough, but this is a fraction of MacDonald. Her beauty was perfect for the times, a svelte redhead look and an endless supply of pouts and smiles. But her voice was her glory, and it never sounded better than in duet with Chevalier, precisely because the two instruments did not match. His was that of a *diseur*, who delivers everything verbally; hers, that of an opera diva, every word a note. He was earthy, she sumptuous—but he was suave as well, and she had It; they met not at the center, but at the edges. In *The Love Parade* they love at first sight, in *One Hour With You* they are married, in *Love Me Tonight* she at first resists him. So in their last picture together—the first in which her name joined his above the title—he has to resist her. This was *The Merry Widow* (1934), Ernst Lubitsch's last completed musical and a fitting third masterpiece to match his *The Love Parade* and Mamoulian's *Love Me Tonight*. Franz Lehár's original was completely revamped with a new plot and lyrics—new not only compared to Adrian Ross' translation, then traditional on English-speaking stages, but offering entirely new ideas on character. The original premise survives: as the widow controls so much of the property in her Ruritanian homeland, she must quickly be married to a native, the womanizing Captain (formerly Count) Danilo. The ensuing romance takes in not only the original's

Paris but Lubitsch's finely extracted middle Europe. The credits set the tone: a magnifying glass hovers over a map of Europe, trying to locate Marshovia. When it does, the film bursts into a synopsis of the love story in a single moment: Chevalier leads marching Marshovian troops in "Girls, Girls, Girls" as village lasses call out his name in a thrill . . . and a glowering carriage passes by with a veiled woman inside, mourning her late husband. Chevalier and MacDonald cross paths at first, at last, again, forever.

Many feel *The Merry Widow* is their best collaboration, but it turns out that Chevalier wanted Grace Moore as the Widow. He had switched over to MGM from Paramount. So had MacDonald, but Chevalier felt a little uncomfortable with her, finding her temperate demeanor something of a down. (For her part, MacDonald later referred to Chevalier as "the fastest derrière pincher in Hollywood.") Moore's life-loving ways would be more fun to work with; moreover, Chevalier resented the implication that he and MacDonald were a team. But Moore, just back in film after a smashing comeback in *One Night of Love*, wanted top billing and that was that. MGM considered Joan Crawford, Lily Pons, and Vivienne Segal among others, but Thalberg pressed MacDonald on Chevalier. With Ernest Vajda and Samson Raphaelson to handle the book and Gus Kahn and Lorenz Hart to write the new lyrics, MGM had one of the spiffiest entries of the decade. Interestingly, the lyricists suppressed the playful and sardonic strains that respectively distinguished them in musical comedy, adapting themselves to Lubitsch's special view of operetta as fleshly romanticism. Remember, MacDonald, like Chevalier, has self-satire; only later, with Nelson Eddy, was she to become the Iron Butterfly, tense with profile and unyielding in duet. Lubitsch brought out the elf in her. In *The Love Parade*, staring down her matchmaking Cabinet, she pulls up her skirt and, as Lubitsch pulls in with a view of her well-turned left leg, announces, "There's only one other leg like that in the whole of Sylvania." She displays her other leg: ". . . And that's it." But to make the vivacious MacDonald believable, operetta must show also the vulnerable MacDonald. All her best roles do. *The Love Parade* had given us "Dream Lover" to complete MacDonald's file; in *The Merry Widow*, her most ravishing moment is "Tonight Will Teach Me to Forget," drawn from a duet, "Sieh dort den kleinen Pavillon," that is sung in the show by two supporting characters. The melody, updated as a fox trot, ripples with arabesques, and MacDonald sings it with winsome resignation, a lonely widow whose marriage was of such little import that we learn virtually nothing about it. "Today only taught me to regret," she sadly admits, letting a violin solo weep for her, and then prepares to close her "book of dreams . . . and forget." But ho! Not long after, to propulsive variations on Léhar, the widow finds a purpose in life. "Get everything ready!" she tells her maid. "We're going to Paris! Tomorrow! Tomorrow morning! As soon as possible." She tosses her head. "There's a limit," she observes, "to every widow."

Less rich environments than these called for less highly embellished persons. Who would play, say, the lovable day-to-day girl that modern-dress musical comedy requires? The odds-on favorite was Nancy Carroll, a fine actress of healthy sweetness who could sing adequately and dance a little better than that—a natural complement to Buddy Rogers. Carroll alone made the insipid, darkly photographed *Honey* (1930) bearable, as a southern girl who rents her house to a vacationing northern family and poses as the live-in maid, with her brother as butler. (This was the film that tried to make an ingenue of Lillian Roth; with Carroll around, Roth hadn't a chance.) A farce that never hits tempo, *Honey* throws in anything to get a laugh, but on its tiny budget there is little to grab. Jobyna Howland plays Roth's snooty mother, Skeets Gallagher Carroll's brother (to court Roth), Stanley Smith Carroll's vis-à-vis, Harry Green a Jewish hanger-on with little charm, ZaSu Pitts a tearful cook, and little Mitzi Green Pitts' bratty daughter. Most of the film takes place in Carroll's house. Suddenly, director Wesley Ruggles takes us to a black jamboree for the film's one production number, "Sing You Sinners," in which Mitzi displays her precocious vocal heft. This is not enough to enliven a dead film. Even Carroll begins to sink after a while, and one ceases to wonder why her career bogged down in mid-decade. Entries like *Honey* murdered her.

In the early 1930s, both MacDonald and Carroll were Paramount girls, demonstrating the considerable character range of the time; and Marlene Dietrich, a third Paramount contractee, blows that range wide. Dietrich's first six American films, five directed by Joseph von Sternberg and one by Rouben Mamoulian, are in no sense musicals, but most of them feature Dietrich in a few songs and are sometimes thought to have influenced musical staging in their erotic approach to the nightclub specialty. It can't be disputed that Dietrich's famous delivery of "Falling in Love Again" in her last German film (also with von Sternberg), *The Blue Angel*, inspired Bob Fosse and Liza Minnelli in her "Mein Herr" number in *Cabaret*, for if Minnelli gambols on her chair with a mania where Dietrich simply toyed with hers, and if Fosse's Groszlike Kit Kat Club is not as unnerving as von Sternberg's more odiously banal Blue Angel, still the two numbers are much alike.

But how influential could the von Sternberg Dietrich be for the American musical, with her mannish outfits and opaque sexuality? In *Morocco* (1930), Dietrich sings the raunchy waltz "What Am I Bid for My Apples?" as a bored Eve, dispensing forbidden fruit to the customers, tasting a man's champagne and his date's lips, taking a flower from her and tossing it to a bored legionnaire (Gary Cooper). They don't stay bored long. Not even Chevalier and MacDonald burned the screen the way Dietrich did—and in *Blonde Venus* (1932), playing a housewife who returns to the nightclub stage to finance her husband's treatments for radiation poisoning, Dietrich begins "Hot Voodoo" to pounding jungle drums in a gorilla suit. The song was the work of studio writers Ralph Rainger and Sam Coslow, but when Dietrich sings "All night long I don't know wight fwom wong," we are hurled far out of the naive idiom in which, just for example, Coslow wrote the words to *Honey*'s "Sing You Sinners."

Dietrich was billed as "the woman all women want to see," if only to learn what stupendously meticulous lighting can do for what was already a once-in-a-lifetime face. The musical sequences in her film were not, in the end, influential; no musical could contain such fatal hedonism. Dietrich is useful here in pointing up the film musical's sensual limitations: it moved from MacDonaldlike fairy princesses with resilient but not unchartable libidos to next-door sweethearts like Nancy Carroll. That left a lot of room, but it was as far as the musical could go. Later, gathering Alice Faye, Betty Grable, Deanna Durbin, and Judy Garland at its center, it would not go even that far.

The men had more latitude, as they did in the culture at the time, especially the comedians, who could take or leave the otherwise obligatory love plot. Jack Oakie actually seemed happier when he didn't get the girl, and Joe E. Brown, a large-mouthed acrobat whose films reveled in athletic settings (he had been a baseball player in a former life) in which Brown would be mistaken for a champion or otherwise lured into getting himself half killed, screamed and yelled more naturally than he kissed. When Brown "stole" Bert Lahr's Broadway part in the adaptation of *Hold Everything* (1930), he drew heavy fire, mainly from Lahr, but in truth this role of a punchy boxer was right up Brown's roller coaster—though giving him Winnie Lightner to play the romance to only underlined Hollywood's confusion as to how best to cast essentially comic personalities.

Eddie Cantor's vehicles institutionalized the comic musical better than those of other comics, not least because Cantor's were among the few musicals to show a steady profit in the slump years. Short and thin, the excitable type, Cantor fell into Chaplin's underdog-outwits-bullies mode, but in verbal patterns. Cantor was something like an uncluttered Jolson, and like him made no attempt to resist the odd Jewish joke when the mood struck him. But where Jolson sublimated his talmudic wail in blackface bathos, Cantor expressed his more discreetly yet more lightheartedly, moaning and cringing when cornered by his enemies in traps we know he's bound to spring out of, singing of how his girl could do a lot better but loves him anyway, and citing instances of his worthlessness, as when in *Roman Scandals* he loses his position as the emperor's food taster: "I'm a failure. I can't even keep a job as a slave." Strongly in Cantor's favor was his collaboration with the independent producer Samuel Goldwyn, for Goldwyn gave Cantor lavish budgets and smart supporting talent. The six Cantor–Goldwyn films make up a kind of series, all featuring Cantor more or less playing himself in some alien setting, eluding menaces, slipping into blackface, and closing in a wild slapstick melee. At intervals, the irrelevant but superb Goldwyn Girls hang around, have a parade, or dance. Cantor's rolling eyes and flibberty hands, clapping at the merest scent of terror or joy, counted among the least irritating of all comedians' mannerisms, and the similarity of one film to another didn't seem to hurt them. In *Whoopee!* (1930) he is Henry Williams, out west for a rest cure; in *Palmy Days* (1931) his Eddie Simpson is plagued by Charlotte Greenwood and hired thugs; in *The Kid From Spain* (1932) Eddie Williams flees a gang of bank robbers south of the border; *Roman Scandals* (1933) puts yet another Eddie, dreaming, in old Rome and wakes him with a blow on the head during a mad chariot race; *Kid Millions* (1934) is Eddie Wilson, Jr., an heir at loose ends in Egypt and back home opening up a mammoth ice-cream parlor in an inserted color sequence dominated by Cantor's extremely green top hat; and *Strike Me Pink* (1936) closed the set with Eddie Pink running an amusement park, getting stuck high up in a Ferris wheel, and eluding gangsters disguised as Keystone Kops.* Throughout, Goldwyn's thriftless approach to moviemaking kept the decor eye-filling, the material top-notch, and the performers worthy of the material. But it was Cantor that made it go with his vivid hysteria and likeable horniness (some of

---

*Cantor took the serviceable format with him when he moved to Twentieth Century-Fox for *Ali Baba Goes to Town* (1937): dream adventure in a dangerous place (ancient Araby), harem girls, blackface number ("Swing Is Here to Sway"), Jewish jokes, references to contemporary politics, and climactic melee (with Cantor on flying carpet).

the lyrics he sang count among the most suggestive of the day). By 1934 he was the highest-paid actor in films, earning $150,000 plus percentage points that took him to $270,000 for a single film.

Whoopee! stands out from the others because it was very closely based on a stage show, a smash Ziegfeld special that might have run as long as Cantor was willing to play it, had the producer, strapped again, not sold the property to Goldwyn, who promptly closed it and readied the cameras. For once, most of the show's cast replayed their Broadway roles; of the leads, only the ingenue, Eleanor Hunt, was new, and even she had been in the show, in the chorus. Ziegfeld himself co-produced with Goldwyn, making *Whoopee!* a historical document as a transcription of the Ziegfeld style—one of the most formative in American theatre. One thing Goldwyn and Ziegfeld had in common was big spending. An expensive film musical cost about $250,000 in 1930, but Goldwyn laid out a million, and it shows, especially in the detailed dance numbers, staged by Busby Berkeley in his first screen assignment. Feeling his way, Berkeley tries out a few of the overhead shots, the symmetrical groupings, and the slow pan of the chorus line, face upon face, that he would perfect a few years later at Warner Brothers. But mainly he had all he could do working out a cinematic replica of the complex rhythmic push he was noted for on Broadway. The Goldwyn Girls were not only dancers, but showgirls who looked fine just standing there beaming. This is where Ziegfeld came in, with his elegant promenade routines that nobody else ever got right.

Good as *Whoopee!* was on stage, some felt the film was better. Goldwyn shot in color, for one thing, and no real-life color show was ever as much fun as two-strip Technicolor. The story was tightened and the score actually improved, Walter Donaldson and Gus Kahn's originals (including "Makin' Whoopee") joined by some new gems including their own ebullient "My Baby Just Cares for Me" and the comic torch song "A Girl Friend of a Boy Friend of Mine" and Nacio Herb Brown and Edward Eliscu's "I'll Still Belong to You." With Betty Grable leading the Goldwyn Girls in a rip-roaring opening number, Ethel Shutta (in her only feature film) launching "Stetson," a hat number with much Berkeleyesque arrangements of the girls' white cowboy hats, and a better-than-average run of choral settings for wedding and Indian scenes, *Whoopee!* is a musical in its fullest sense, its only drawback being the poor quality of the sound, which makes the lyrics of the first number unintelligible even on repeated hearings. However, George Olsen and his band, another holdover from the Broadway

Whoopee!, came through most effectively with some of the most virtuoso playing ever recorded. Too many musicals went in for large orchestrations which, when fed into the track, came out all highs and lows, woefully depleted of body. Olsen's smaller group has an insane immediacy, its rampaging saxophone and savage banjo right in keeping with Cantor's nerve-wracked craziness.

What is most amusing about the star-comic vehicle is the utter seriousness with which the lovers and villains go about the plot business in the face of the top banana's constant immaterial tricks. They seem not to "get" him, as if they were frozen senseless during his lines, like the characters in *Strange Interlude* during the interior monologues. Cantor is locked into *Whoopee!*'s action to a certain degree, as he helps a young couple (she white and he Indian) when the girl is about to be married to the local sheriff, and thus gets into trouble with the neighboring he-men. Yet Cantor plays around the story as well as in it, and sometimes drops all pretense of character, as when the heroine breathlessly tells Cantor that she and the Indian are going to elope and entrain east for their honeymoon. Cantor immediately chimes in—on a tangent: "Honeymoon! That reminds me. You know, my sister's husband wanted to take her to Florida on their honeymoon, but she's been to Florida, so she sent a girlfriend. Ha-ha, ha-*ha!*"

Truth to tell, these ad lib-like digressions had been holding the American musical back artistically for decades. If we don't take Cantor's character seriously—and how can we, when he doesn't?—then neither we nor the authors take the story seriously. So *Whoopee!* is resolved in nonsense: (1) the Indian turns out to have been a white foundling raised by Indians, which removes all objections to the marriage, and (2) Cantor decides, for absolutely no reason, to cease resisting his amorous battleaxe nurse Shutta and marry her. Yet, idle as the story is, Cantor's character does leave an impression: he is the little guy who tames a boisterous world with subterfuge. If the plot is an excuse for bits, the bits are choice, as when Cantor, masquerading as a singing cook, is ordered to prove his identity to a menacing posse. "Go on," snarls the heavy. "Let's hear ya. Now!" And with scarcely a breath, Cantor pours himself into "My Baby Just Cares for Me," Olsen's combo pointing up his anxiety with syncopated brass notes bumped in just after the downbeat of each phrase. Is Cantor really anxious? The character should be, but this is a big star number, and Cantor gives it all it needs as fun, not illumination. In the second chorus, accompanied by a percussively swinging two-piano solo, Cantor elaborates on the theme, asserting, in a Charleston rhythm, "My baby don't care for Lawrence Tibbetts." Why? "She'd rather have me around to *kibbitz.*" What baby? Surely not Shutta. And who, outside of a few New Yorkers, knew what *kibbitz* meant? No matter. Jolson helped Cantor instill in film the free-and-easy Broadway approach to plot, and it held on.

The personalities useful to the musical were a varied lot. But so were the musical forms themselves—Lubitschian operetta and heavy-handed operetta, collegiates and backstagers, star-comic farces and slightly comic romances all called for different voices, looks, movement. There was room for Chevalier and Cantor and Buddy Rogers, for Nancy Carroll and Jeanette MacDonald. But already, performers of undeniable talent were being found wrong by type or at best of subsidiary possibilities: Fanny Brice, Winnie Lightner, Lillian Roth, Ethel Merman, Bernice Claire, Evelyn Laye, Charlotte Greenwood, Gertrude Lawrence, Ramon Novarro, Rudy Vallee, Alexander Gray, Jack Whiting, Paul Gregory, and Ted Lewis. Whether they had been overexposed, cast in the wrong parts, defeated by poor writing or direction, or victimized by the public's impatience with musicals in the very early 1930s, it was all the same to producers. Either you clicked or you thudded. And the producers added a corollary to the rule: whoever clicked should be succeeded by more like him or her. No one could follow Chevalier or Cantor or Jolson. But eventually the certain Something was settled on in such contract players as Alice Faye, Betty Grable, Deanna Durbin, Bing Crosby, Dennis Morgan, and Howard Keel—people of popularity and impact but chosen for kinds of go-everywhere, mid-American charm that would cause no offense. No American hero was allowed to do what Chevalier did. He was foreign; they're supposed to be quaint when they're sexy. No American heroine was supposed to express her lighter side with Fanny Brice's daffiness; you can't make love to a lampoon.

The sifting period is over. Art is transformation, and transformation feeds on idiosyncrasy. But the studios will as much as possible consolidate a series of genres around Something as often chosen for its lack of idiosyncrasy as for its talent. Before *42nd Street,* musicals were conceived in chaos, but they were rich in spontaneity. From now on, many of them will come forth with a touch of the assembly line about them.

☆ 5 ☆
The Texture of
Popular Music

THE CLOSEST CONNECTION between film and stage musicals lay in their songs, as Tin Pan Alley (meaning the community, bylaws, traditions, and economics of the American songwriting industry) supplied composers and lyricists for both mediums. Almost all the major Broadway songwriters worked in Hollywood in the 1930s on at least one project, and in later years a few of Hollywood's regulars moved to Broadway (notably Frank Loesser and Jule Styne). Then, too, the constant filming of stage shows kept the two schools in tune.

But two schools they were, separated by aesthetic imperatives while creating for the same national audience. Some songs "feel" theatre, others feel Hollywood, and still others could belong to either—Harold Arlen and E. Y. Harburg's "It's Only a Paper Moon,"* for instance, which actually fills all the above conditions. It was written for a non-musical play, Ben Hecht and Gene Fowler's *The Great Magoo*, in 1932, but did not find an audience until it was used in the film *Take a Chance* a year later. On first hearing, it has the artless appeal of a movie ballad. But on investigation it shows the sophisticated craftsmanship normally associated with Broadway, especially in Arlen's incisively compressed melody.

Was the Hollywood score simple where the Broadway score was wily? It was in some ways. For one thing, it had fewer numbers, generally four or five to Broadway's twelve or fourteen. For another, Holly-

---

*Billy Rose's name appears on the song's byline, but historians have questioned his contribution.

66 ☆

wood feared contextual plot or character songs, always hoping for hit tunes that transferred effortlessly to radio or recordings. Someone like Irving Berlin should have made the most comfortable transition from Broadway to Hollywood by virtue of his ease in all-purpose pop—yet Berlin's earliest efforts were not his best. Neither *Hallelujah* nor *Mammy* seems to have inspired him; only the title song in *Puttin' on the Ritz* (1929), a backstager featuring the extremely ill-received Harry Richman, suggested the great Berlin who put individual bite into conventional pop structures. Not till he wrote *Top Hat* (1935) for Fred Astaire and Ginger Rogers was Berlin in fettle. *Top Hat's* five songs float on the film's dressy style with a chic that never loses its roots on earth—exactly the tone that the Astaire–Rogers films purvey. "Cheek to Cheek" is an especially long-lined ballad with a main phrase that strains upward and glides down and a release (the middle section) that screams for motion. "Dance with me!" Astaire begs; and it is this same section that prompts the most athletic moment in the dance that immediately follows. As on Broadway, Berlin is writing for the work, for the people in it. "Isn't This a Lovely Day (to be caught in the rain)?" is as confidently persuasive as Astaire always is when courting Rogers, "The Piccolino" grins and preens because the love plot is running smoothly, and "Top Hat, White Tie, and Tails" might well have served as the theme song of the whole Astaire–Rogers era. Most interesting of all is "No Strings," *Top Hat's* first number, which trips into song literally in mid-phrase. "No yens, no yearning," Astaire tells Edward Everett Horton about himself, "no strings and no connections," and suddenly he's singing "no ties to my affections . . ."

George and Ira Gershwin, too, failed to make film work for them at first, though their score for *Delicious* (1931), another Gaynor–Farrell romance, did serve to introduce George's *Second Rhapsody,* a kind of sequel to the *Rhapsody in Blue,* meant to accompany Scottish waif Gaynor's walking tour of Manhattan but cut to a few minutes in final editing. Like Berlin, the Gershwins came through in an Astaire–Rogers item, *Shall We Dance?* (1937), extrapolating the moods of boy-meets-girl in "Beginner's Luck" (the meeting), "Let's Call the Whole Thing Off" (mock trouble), "They Can't Take That Away From Me" (real trouble), and "Shall We Dance" (the getting).

Some of Broadway's most adept songwriters never found a place in film. Sigmund Romberg and Rudolf Friml bombed out with their original scores and saw their strongest Broadway efforts reduced to a few numbers in the MacDonald–Eddy adaptations. But one Broadway songwriter found Hollywood so congenial that he gave up songwriting. This was B. G. DeSylva, the "idea" man in DeSylva, Brown, and Henderson, who turned producer at Fox and Paramount, leaving his partners without a foundation.

Of them all, Richard Rodgers and Lorenz Hart must have had the most fun in Hollywood, for they alone carried out experiments that rivaled Broadway at its most audacious. Their first original film score, for *The Hot Heiress* (1931), opens with construction worker Ben Lyon singing, "A girl can love an actor, a lawyer, or contractor, but nobody loves a riveter but his mother." Somebody loves him—heiress Ona Munson, who lives in the building next to his site. As his work proceeds from floor to floor, she moves up from flat to flat to keep him in view, and strikes the democratic chord by singing one chorus of "Like Ordinary People Do" in a takeoff on a ritzy accent. There are only three songs, but each makes its point. In "You're the Cats," she wonders what makes him so irresistible. "You're unconventional, and I'm very glad," she says. "No, I'm American," he answers; "so's my ma and dad."

Rodgers and Hart were unconventional, not at first in their subjects so much as in the odd combination of Hart's savvy wit and Rodgers' even-lined, sentimental tunes. This interior contradiction set them apart from others; perhaps that was why Hollywood let them do such bizarre things—such as composing the *Love Me Tonight* score before the script was written (no wonder: the songs *are* the script). They could be conventional, too. Like many of their colleagues, they appeared in a short to showcase their stuff, and as *Masters of Melody* (1929) sketch out the ideas that gave birth to three hits, letting singers deliver the songs. ("The Girl Friend" is murdered by two of the worst performers ever, who also leave out the no-no word in the line, "Hell, the girl's ideal.") But hits were not on the Rodgers–Hart mind necessarily, and with the invention of their "rhythmic dialogue"—rhymed passages delivered as speech in time to music—they made it difficult for the average ear to follow the shape of their musical sequences. In *Love Me Tonight* they used it sparingly, mainly in a doctor's examination of despondent Jeanette MacDonald; presumably Rouben Mamoulian contributed to this collaboration of speaking, singing, accompaniment, and sound effects, for little operas were his thing. MacDonald is a widow. The doctor asks her, "Were you very happy with your spouse?" "He was the son of a noble house," she replies. "It was the happiness of great peace." Now we see why. To the strains of Mendelssohn's sappy "Spring Song" MacDonald presents a photograph of her late husband. Not only does he look repulsive—he *sounds* it: Mendelssohn goes sour as we look and the tune staggers down into the bassoon like a drunk.

In the same year, 1932, Rodgers and Hart extended the rhythmic dialogue technique in *The Phantom President*, George M. Cohan's talkie debut in a double role as a stodgy candidate and the medicine-show salesman who impersonates him during the campaign. Many critics were reminded of the Gershwin stage musical *Of Thee I Sing* of the year before, because it treated the same general subject similarly, pushing beyond the borders of the AABA pop song form to raise up whole scenes in music. The structure was operatic, but the sound style was musical comedy. This marked a terrific breakthrough for the American musical—as Walt Disney pointed out by implication in his cartoon short *The Three Little Pigs* (1933), which takes the form of a one-act opera: sung throughout. At the same time, Rodgers and Hart also leaped the verge, playing about half of *Hallelujah, I'm a Bum* (1933) in rhythmic dialogue.*

Hallelujah, I'm a Bum is a curious item. It's a Depression tale, set almost entirely among the citizenry of Central Park, hoboes with a home. It's also a Jolson tale, though here he is not protected by his usual shtick, and never even gets a real Number in the Jolson style. It's surprising that he did the film at all, for he liked confrontational entertainment wherein the audience either loves you or hates you—few spectators knew what to make of this tale of a tramp who falls in love with the mayor's girlfriend when she gets amnesia and has to give her up when she comes out of it. Not only is the story unusual, but the treatment keeps promising tunes that it delivers only once, in the ballad "You Are Too Beautiful," which Jolson renders with what is for him astonishingly good taste. Perhaps he felt defeated by the continually blown opportunities to implant the music in the public's lazy ear. The wonderful "I Gotta Get Back to New York" isn't heard even once straight through, and a jazzily lyrical melody, "I'd Do It Again," makes more of an effect when played instrumentally in the opening credits than it does in the action—because it is so well integrated into the action that one hardly notices it. Moreover, the most dramatic scenes, normally the ones set to music in a musical, are played in plain speech. It is the in-between incidentals that are sung. Hart and his co-librettist S. N. Behrman did a splendid job in characterizing Bumper

---

*Actually, Sigmund Romberg and Oscar Hammerstein wrote a film opera as early as 1931 in *Children of Dreams*, the action carried through in song and accompanied dialogue. A quick failure, the movie had little discernible influence.

(Jolson), the irresponsible mayor (Frank Morgan), the girl (Madge Evans), Bumper's black sidekick Acorn (Edgar Connor), the Communist sanitation man Egghead (Harry Langdon), and the smaller parts (Rodgers and Hart each appear in a walk-on), but while the roles are clear, the musical passages aren't, not on first hearing. The authors make a tour de force of a scene in which Bumper finds a purse with a thousand-dollar bill in it ("the aristocratic rag," sneers Egghead, "of a plutocratic hag"), but who would attend this film the two or three times it takes to catch all the rhymes and absorb the volatile flow of melody?

Composer Vincent Youmans had less provocative notions about what comprises a film score; he also had the unpleasant experience of seeing his *Great Day!*, a Joan Crawford vehicle, closed down by MGM after ten days' shooting in 1930. Three of his shows, including *No, No, Nanette* and *Hit the Deck*, became films that year, but his first original score came in 1933, for *Flying Down to Rio*, the film in which Fred Astaire and Ginger Rogers were first teamed up. Youmans was careful. He sat down and wrote four very first-rate examples of pop prototypes. With no established Astaire–Rogers ambience to worry about, Youmans and his lyricists Gus Kahn and Edward Eliscu wrote outside of any characterological reference. "Music Makes Me (do the things I never should do)" is upbeat and syncopated, the sort of thing hundreds of belters might sing with a band (as Rogers does here). The "Carioca" is another of the Latin dances that were trying to sweep the country as of Roosevelt's Good Neighbor Policy. "Orchids in the Moonlight" tells of tango in the minor key, with a major-key middle section of slithering harmonies. And the title song would have been the theme song, done to death, only a few years before.

Youmans was a tricky composer when he wanted to be, and he builds "Flying Down to Rio" out of a single phrase varied with an intent rhythmic drive that makes it a natural for a big dance number. As it happens, however, choreographer Dave Gould made the "Carioca" the big floor number. "Flying Down to Rio," sung by Astaire, accompanies an aerial ballet of girls on planes, the machines themselves doing what "dancing" there is and the girls doing little more than hanging on. There is some movement—wing-walking and a few kicks—and at one point a girl falls off a wing and is caught on a plane below—*very* realistic in effect, though the whole business was filmed on planes suspended a few feet off the ground and the horizon and terrain added through back projections of Rio de Janiero and, yes, Malibu Beach.

Are four songs a musical? Even four as good as these, counting lengthy "Carioca" dancing and Astaire's tap reprise of "Music Makes Me"? Rodgers and Hart's Chevalier–MacDonald operetta *Love Me Tonight* had nine numbers, and this seems a more comfortable proportion, especially because they are more necessary to the action than Youmans' *Flying Down to Rio* quartet. Rodgers and Hart are lithe where Youmans is effusive. Cole Porter, too, was lithe. On the coast he could not employ the horny double meanings of his Broadway lyrics (most of them sorrowful gay *mots* masquerading as carefree hedonism), especially after the Production Code clamped down in 1934. But he could spend freely of his musical eroticism, always looking for the odd note or a chromatic run cut into the heart of a tune to bring out the beast in love. Porter got to Hollywood early, in *The Battle of Paris* (1929), the flop that ruined Gertrude Lawrence's hopes of a career in Hollywood musicals; at least Lawrence did manage to get in on one of Porter's more suggestive lyrics, "They All Fall in Love."

In the late 1930s, Porter wrote his first full-length film scores, and like Gershwin and Rodgers showed how much spryer Tin Pan Alley's eastern office could sound compared to the midcult approach of the western branch. Hollywood teams often wrote songs without knowing much about a film. The Broadway bunch wrote for story. *Born to Dance* (1936) and *Rosalie* (1937) were dancing musicals starring Eleanor Powell, so Porter wrote her highly rhythmic "up" tunes that cull their energy from her stunning tap. *Born to Dance* gives her "Rap-Tap on Wood," a jiver whose melodic kernel repeats itself obsessively as a tap routine might; *Rosalie*'s "I've a Strange New Rhythm in My Heart" locks that strange rhythm into its tune, cross-metered from fox trot to waltz and back again. Broadway people are also attuned to *styles* of pop. *Born to Dance*, with sailors and chorus girls in its cast, calls for modern spunk—"Hey, Babe, Hey" and "Swingin' the Jinx Away." *Rosalie*, a modern-dress operetta about a West Point cadet (Nelson Eddy) in love with the Princess of Romanza (Powell), calls for a savor of middle Europe—"Spring Love Is in the Air," assigned to Ilona Massey, who has more voice than Powell as well as an amusing Graustarkian accent, and who looks neat in the company of balalaikas, gypsy fiddles, and dirndl dancers.

Porter is trying to meet Hollywood on its terms, it seems. *Rosalie* has a title song, which Eddy uses, along with "M'appari" (from *Martha*), to serenade Powell outside her Vassar dormitory, and Porter worked especially hard on it, turning out some half-dozen versions before he hit on the right one. How right is it, though? The melody is jovially antique, almost a satire on banality, and it sounds great on Eddy. But the words suggest Porter's embarrassment—"I date, I suppose"—rather than the character's confident virility. So Porter remains Porter, hating love because he can't find it, yet needing to believe in it because what else is there?* Accordingly, Virginia Bruce delivers "I've Got You Under My Skin" in *Born to Dance* and in *Rosalie* Eddy tries "In the Still of the Night," and a haunting waltz called "Close" (written for *Rosalie* but used only in underscoring) tells of a kiss "so soft, so sweet, so warm." Hollywood, however, is sloppy about style, and fills out Porter's *Rosalie* score with filchings from Sousa, Borodin, and Chaikofsky (the second movement of the "Pathétique" Symphony—which oddly bears a slight resemblance to the first phrase of "I've a Strange New Rhythm in My Heart").

Integrity of style is essential to the Broadway score, incidental in film. As far back as Gilbert and Sullivan and Offenbach, musical comedy has reveled in parody, and ersatz recreations abound, sometimes to set time and place and sometimes for satire's sake. Victor Herbert found ragtime takeoffs and military marches indispensable; Romberg and Friml were always faking locale melodically. Broadway composers introduced this practice into film, as in Irving Berlin's "Waiting at the End of the Road" in *Hallelujah*, Walter Donaldson's Indian pastiche in *Whoopee,* or Romberg's Johann Straussian "You Will Remember Vienna" in *Viennese Nights.* By the late 1930s, the imitations grew prankish, and whoever arranged the dance music in *Born to Dance* developed Eleanor Powell's big turn after "Easy to Love" into a balletlike affair that keeps sounding like certain pensive moments of "The Dance of the Hours" from Ponchielli's *La Gioconda* until at last it bursts into a whirlwind can-can that combines Porter's tune with Ponchielli's orchestration. Hot dog!

Though the Broadway émigrés outclassed the Hollywood regulars, most of these came from the east, too: they simply weren't well-known. Nacio Herb Brown and Arthur Freed were a rare team for their experience logged in west coast theatre circuits, but they helped set the style for Hollywood film songs with as little rarity in them as possible. Brown's harmonies favor the simplistic and Freed's lyrics go for the easy rhyme. Such a tune as "You Were Meant for Me," the love song in *The Broadway Melody*, derives its strength from simple

---

*Porter wrote one of his most honest, even autobiographical songs in "I Know It's Not Meant For Me," for *Rosalie*. It would have been Ray Bolger's solo spot, but was cut from the score during production.

repetition, and the title song has nothing but an emphatic final line ("That's the *Broad*-way *mel*-o-(bum-bum)-*dy*!") to paint it bold. The only interesting item in the whole score is "The Wedding of the Painted Doll," mainly because the melody jitters back and forth from major to minor in a jumpy vocal line suggestive of dancing puppets. Anyway, the "Painted Doll" number is the highlight of *The Broadway Melody* for a number of reasons—the oddball xylophone in its orchestration; the important first use of color in a sound feature; the careful attempt to root the visuals on a literal Broadway stage while doing things that only Hollywood's sound stages could do, with electrified trap doors and spatial relations; and the effete *tenorino* who sings the number. All this collides perfectly in a scene as weird as it is straightforward: it's inventive, yes, but it's also simple.* Moving on through the years, Brown and Freed could be counted on for novelty numbers like Joan Crawford's "Chant of the Jungle" in *Untamed* (1929) or ballads like "You Are My Lucky Star" from *Broadway Melody of 1936*, both as simple as pie. But the latter has a sweet tang, while the former is rotten with drum-drum and "exotic" flatted notes. Sounding *appropriately* simple is not as easy as it sounds.

But simple—let's say direct—was what Hollywood wanted; *direct* sold sheet music and records in the millions. When the *Fox Movietone Follies* opened in mid-1929 in saturation bookings, it swept the nation with three song hits by Con Conrad, Sidney D. Mitchell, and Archie Gottler: "Breakaway," "Walking With Susie," and "That's You, Baby," pushing some 100,000 sheets and discs. Yet these are almost irritatingly puerile numbers. "Breakaway," another of those "new" dance sensations comprising down on the heels and up on the toes, claims "it's got the snappiest syncopation" yet has little syncopation at all. "Walking With Susie" is cliché melody that stutters for novelty. "That's You, Baby" nauseates with its baby-talk flirtation. But, as William Fox might have pointed out, you can't argue with a bank account.

Despite the fortunes that songwriters made for them, the producers treated their tunesmiths as laborers, expecting hits to be turned out like cut cookies, light, medium, well. And there was something just in this: if the ballads, dance numbers, and comedy songs are all interchangeable, then what difference does it make who writes them? The

---

*Brown and Freed liked the "Painted Doll" so much they rewrote it at least twice—in "The Woman in the Shoe" in *Lord Byron of Broadway* (1929) and "Hot Chocolate Soldiers" in *Hollywood Party* (1934).

☆ *THE BERKELEY EFFECT: top to bottom:*
"The Words Are in My Heart" from Gold Diggers
of 1935 *(fifty girls, fifty hollow pianos, fifty men in*
black moving the pianos from underneath); Rogers
sings "We're in the Money" in pig latin in Gold
Diggers of 1933; *"Lullaby of Broadway" (Powell*
and Shaw, center) in Gold Diggers of 1935.

☆ *THE BERKELEY IMITATION: above,* Warners' Ready, Willing and Able *had Keeler and Shaw but lacked the Berkeley zip, except momentarily in the Whiting–Mercer "Too Marvelous for Words" (Keeler with Lee Dixon); below, MGM's* The Great Ziegfeld: *Ray Bolger leads "You Gotta Pull Strings."*

producers respected fame and thus approached the great Broadway creators with respect, at least in person (and Cole Porter's elegance, backed by an independent fortune, really did impress them). But the producers did not especially respect the work that had prompted the fame, and never thought of a given work as being particularly right for a given team—as for example, on Broadway, Kern and Hammerstein would be right for a Marilyn Miller show or the Gershwins for Fred and Adele Astaire. Nor did Hollywood promote its songwriters in the ads. "Who writes the words and music to all the girly shows?" Dick Powell sings in *Dames*, and tells us: "No one cares and no one knows." For sure—the *Dames* credits don't even bother to spell out the six songwriters' first names.

Richard A. Whiting, a composer who worked with too many different librettists for even the cognoscenti to get his name straight, had versatility—perhaps too much: his autograph is not as easy to pin down as Porter's, Gershwin's, Kern's. His oeuvre as a whole, from 1929 to his death in 1938, has no stylistic distinction, yet individual scores and tunes do. *Monte Carlo*, which Whiting wrote with co-composer W. Franke Harling and lyricist Leo Robin, could have been expanded for Broadway, with its prudent observation of character—trivial ("She'll Love Me and Like It") for MacDonald's odious fiancé, irreverent ("Trimmin' the Women") and sincere ("Give Me a Moment Please") for her vis-á-vis Jack Buchanan, and of course the famous train sequence would be nothing, despite Lubitsch's flying camera, without the driving rhythm of "Beyond the Blue Horizon." Whiting wrote equally well for the salacious Chevalier and the circumspect Buddy Rogers, the lush MacDonald and the squirty Nancy Carroll and the even squirtier Shirley Temple (only once, but it was a long one: "On the Good Ship Lollipop").

Composer Ralph Rainger, who worked mainly at Paramount with Leo Robin, was less story-oriented than Whiting, but like him Rainger disproves the simplicity rule maintained by too many of his colleagues. He, too, worked on a Chevalier film, *A Bedtime Story* (1933), in which Chevalier adopts a foundling whom he calls Monsieur Baby, played winningly by six-month-old Ronald Leroy Overacker, billed as Baby Leroy. Who was stalwart enough to resist Baby Leroy's delightedly arching his back whenever someone picked him up or clutching the edge of his crib in wonder and worry? A popular publicity still showed Baby sucking his bottle in Chevalier's arms, wearing a little copy of Chevalier's boater; this was perhaps the last straw. Still, nobody upstages Chevalier,* and Rainger defended the star with four songs in the official Chevalieresque style. When Chevalier sings, the world watches, but he must sing *his* songs.

Hollywood scores were not only simple, but also failed to engage their stories with context songs. Never, *never* did Hollywood get over its horror of characters singing for purposes of plot—somewhere, there has to be a band, or a microphone, or an audience, or even just a guitar, to reassure the public that of course real-life people don't sing. There were countless exceptions, such as the Astaire–Rogers or Mac-Donald–Eddy series. If you're in love, you'll waltz. But the horror does explain the proliferation of theatre, nightclub, and radio settings.

And this led to a lack of context. Pop songwriters, which is what most of the Hollywood regulars were, suffered institutional pressures to make every song a hit. To do this, they had to express what most people feel but are too inarticulate to say: to generalize. The subjects are banal but the lyrics set up a vernacular poetry and the music enhances the communication. The right mating of words, music, and image—no matter how overworked that image may be—is what gives pop music its stimulation, and explains why so many film scores could be written without the authors' knowing much about the character who would sing them. In film musicals there is always someone who wants, finds, loses, and reclaims romance; there is always a spot for a new dance sensation; there are bands to sing with, a football team to cheer up, a newlyweds' kitchen to cook breakfast in, a magic moon to address; if not, we can fit one in. With no plot songs to write, who needs to know the details of a plot?

Thus, a prolific team such as Harry Revel and Mack Gordon could turn out upwards of a hundred love songs, script unseen. How to make each sound different? Composer Revel bore the brunt of the work, distilling a sense of everyday American sensitivity in his melodies while Gordon plucked his titles out of the colloquial ozone. The Revel–Gordon songs sound like cuttings from conversations: "Never in a Million Years," "It's Swell of You," "Love Thy Neighbor," "May I?," "Stay as Sweet as You Are," "You Say the Sweetest Things." The team appears briefly in *Sitting Pretty*, one of the nine movies that Ginger Rogers made for release in 1933, with Jack Haley and Jack Oakie as

---

*Not long after, W. C. Fields attempted to block Baby Leroy's scene-stealing by feeding him alcohol. "The boy's no trouper," he then said. "Anyone who can't hold his liquor shouldn't drink on the job."

songwriters, Rogers as their fervent supporter, and some very gentle burlesque of the film colony, including one of Thelma Todd's best parts as man-eating star Gloria Duvall. Here, Revel and Gordon test themselves by writing three uptempo love songs, but Revel's harmonically defined vocal lines, which always seem to be pursuing a chord, and Gordon's right-on titles bring them home. "You're Such a Comfort to Me" is a list of clichés ("like a port in a storm," "like honey to a bee"), yet Revel finds something odd to do in the release, and the song works. "Good Morning Glory" suggests the treat of waking up to thoughts of one's boy- or girlfriend. "Did You Ever See a Dream Walking?", the film's hit, pushes simplicity to the brink of emptiness, yet these craftsmen make it sound fresh. Again, it is more directness than simplicity.

Revel was the craftsman, espcially good in leading the main strain of his tunes into an expansive release. If Gordon held to the surface of things, Revel found the idiosyncratic edge in the universal. In an Alice Faye–Don Ameche picture, *You Can't Have Everything* (1937), Gordon lectures the impatient among us in his lyrics to the title song, another of those messages that purport to equalize inequity yet basically support the status quo: "Don't envy neighbors and the fortunes that they get." Revel makes it swing in a long-lined rising phrase that hops at its crest, and then he pulls off a nifty syncopation in the release. "The Loveliness of You" works even better, for here Gordon's ear for natural dialogue glides along with Revel's tricky melodic phraseology in a perfect fit. Speaking of "cheek to cheeking," the singer admits he is not articulate in love talk—"But, unaccustomed as I am to public speaking," his girl's beauty will inspire his tongue. Thus the song contains a self-fulfilling prophecy: she *is* beautiful, so he *can* sing.

Without question, the standout of all the Hollywood songwriters was composer Harry Warren, who worked with a number of lyricists for a number of studios after a few years on Broadway writing revues or very loosely structured book musicals. His was just the background for Hollywood, and Warren, teamed with Al Dubin on the four songs in *42nd Street*, fit right. They worked right through the series of Warners backstagers with Busby Berkeley dance numbers, sometimes being called in to bolster other men's scores when Berkeley found these lacking in big-number potential. Dubin was irreplaceable for the way his lyrics prompted pictures from Berkeley; Warren was irreplaceable because his tunes were so strong. Of all the Hollywood teams, Warren and Dubin caught the most basic images in the most unusual patterns. Few others extrapolated the mixed buoyancy and bitterness of the Depression years as well as they did in two songs from *Gold Diggers of 1933*, the opening "We're in the Money," square-cut and kicky in the major key, and the closing "Remember My Forgotten Man," angular and drooping in the minor.

One can see why Berkeley depended so much on the Warren–Dubin numbers, and why they probably would not have fared as well on Broadway as in film: their songs don't fit a context, but rather invent one. A song like "Lullaby of Broadway" from *Gold Diggers of 1935* is not in the "Broadway Melody" line of smiles and tears in the old show town. This song is more specific, almost a day in the life: activity ("the hip hooray and ballyhoo"), sound ("the rumble of a subway train"), people ("the daffydils who entertain"), and place ("Angelo's and Maxie's"). And while it opens with a jazzy, stepping strain, it does indeed work up to a lullaby. Musicians delight to point out that this most artless of tunes is constructed harmonically on a generous plan: where most pop songs assert a home key, leave it in the release, and return to it for the close, the first half of this song, the Broadway jazz, actually sets up a modulation *into* the home key, which is not established till the second, lullaby, half.

Warren and Dubin could write to order, as in *Go Into Your Dance* (1935), a Jolson film. This was probably Jolson's most autobiographical role, that of an irresponsible Broadway star mixed up with the underworld and in love with Ruby Keeler. Jolson's career had been on the decline for some time and Warners hoped to attract crowds for him by pairing him with his wife, Keeler. Good thinking. But Jolson didn't like to admit that he needed help from anyone, and not only did he refuse to do another film with Keeler, he also hogs the screen in *Go Into Your Dance*. Of the seven songs Warren and Dubin wrote for the film, Jolson takes five of them (plus "Cielito Lindo"), gives one to Helen Morgan as an actress in love with Jolson, and allots another to Keeler and the chorus girls in a nightclub scene but talks through most of it while trying to make time with one of the girls. It's just as well. Morgan's "The Little Things You Used to Do" is so perfect for her that she really takes the stage with it, and Keeler was no singer. She taps like a zealot in "She's a Latin from Manhattan," wherein Jolson unmasks the would-be *flamenca* as "Senorita Donahue," and she makes a lovely entrance down a stairway between rows of men in tails to Jolson's salute in "About a Quarter to Nine." To complete the survey, Warren and Dubin hand over the inevitable "Mammy, I'll Sing

About You" and the cheer-up rouser, "Go Into Your Dance." What's amazing is that the authors tailored the score for Jolson (and Morgan) without betraying their own style.

Is it because they didn't have a style—they and all Hollywood? AS-CAP* ranks Warren seventh in the list of the biggest-selling songwriters, and the specialists parse him for days, yet he is unknown outside the business. Why? Possibly it is because of that tricky simplicity, which kept film scores focused on the center of human universals, away from the peculiar, individual edges that produced, for example, Porter's tortured, Hart's puzzled, Berlin's incurious, or Ira Gershwin's chaste love lyrics on Broadway. Hollywood most certainly did have a style, too tight a one. When Warren and Dubin wrote a love song— and they were the best in the industry—it loved love, period. If you have love, you're cheery; if you've lost it, you're blue. Thus even Warren and Dubin were held back, not from writing great songs, but from testing themselves with the challenge of art. To study Warren's setting of Dubin is to delight in the confidence of an astonishing spontaneity. "About a Quarter to Nine," which simply suggests a man's looking forward to a date, uses a minor key in the verse (the introduction, so to speak) for expectation, blows it open in the main theme, takes a swinging strut in the major, revs up in the marchlike release, and sails straight home. The verbal idea produces the sound, dynamite. But the idea is old and Dubin's lyric thinly spread; only Warren makes it go. This is pop music at its heart, so universal in appeal that it lacks the penetration of individuality. And this universalism is what Hollywood based its dynamic on: a paper moon.

---

*The American Society of Composers, Authors, and Publishers, the major union of the Tin Pan Alley giants.

☆ 6 ☆
The Allure of Genre

$\mathbb{A}$MERICAN FILM is unique in the arts in that it went freelance only after its first fifty years. Until then, except for the films of a few rugged individualists in the early silent days and such self-capitalized auteurs as D. W. Griffith and Douglas Fairbanks, movies were produced not by freely collaborating individuals but in factories—the studios—where executive pressures hampered individuality. The oppression was not consistent. Many distinctive talents were given latitude—directors King Vidor, F. W. Murnau, and Victor Sjöstrom, for instance. Even the stubbornly improvident (but brilliant) Erich von Stroheim got several chances to create till his gamey eroticism made him outlaw. Moreover, even assembly-line production encouraged qualities of diverse character—innocence (*Sunny Side Up*), sophistication (*Love Me Tonight*), aggressiveness (*Puttin' on the Ritz*), earthiness (*42nd Street*), anarchy (*Hallelujah, I'm a Bum*), and ironic downfall (*Applause*).

Still, as flop musicals and—therefore—flop personalities were weeded out in the first years, the studios realized that the musical worked best within certain emotional categories. Each studio defined the categories differently, however, and originality somehow thrived in this environment, as long as it took some form that either created or maintained a profit-making genre of musical. Thus, Jeanette MacDonald moved comfortably into operetta, which already existed; Fred Astaire just as comfortably invented the art deco society-put-on dance musical.

The smash success of *42nd Street* prompted its studio, Warner Brothers, to institute a series of backstagers in which cynical show people find something to believe in: their jobs. Warners favored stories about the working class, about boxing, racing, organized crime, and organized societal brutality, and naturally the studio brought the musical into line as well. The Warners outlook was less political than socio-cultural—Warners writers pointed out inequities in the system without urging partisan solutions. It was the Depression studio, saturated with the feelings of the time and anything but escapist, and it is notable that one of Hollywood's most bitter arraignments of economic injustice was heard in a Warners musical—the "Remember My Forgotten Man" number in *Gold Diggers of 1933.*

If Warners had an opposite, it was Paramount, where escapist fare was an old tradition, not an antidote to the Depression. Paramount was the place where the deftest designers experimented, where Lubitsch, Mamoulian, and von Sternberg worked, continentally droll and extreme. Warners' musicals were bold and their characters raw. Paramount's were witty and prankish. MGM had the biggest stars, but Paramount colored in a broader spectrum, taking in Mae West and Nancy Carroll, Bing Crosby and Maurice Chevalier.

MGM was the gala studio, where more money meant polish. Its workers, from expert to laborer, were well paid and never rushed; this allowed for high gloss in every A-budget feature. Even the B pictures were better produced than some studios' A films. Paramount couldn't have afforded the outlay that MGM spent on its many operettas, and Warners wouldn't have wanted to. And when MGM produced modern-dress musical comedy, it avoided the rooming houses and back alleys of the Warners backstagers, instead haunting the country mansions and flashy nightclubs of the privileged.

William Fox lost control of his studio in 1929, but it hung on in financial chaos until Darryl F. Zanuck, who left Warners in 1933 to form Twentieth Century Pictures, merged with Fox in the middle of the decade. Zanuck was the man whose brainstorm had produced *42nd Street* and revived the moribund musical film, but Twentieth Century-Fox turned out the most formula-oriented musicals, centering on series built around Alice Faye, Shirley Temple, and skater Sonja Henie. Faye's films had a plot—the same one—and were loosely constructed to allow room for vaudeville by dancers and comics. Temple's films were tighter, and Henie's consisted largely of ice. There was little of the proletarian self-belief that marked Warners' output, little of Paramount's verve or MGM's sheen. Fox, more than the others, honored genre above all.

The other major studios released fewer musicals. RKO concentrated on Astaire and Rogers, Universal's thirties releases peaked in its horror cycle turned out by James Whale, Tod Browning, and Karl Freund, and Columbia wasn't interested in musicals. There are exceptions, but it is true that procedures for mass production supplanted the helter-skelter of the early years—and the public apparently preferred to settle down with something steady. Some of these series stand among the most lasting contributions to American art. In the Astaire–Rogers films, Astaire's offhand manipulation of elegance from a non-social viewpoint—his films seem aware of an American class system but Astaire functions outside it—tells us something about the American social outlook. And the Warners backstagers are not only aware of the system but are clearly fighting it from the outside pushing in. The Astaire–Rogers films are backstagers too, in a way, though they deal mainly with the offstage love life of two characters rather than the efforts of a whole cast to get a show on. But the difference points up the two series' very different outlooks. Astaire and Rogers never mention the Depression; they're too busy dancing. The Warners characters are obsessed with the Depression: that's why they dance.

In late 1932, before *42nd Street* had come out, Warners was already working on the second *42nd Street*, *Gold Diggers of 1933*, a remake of *The Gold Diggers of Broadway* which in turn had been a remake of *The Gold Diggers* (1923), a silent with Hope Hampton and Louise Fazenda. All are based on Avery Hopwood's play of 1919, telling of a stuffy aristocrat who attempts to break up his nephew's engagement to a chorus girl. The girl's best friend poses as the woman in the case, the uncle falls for her himself, and all ends well in a double marriage. Hopwood specialized in sentimental stories painted with coy ribaldry, but *Gold Diggers of 1933* took its tone from *42nd Street*. The screenwriters, Erwin Gelsey and James Seymour, liked Hopwood's ersatz erotica as little as they liked his sentimentality, and while they honor true romance they otherwise stick to the blunt realities of hard times on the mean streets. This has to be one of the most honest musicals Hollywood ever produced.

Mervyn LeRoy directed, shooting on an outlay of $300,000 in forty-five days with a team that typifies the Warners thirties backstager: Warren and Dubin writing the songs, Busby Berkeley staging the numbers, and a cast including Joan Blondell, Aline MacMahon, Ruby Keeler, and Ginger Rogers as chorus girls; Dick Powell as the young Boston blueblood involved with Keeler; Warren William as his guardian (brother this time around) who first takes Blondell for the "gold digger" and finally for his wife; fat, ludicrous Guy Kibbee as a Boston lawyer; and deadpan, pop-eyed, buzz-saw-voiced Ned Sparks as a producer. All of them are at their sharpest; they spit out angry jokes and deliver more feeling lines with a hint of the same anger, all the world of money, love, and ambition snapped out in the black and white of success or unemployment.

The film opens in a lavish burst of optimism that dissolves as we watch. Rogers, Blondell, and Keeler lead the Berkeley girls in "We're in the Money" in costumes made of coins, flanked by piles of coins, against a backdrop of huge coins, and waving a line of coins in precise oscillation, all smiles. Rogers gets off one chorus in pig Latin and Berkeley pulls in so close on her that one can almost lick her teeth. But we're not in the money and the movie knows it. The producer has not paid his bills and the number fades out unfinished as the sheriff and his men clomp in to cart away the scenery and costumes, the girls' coins included. "You can at least leave me carfare!" Rogers wails as some oaf yanks off her gilt. The girls' vitality revs up again when Powell decides to back Sparks' show. He's not only rich; he's a songwriter. "I'll cancel my contract with Warren and Dubin!" says Sparks. The show is on, with a part for everyone. MacMahon, the wisecracker of the group, will be the comedienne. "It'll be the funniest thing you ever did," Sparks tells her. MacMahon replies, "Didja ever see me ride a pony?"

As the film proceeds, the show opens and loses our interest—except insofar as it provides the film's three big numbers—and we instead follow the love plots as the girls and Powell conspire to win his brother's approval for his and Keeler's engagement. Then Powell and Keeler lose our interest: Blondell and William dominate the film as they toy with and then genuinely find each other. In the general glow even MacMahon and Kibbee end up as a couple, and we wonder what happened to the gold diggers we were promised. The worst we see is Mac-Mahon stealing milk ("That's all right," she observes grimly; "The farmer stole it from a cow") and Rogers making a play for Kibbee. We do see Blondell and MacMahon tricking the two Bostonians into buying them expensive hats, but this is treated as fair revenge for the two men's snobbishness. Anyone who would stand between Powell and Keeler in a backstager is The Enemy.

The pushing earnestness about The Show that drove *42nd Street* does not dominate *Gold Diggers of 1933*, then, but when it's felt it's wild. Blondell is literally hysterical with relief on the phone as she tells her friends that they all have jobs, and we get another of those last-minute opening-night substitutions when Sparks' aging juvenile comes down with lumbago, and tunesmith Powell is implored to go on for him. Powell refuses—he's still incognito and fears that someone will recognize him if he appears on stage—and MacMahon hammers at him impressively on his obligation to "the kids" who need the work. This changes his mind, of course, and as he is hustled off into costume, MacMahon keys us into Hollywood's admiration for Broadway grit: "He's got nerve. He's regular. He belongs in the show business." Because he shares.

All we see of the show, *Forgotten Melody*, are three numbers that bear no relation to each other*: a risqué scherzo, a romantic idyll, and a stunning Marxist tableau of common-man disillusionment. Just as the numbers in *42nd Street* progressively grew beyond the boundaries of a theatre stage, in *Gold Diggers of 1933* Berkeley disbands any attempt to formulate a theatre style for more than a few minutes at the beginnings and ends of numbers. Hollywood has been criticized for this unreal view of theatre production, but Berkeley and his disciples do not pretend to be filming theatre: they give us the cinematic equivalent of what theatre does. The same imagination and energy ignite both forms, but each employs them differently; with film one must step through the looking glass, not just gaze into it. "I edit in the camera," Berkeley said. His camera doesn't follow his choreography but rather initiates it in overhead holds, fast tracking shots, slow pans. Other directors might use four cameras at once on a dance number, to choose later from the different views. Berkeley used one camera. The way he used it, one is all you need.

"Pettin' in the Park," the first of *Gold Diggers of 1933*'s three big ones, is a "story" number, following flirtations through the four seasons. It starts small, on stage, with a sleek vocal from summer petters Keeler and Powell and Keeler's energetic tap, but soon opens up into an expanse of sound-stage park with lounging couples, policemen, and a sinister baby. (One of Berkeley's most famous quirky bits, the kid was played by a midget, Billy Barty.) As the seasons change, so do the activities, from fall rollerskating to snowball throwing to summer

---

*The Broadway Melody established the rule in backstagers that The Show be a revue rather than a story musical. That way, no one has to work around a plot, set characters, or context songs; in a revue, anything—from solo specialty to big number—goes. Every rule has its exceptions, however, and *On With the Show!*'s onstager, *The Phantom Sweetheart*, has so much in the way of story that if Warners had only filled in the missing scenes it might literally have been staged.

swimming in an art deco pool. Rain sends the girls scurrying into a pavilion, where they undress in silhouette. The baby, grinning in a slicker, pulls up a shade and peeks. The petting, meanwhile, goes on, the boys in raincoats and the girls in armor-plated bathing suits. For the finish, the baby hands Powell a can opener and he sets about "opening" Keeler.

"The Shadow Waltz" takes one onto a more delicate plane. "In the shadows let me come and sing to you," the song begins, and that's about all that occurs. In darkness, girls costumed in stiff, layered white skirts billow around Keeler (in an unconvincing blond wig), all playing white violins. For the climax, Berkeley ascends on his boom to shoot the violins, glowing in neon outline and grouped to form one huge violin, bow and all. Reaching back a few years, Warren rescues the "hesitation waltz," pushed out of fashion by jazz; it sounds an odd note amid the realistic bite of the rest of the film.

The realism runs especially heavy in the finale, "Remember My Forgotten Man." Even now, five decades later, this sequence has terrific impact. It was probably inspired by the desperate march on Washington by the "bonus army" of World War I veterans, tired of waiting for promised benefits in the worst of times, and by Franklin Roosevelt's reference on a radio address to "the forgotten man at the bottom of the economic pyramid," both events of spring 1932. The scene sneaks up on us, for the love plots are still being resolved backstage as assistants knock on dressing-room doors calling for all hands in the "Forgotten Man" number, and Blondell misses her cue. We are still in the theatre, looking straight-on at the stage; at last in place, Blondell lights a bum's cigarette, leans against a lamppost, and launches the number, which passes to a black woman (Etta Moten) and takes in a vignette of a cop hassling the bum till Blondell points out his medal of honor, all this still on stage. Now Berkeley pulls out of physical reality to collect a collage of war and postwar, from heroism on the field to breadlines curling around the block. At the end, Berkeley returns to the stage, showing files of soldiers marching along metalwork ramps and a civilian population arranged along steps that run from wing to wing, with Blondell in the center, all raising their arms in supplication. Commentators have questioned the number's inclusion while praising its power—but it seems that *Forgotten Melody* is supposed to be the kind of show that might contain such a number, despite the frothy atmosphere of "Pettin' in the Park" and "The Shadow Waltz." When Powell first describes the number to Sparks, the producer is thrilled: "That's just what this show's about—the Depression—men marching—marching in the rain—doughnuts and crullers—men marching—jobs—jobs . . . a blue song—no, not a blue song, but a wailing—a wailing . . . the big parade—the big parade of tears. . . ."

Like *42nd Street, Gold Diggers of 1933* thrilled the public and helped ensure a future for backstagers with naturalistic bite, and as Warners had signed Berkeley to a seven-year contract, he continued to complement the tough-talking scripts with his expressionistic whimsey. The third Warners backstager of 1933, *Footlight Parade*, confirmed Berkeley's fondness for matching patterns, fluently metamorphic sets, and panning shots of girl upon girl. With Lloyd Bacon as director and James Seymour working with Manuel Seff on the screenplay, the *42nd Street* style remains sound. James Cagney, in one of his few musical roles, gives it distinction as a Broadway showman thrown out of work by talkies who recovers by producing short stage shows to accompany the films. And what shows! *Footlight Parade*'s first hour concerns the rehearsals and the love plot, involving Cagney and Blondell as his neglected secretary, and each of the last three reels presents a Berkeley special as Cagney's troupe scrambles from theatre to theatre putting on their "prologues." Warren and Dubin again came through: with "Honeymoon Hotel," a story sequence that brings back the fascinatingly unpleasant Billy Barty as a tot who harasses Powell and Keeler, and with "Shanghai Lil," in which an American serviceman seeks and finds his Oriental sweetheart. Cagney himself ends up in the number by accident, shoved onstage in his first-night duds by a soused actor. As before, Berkeley abandons the theatre environment immediately, putting Cagney and company—including an endearingly out-of-place Keeler as Shanghai Lil—through changes of costume and decor for a grand finale of marching troups. *Footlight Parade*'s biggest number is the centerpiece of the trio, "By a Waterfall." This time, the idea came before the song: hundreds of girls frisking in an aquacade. Warren and Dubin were on vacation when Berkeley planned the number, and he introduced a new sound to the series, that of Sammy Fain and Irving Kahal. With the girls diving, splashing, floating, and sliding, with pools, fountains, and spills, and with hydraulic lifts and pumps sending 20,000 gallons of water a minute over the falls, the number represents Berkeley's most extended variation on nothing.

After three Broadway backstagers in a row, Warners felt something new was indicated, so the next in the series, *Wonder Bar* (1934), moved to a Paris nightclub. Old hands Lloyd Bacon, Berkeley, Warren and Dubin, Dick Powell, Guy Kibbee, Hugh Herbert, and Ruth Donnelly held their form, but new recruits Al Jolson, Delores Del Rio, Kay Francis, and Ricardo Cortez supply a change in tone. *Wonder Bar* is a *Grand Hotel* set in Jolson's club, where jealousy prompts Del Rio to stab Cortez. Despite the Production Code, Jolson disposes of the corpse so Del Rio can pair off with Powell. Warren and Dubin provided a haunting theme song with a continental flavor (Powell sings it straight American, however) and of course provisioned Jolson's blackface spot, "Goin' to Heaven on a Mule." Berkeley is at his best in "Don't Say Goodnight," which grows out of Del Rio and Cortez's pas de deux into a staggering geometry of whiteclad dancers and columns (which turn into trees), set off by a Cinderella bit involving a woman's lost slipper. At the height of it all, eight mirrors enclose a circle of dancers, the reflections turning a hundred people into a thousand, the whole shot from an overhead angle so the mirrors can't pick up the camera. The "mule" number has been attacked as racist for its picture of a black heaven out of *The Green Pastures*, with an instant fried-chicken machine and a celestial Cotton Club (plus, for Jolson's sake, a Yiddish newspaper), but the brief shot of Jolson and mule trekking across a thin arched bridge to the fortress of heaven is stupendous.

By this time, the name Berkeley had become a byword of imagistic spectacle, using people as objects and objects as people. Some few doubters noted similarities between his exhibitions and those thrown by dictators in Germany and Italy and called the Berkeley numbers a naive American fascism, with their anonymous multitudes and lock-step precision routines. But no fascist would have raised such pointlessly fanciful parades as Berkeley's. One mother made a stir with a magazine article entitled "I Don't Want My Daughter Growing Up to Be a Human Harp," after seeing the big number in *Fashions of 1934*—in which, indeed, the front of the harp frames were hung with Berkeley girls. But the article was taken as part of the fun rather than as serious dissent, and Berkeley's kaleidoscopes became part of the era's autograph, their fantasy a science-fiction of beauty and their exaggeration a quaint comix.

However. A sameness was creeping into the series. *Dames* was *Gold Diggers of 1934* in all but name—Dick Powell again a songwriter, Keeler again his girl, Blondell and Kibbee as the hustling chorus girl and her mark. Other men were writing the scores, but Berkeley needed the story guides that sparked him in "Shuffle off to Buffalo" and "Pettin' in the Park," and Dubin and Warren were socked in to do the songs for the three big numbers, "I Only Have Eyes for You," "The Girl at the Ironing Board," and the title song. The first is the usual variations on a theme—that Powell sees Keeler everywhere—which lead from girls in Keeler masks to girls forming a Keeler jigsaw puzzle. "The Girl at the Ironing Board," however, is a production number largely using one person: Blondell dances with laundry animated puppet-style. "Dames" is choice Berkeley, girls in black and white bent through a prism of patterns and pictures on the question, "What do you go for? Go see a show for?" At the climax, they fly high to dazzle in close-up. (The scene was shot with the girls starting at camera level and gently being lowered on a wire; the film was then speeded up and run backwards.)

So the numbers stayed inventive; but the plots and characters were tired. *Gold Diggers of 1935*, with Powell again and an amateur charity show and some ridiculous plutocrats for novelty, marked Berkeley's debut as sole director of a film. We finally get our first hardcore gold digger in Glenda Farrell, a stenographer who has snuffbox expert Hugh Herbert sign a love lyric so she can blackmail him with the threat of a breach-of-promise suit. We also get a look at the gold digger's night world in "Lullaby of Broadway," Berkeley's most sensational number. It opens with the face of Wini Shaw singing the tune, a dot approaching from the distance. As her face tilts upside down and she smokes a cigarette, Manhattan shows through her skull. Morning. A lone cop dwarfed by the buildings, coffee in the pot, newspapers in bales, crowds rushing the subway, fancy-dress people staggering home from their parties—and the city is seen at a tilt: alienation, dizziness, drunkenness. We focus on Shaw, a Broadway baby. She hits the sack and after a full day's sleep is up and at 'em. We cut to a huge, empty nightclub with a tiered dance floor. As one Latin couple in white dance, Powell and Shaw watch at a table. Now an entire dancing corps in gray and black stamp in, and the music pulls out under the assault of the tapping. The number treats size and coldness and hysteria as the modes of the city, catching them with a rightness that smashes Hollywood's emotional categories and codes for starry Something. "Come and dance!" the men beg Shaw, their refrain and her answers set right into the melody. She joins them and Powell joins her, but suddenly, with a scream, she plunges off a balcony to her death. As a men's chorus quietly restates the song, the dream runs backwards, the Manhattan skyline dissolving back into Shaw's face and the face slipping back into darkness.

Where did Berkeley get his ideas? Warren and Dubin provided the springboard, but no one knew when the leap into a picture plan might land. With salaries at rock bottom (Powell was getting less than $200 a week at the time of *42nd Street*) and working hours virtually unlimited, Berkeley could rehearse his people for weeks on one number till it was perfect, and then shoot—sometimes in one take. To the executives who pressed him for details in advance, Harry Warren later recalled, Berkeley would give "long-winded explanations in doubletalk . . . He was the bane of the production chiefs. They would come onto his sets and see a hundred girls sitting around doing their knitting while he thought up his ideas."

"Lullaby of Broadway" marked the apex of the Warners backstage series; few of the numbers and none of the films as wholes rivaled what had preceded them. But a uniquely American style had been set in the film musical, one that owed little to the Broadway model. "Lullaby of Broadway" for instance, is pure film and pure Hollywood: visually, in its real-life montage; physically, in its cavernous nightclub; musically, in its seedy populist jive; and ideologically, in its horrified fascination with New York night life. Berkeley went on to such events as *Bright Lights* (1935), a Broadway backstager with Joe E. Brown; *In Caliente* (1935), a nightclubber set in Mexico; *Stage Struck*, more or less the *Gold Diggers of 1936* with Powell, Blondell, Warren William, and a Harold Arlen–E. Y. Harburg score; and *Gold Diggers of 1937*, with Powell and Blondell and one of Berkeley's best numbers, "All's Fair in Love and War," in which whiteclad sexist troops do battle, having made peace in huge rocking chairs.

The Warners backstager was created for the Depression and couldn't outlast it, but when fresh it had tremendous impact. Every studio had to put on its own *42nd Street* in 1933. MGM typically hued its entry, *Dancing Lady*, in starry glow, casting Clark Gable as the showman and Joan Crawford as the chorus girl whose determination to dance takes her from burlesque to a triumphant Broadway debut. This was a David O. Selznick production, and it shows the good taste of the well-meaning Hollywood honcho rather than the guts of a Warners man. We have no trouble believing the Gable–Crawford romance (complicated by Franchot Tone as a playboy who wants to buy Crawford). But New York naturalism is hard to fake and Selznick, who didn't understand or like the musical as a form, seems to have tried to soften the Warners genre. The result is a hybrid at war with itself. Like *42nd Street*, *Dancing Lady* shows us a real New York—we take the A train uptown with Crawford, riding through a tunnel to the bright land of Broadway. Like *42nd Street*, *Dancing Lady* has the ironman director with the hidden heart (Gable even looks like Warner Baxter). But MGM's director Robert Z. Leonard hasn't Lloyd Bacon's sense of pace, and we don't feel Crawford's drive to succeed as strongly as we feel Blondell's drive to stay off the breadline. Unwilling to trust the public to enjoy nonstop seedy Broadway, MGM gazes admiringly on Tone's country mansion and penthouse.

The support is fine—Winnie Lightner as Crawford's roommate, May Robson as Tone's eccentric grandmother, the Three Stooges as backstage help, Fred Astaire in his film debut as Crawford's partner in Gable's show, Nelson Eddy, Robert Benchley, and Gloria Foy as the girl who is callously thrown out of, back into, and out of the lead to make way for, replace, and make definitive way for Crawford. Berkeley made the big number obligatory, and *Dancing Lady* places it near the film's end, just before Crawford dismisses Tone and embraces Gable. As several teams supplied the score, the big number is a patchwork, starting with the lavish "Hi ho! The Gang's All Here," moving to a Bavarian locale for a ripoff of Arthur Schwartz and Howard Dietz' "I Love Louisa" in the stage revue *The Band Wagon,** and then showing an antique minuet, which Eddy interrupts to sing a Rodgers–Hart song, "That's the Rhythm of the Day," a strange item written more for beat than melody. Everyone takes to the beat, the costumes magically turning current and a horse-drawn cab becoming a lush open limousine. As in Berkeley, some of this is stage-possible and some cinematic, as when Crawford and Astaire are transported from "Hi ho" to Bavaria on a flying disc.

Dancing Lady was a huge hit, thanks to its polish. Other imitations of *42nd Street*, however, retained the grime: cheaper. United Artists' *Broadway Thru a Keyhole*, also in 1933, uses Walter Winchell's voice for authentic report, and claims that its story is based on an idea of Winchell's, though it seems drawn from the personal lives of Al Jolson and Ruby Keeler. There is no attempt to duplicate Berkeley's spectacle, but the casting goes for color and diversity in the Warners manner, with Constance Cummings as the shy chorine, Paul Kelly as the gangster who loves her, Russ Colombo as her true love, and Blossom Seeley, Texas Guinan, Eddie Foy, Jr., Gregory Ratoff, and Abe Lyman and his band for Broadway smarts. The dialogue is not as sharp as it needs to be and only Cummings can act. Guinan in particular is

---

*Trivium Footnote no. 3: the beer-and-blondes number is announced as "Let's Go Bavarian" in the film itself but the opening credits call it "In Bavaria."

embarrassing as Tex Kaley, sporting her "Hello, sucker!" and "Give that little girl a great big hand." At one point, she says she weighs 138 pounds. "Stripped?" she is asked. "I don't know," she replies. "The drugstore was pretty crowded." I don't get it. Seeley comes off no better, though she accords with the Warners realism in a last-minute pep talk to Cummings. She begins almost bitterly on a "Why should the show go on?" theme: you work and hope and a day later you're forgotten. The speech seems genuine, but then Cummings' call comes and Seeley is a thrilled comic going for the boff. "The show must go on!" she exults.

Not all the Warnerslike backstagers subscribed to the Warners belief that guts makes a star. Universal's *Moonlight and Pretzels* (1933 again) teaches a youngster that she has no business Going Out There if she lacks training and talent: grit isn't everything. *Moonlight and Pretzels* is the most theatrical of this group, Bobby Connolly's dance numbers more comfortable when aping the stage than aping Berkeley, and Monte Brice and Sig Herzig's script working hard for backstage sassiness. They thought of one thing Warners didn't: the effeminate choreographer, played by Brice himself in beret and gummy grin. But something is very wrong with *Moonlight and Pretzels*—several things, actually; they take turns. One number will be fine, another ghastly. A character will play realistically here, get mannered there. Director Karl Freund had served as cameraman in such classic silents as Murnau's *The Last Laugh* and Lang's *Metropolis* and had directed a superb piece of horror in *The Mummy* a year before *Moonlight and Pretzels*, but his sense of the grotesque does not suit this material, especially in the appalling staging of the title song (another "I Love Louisa" beer garden spinoff) as a pretext for pointless comic violence. It's a big scene, and ruins the film. The plot is acceptable, taking an unknown songwriter (Roger Pryor) to glory as a Broadway producer despite problems of love (with smalltown girl Mary Brian), of temperament (star Lillian Miles), and of money (his backers, including Leo Carillo as Nick, a Greek Gambler, keep selling or sporting away their interest). But the score, by Jay Gorney and E. Y. Harburg, runs limp. Herman Hupfeld, a specialist in crazy novelty songs, bolstered it with "I Gotta Get Up and Go to Work" and "Are You Makin' Any Money?", both presented straight-on in stage style with a few dull overhead shots of girls glumly spinning on a turntable for "I Gotta Get Up" and with Lillian Miles alone before the curtain for "Are You Makin' Any Money?", relying on a repellent grabby-fingers gesture to put it over.

Freund and Connolly get cinematically ambitious only twice, but these scenes save the film. We see Pryor compose "Ah, But Is It Love?" at the piano, speaking admiringly of Beethoven's and Liszt's staying power; the schmaltzy melody is supposed to represent a cross between pop and legit. Miles hates it. She wants jive. Pryor gives her both, and the camera cuts over to a model of the proposed set, which then comes alive with the number. For a finale, Harburg and Gorney offer an uplifting antidote to their "Brother, Can You Spare a Dime?", written the year before for a stage revue: "Dusty Shoes" looks forward to the end of the Troubles with the election of FDR. Something of a commercial for the New Deal, the song begins as Alexander Gray sings it to his fellow tramps around a campfire, and then goes into a review of the twenties boom and crash in newsreel footage as well as a staged production number, culminating in the kind of pageant Harburg loved, everyone jubilant in an implied share-the-wealth apotheosis—Gray, for example, now beams in a business suit, his jutting chin clean shaven and his eyes sighting a braver world.

Where *Moonlight and Pretzels* really defies the mold is in its treatment of ingenue Mary Brian. This is the Ruby Keeler role, pure girl amid the gold diggers, and Brian has the Keeler style, more charm than talent. We have to like Keeler to believe in her, because people with her limited gifts don't become theatre stars (including Keeler, who had to come to Hollywood to make it big). Her distinction in tap is not enough to offset her amateur singing and line delivery; so we are pleasantly surprised when *Moonlight and Pretzels*' Brian, thrust into the star part by her rich *protégeur*, is rejected even by Pryor. "You and I can't make stars," he tells the backer, his hand waving at the audience where life watches art and knows what's real. "The people out there do." Kern and Hammerstein made a point of rebutting the youngster-to-star device in their stage show *Music in the Air*, wherein the youngster is fired at the dress rehearsal and replaced by a pro. Hollywood dutifully kept this in for the film version of *Music in the Air* (1934), and with *Moonlight and Pretzels* it somewhat mitigates the fantasy that camp collectors delight in in these thirties backstagers.

The camp element in all these films is, of course, applied externally by certain of today's moviegoers. Warners' writers used the word "swell" because people used it then, not to raise giggles, and Zanuck made Keeler *42nd Street*'s youngster because she had the sweetness the role calls for. The slang has dated, the Berkeley look has become a cliché, and few people today remember what it was like to live through an apparently bottomless depth of hunger and despair and to have to look for symbolic redemption in art. So this whole backstage series has lost its edge, granted. But to sit through these films today braying like donkeys has more to do with the currently gathering vogue for solipsistic smugness than with anything in the films themselves. Otherwise, how can a form that struck off a universal response fifty years ago have lost all its persuasive potency? It is outmoded—but not inarticulate.

Less interesting but undeniably popular were the films with a radio setting. The public was very used to radio, and enjoyed *seeing* it, for once, in action. Hollywood loathed radio, for it gave the citizenry something (free) to do besides pack the cinemas; but it gave exposure to film singing stars. It has been suggested that studio executives enjoyed picturing the blunders and flukes that supposedly plagued radio, but in fact the radio films tended to look much more benignly upon the airwaves than the backstagers did upon show biz. Paramount ran an annual radio series in the late middle 1930s, known as *The Big Broadcasts*. The original *Big Broadcast* (1932) built itself around an irresponsible radio singer (Bing Crosby, in his first lead) who loses job and girl but is bailed out by heir Stuart Erwin to preside over a "big broadcast" on a national hookup. This served roughly as the form for the later entries: trouble at station, trouble resolved, and a glorious vaudeville finale. Crosby was on hand for *The Big Broadcast of 1936* (1935), this time in a one-song spot; Jack Oakie led the plot scenes as a bankrupt station owner. *The Big Broadcast of 1937* (1936) went all out with Jack Benny, Burns and Allen, Martha Raye, Larry Adler, Benny Goodman and his Orchestra, and Leopold Stokowski and *his*; and *The Big Broadcast of 1938* (1937) offered two ocean liners, W. C. Fields twice (as twin brothers), and Bob Hope and Shirley Ross singing "Thanks for the Memory."

Story-oriented radio musicals had no big broadcast but more consistency. Mike fright was a favorite ruse for pushing plot, as was poking fun at commercials and announcers' oleaginous delivery. Oddly, many of the actors used in these satires were also prominent in radio, which must have put something of a punk on the satire. Dick Powell made his film debut in a featured role playing an asinine radio star in *Blessed Event* (1932), as enthusiastic in his hymn to Shapiro's Shoes as in "How Can You Say No (when all the world is saying yes)?" But he was a sympathetic hero in *Twenty Million Sweethearts* (1934) as a waiter tapped for stardom by agent Pat O'Brien and coached through his nervousness by Ginger Rogers. The film's theme song, Warren and Dubin's "I'll String Along With You," is heard much too often, and Rogers doesn't sing enough, but the lack of pretension is winning. *Wake Up and Live* (1937) was more high powered, tying its tale of a mike-spooked singer around the alleged real-life feud between Walter Winchell and bandleader Ben Bernie and peppering the results with assorted specialty singers, dancers, and comics—"I don't know whether to marry you tomorrow or go to the dentist," barks Ned Sparks to Patsy Kelly, and she replies, "It's a date!" As the singer, Jack Haley creates a sensation when he unknowingly sings baritone velvet into a mike plugged into a radio show. Haley's breathy tenor was dubbed by Buddy Clark, who really does sound terrific, and as Rogers did for Powell in *Twenty Million Sweethearts,* Alice Faye helps Haley assert himself as fame threatens to unnerve him. But *Wake Up and Live* makes a bigger impression for the most basic of reasons: a solid score. Harry Revel and Mack Gordon say the same old things, but with *such* grand ease; Faye's "There's a Lull in My Life" has become one of the classic love ballads, an "Un bel dì" of the swing era in that singers' reputations are made or shredded in it.

Then there was the college musical, made entirely of quartets, student bands, and devout dancers. The film musical pursued youth and candor, and academe promised a great deal of it: students have no grandeur, no bitterness, and, in the Hollywood version, they spend so little time in classes that there's plenty of time for flirting, proms, and football. Then, too, there are fine opportunities for dizzy deans, nutty professors, perhaps a college widow. Paramount's *College Swing* (1938) has more staff in it than students. Betty Grable (the *New York Times* said "She shags through the entire action"), Ben Blue, Florence George, and John Payne were still young enough to matriculate at a median age of about thirty-two, but Martha Raye (as "Professor of Applied Romance"), Bob Hope, Burns and Allen, Jackie Coogan, and Edward Everett Horton got top billing as the academics.

Of all the college musicals, Twentieth Century-Fox's *Pigskin Parade* (1936) may be the most typical, though it's hard to single out one film when they are all so alike. Here, the big game pits a small Texas school against Yale through some mistake; Jack Haley is the ineffective coach, Patsy Kelly his wife who accidentally incapacitates the star player with a bar bell, Stuart Erwin the new star plucked from the watermelon patches of Arkansas, Judy Garland his sister Sairy who has renamed herself Murine ("I got it off'n a bottle"), Anthony (later Tony) Martin the campus bandleader, and Betty Grable, Johnny Downs, Dixie Dunbar, and the Yacht Club Boys fill in as students.

Never was a campus so innocent, though the Yacht Club Boys in "Down With Everything" call themselves the "Anti-super-boopa-doopa-commu-bolsha radicals," turn a grind into a maniac, and send him off to heave a brick through a bank window. Otherwise, all is an American fairyland where an obscure Texas college that builds its football hopes on wimpy Erwin can actually beat Yale, and where everybody majors in romance. Launching the verse to "You're Slightly Terrific," Martin informs us that movies teach greater truths than any college can, and near the end Garland presents the movies' greatest truth at halftime of the big game in "It's Love I'm After (I don't want to be a millionaire)."

Garland, fourteen years old, out on loan from MGM (which didn't know what to do with her), and billed ninth, is wonderful, raw exuberance. She looks dowdy till she acclimatizes herself to undergraduate life, and then suddenly blossoms. No: explodes. The train ready to leave Texas for New Haven and the scene packed with wellwishers, everybody screams for a song. Garland momentarily unveils the trembly insecurity that would survive her in legend. "I've got a song," she says. "Can I sing it?" "Would it make you happy, honey?" she is asked; she knows she's in and beams, "Oh, it sure would!" and belts out "The Texas Tornado," her ease and power spreading the voice out in sound waves thick enough to see. *Pigskin Parade* didn't break any house records, but it told MGM what to do with Judy Garland.

Unlike the backstage, radio, and college musicals, operetta had little comedy, few leads, and a lot of pretension. As genres go, this was the tricky one: expensive, temperamental, and too quaintly non-American. So few costume operettas succeeded in the first sound years that the form had been almost discontinued, but Columbia reorganized the movement with *One Night of Love* (1934), Grace Moore's comeback as an American girl who goes to Europe to learn her craft and falls in love with her impresario (Tullio Carminati). Moore had learned from her earlier film failures, setting a new personal style for operetta on Broadway in *The DuBarry*, an engagement that she apparently promoted specifically so that Hollywood could rediscover her. Columbia's standing in the industry placed it somewhere between the major studios and the quickie garages of Gower Gulch (known as Poverty Row), and *One Night of Love* is a small piece in modern dress. All it has is Grace Moore singing opera: all it needed. Moore was an exciting soprano who communicated not through acting but through musical intensity; here, in "Sempre Libera" from *La Traviata*, the Habañera from *Carmen*, "None But the Lonely Heart," the title song, and others such, Moore is slim and confident; her phrasing caresses and her high notes blaze. The opera selections are not in English, the *Traviata* excerpt is horribly scrappy, and a rehearsal of the sextet from *Lucia di Lammermoor* is covered by dialogue. But Moore makes all the points, especially in "Ciribiribin," an Italian pop song sung in a tavern to a rapt gathering who join in for the last chorus while Moore flies high on an extravagant obbligato.

One Night of Love's huge profits heartened Hollywood to try operetta all over again, each studio sending to New York for legit singers. MGM, with its ample contract pool, already had the goods on hand in Jeanette MacDonald and Nelson Eddy. The pairing seemed unlikely: MacDonald, the boudoir dazzler of the Chevalier films opposite Eddy, the nonactor whose movie experience consisted of singing spots in three films? Allan Jones was suggested—but he was under contract to the Shuberts and couldn't cut free. So it was MacDonald and Eddy. MGM was hoping to launch not just a film but a whole series, and the sense of a team in the making was essential to the scheme, so the little-known Eddy shared billing with the famed MacDonald, his stolidity side by side with her vivacity. Eddy was the singing tree, immobile, and MacDonald the ornate kite trapped in its branches. Either one alone was a still picture; together they told a story.

MGM gave them a smart vehicle, Victor Herbert's 1910 stage hit, *Naughty Marietta*. Twenty-five years old, its score—"The Italian Street Song," "I'm Falling in Love With Someone," " 'Neath the Southern Moon," "Tramp, Tramp, Tramp," and "Ah! Sweet Mystery of Life"—still treated those who thrill to operetta, and its tale of a French noblewoman and a backwoods soldier of fortune in old New Orleans was still serviceable. The original *Naughty Marietta* had two opera-trained stars, Emma Trentini and Orville Harold (Eddy had sung opera and MacDonald was eventually to do so), and the music sounds it, with lots of coloratura embellishment for her in "The Italian Street Song" (the one with "Zing! Zing! Zi-zi-zi-zi-zing-zing! Boom! Boom! Ay!") and an all-out lyrical bazooka for him in "I'm Falling in Love With Someone"—the words say "Aw, shucks" but the notes carol lustily. Possibly the two stars had some inkling of how well the experiment would turn out; they're so glad to be in on it that they're already singing an overture before the story has begun.

We quickly learn that MGM has determined not to make another continental operetta in the Lubitsch style. His *Merry Widow* in 1934 had done acceptable business only in the metropolitan centers. *Naughty Marietta* in 1935, directed by W. S. Van Dyke II, would be national, something everyone can cotton to right off. Jeanette is popular, high-born, generous, and creative. She helps an old musician tap out a mystically romantic tune on the piano, inspired by the bells that rang out at the end of the title credits. "It's like the music of the spheres," MacDonald coos. "The melody of the universe, everything." Moments later, she is editing the tune—"Let's give it rhythm and move it up a tone." Presto! "Ah! Sweet Mystery of Life" is in gestation. It's not the heroine we love in Lubitsch, but a flash of the old MacDonald brightens the scene in which her unwanted suitor and his sisters present her with her proposed trousseau—all black. "Has there been a death in your family?" MacDonald snaps.

Nelson is popular, low-born, generous, and stalwart. Fleeing the diplomatic marriage disguised as a casquette girl, MacDonald and the other casquettes are captured by pirates; Nelson and his men rescue them. Immediately, the two stars bicker, but seriously: romantically. There is none of the self-spoof Lubitsch found in such plots, and it turns out that the public preferred the new MacDonald. They didn't want spoof. They wanted romance—spectacle, adventure, crinolines and uniforms, broad comedy from the comedians, as little as possible from the stars, and *lots* of voice.

MGM provided it all, reinventing the operetta genre all over again. Spectacle: the scene in which MacDonald departs France is a grand one, with a real harbor, a real ship, and a huge chorus with a fun tune, and then a hymn as the boat pulls out. Adventure: the pirates are really menacing (one of them coldbloodedly shoots the duenna who attempts to protect the girls) and Eddy's cohort intervenes when they are on the verge of raping their prisoners. The villain, MacDonald's French fiancé (Douglas Dumbrille), is nasty and haughty. MacDonald's outfits before she changes her identity and after she is unmasked are lavish. The comedians (Frank Morgan and Elsa Lanchester) don't intrude on the love plot and the lovers don't intrude on the comedy, contenting themselves with getting on each other's nerves in coy ways. (Eddy calls MacDonald "Bright Eyes." Try to imagine Chevalier doing that.) And the score pays full measure in vocal splendor. Eddy is in spectacular voice for "The Owl and the Bobcat," pumping tone out in exposed high lines as if it were the easiest thing in the world.

For him, it was; certainly it was easier than acting. Eddy's baritone boasted a phenomenal upper register that took him well into tenor territory, and he sang so grandly so casually that his numbers alone put his characters over. It's unfair to belabor the joke about his wooden acting, but he never did get the hang of reading lines, and it robs his roles of the panache they need. His inflection is not wrong so much as weak. MacDonald has to carry their dialogue, playing both their parts. She projects her insulted dignity and, by a kind of reflection, his braggadocio. That was their secret.

More about this team later. Let's consider other Broadway adaptations in these years of stabilizing genre-ism, especially in light of what the post-*42nd Street* Hollywood thought too sophisticated to use. The 1930s bring us into extremes of type, Warners' backstage guts or MGM's operetta glister. But Broadway always finds vitality in a combination of the two—*Of Thee I Sing*, for instance, with its taut political satire heightened by Gershwin's operatic structures. There was no *Of Thee I Sing* film, needless to say. *Naughty Marietta*, on the other hand, was an MGM cinch, once the two leads were cast, with sensible, "One Take" Van Dyke in charge and Herbert Stothart, himself a veteran of Broadway operetta (he collaborated with Rudolf Friml in composing the *Rose-Marie* score) shaving off outdated or unwanted numbers and rearranging others. Half the original Victor Herbert–Rida Johnson Young score remains in some form, beefed up by two interpolations from other Herbert works, and not a note is out of place. But Paramount brought *Anything Goes* to the screen in 1936 with its sharp comedy dulled, its characters prettied, and its Cole Porter score trimmed to "You're the Top," "I Get a Kick Out of You," and the minor "There'll Always Be a Lady Fair." Yet *Anything Goes*, a shipboard farce involving a nightclub singer, a stowaway, an heiress, and a mild-mannered public enemy no. 13, should have been right for the screen as it was. Letting Bing Crosby and Ida Lupino play the roles originated by William Gaxton and Bettina Hall was good thinking, as Crosby was more amiable and Lupino more exciting than their predecessors, and at least Ethel Merman was held over from Broadway, though setting her in a revolving swing for "I Get a Kick Out of You" was somebody's very strange anticipation of high-tech camp.

Hollywood did better with operettas like *Naughty Marietta* because operetta flattered the sentimentality that Hollywood liked to flatter— musical comedy too often degraded it. A piece like Kern and Hammerstein's *Sweet Adeline* lay right up Hollywood's alley, with its 1890s nostalgia, backstage whoop-de-do, and Cinderella romance of a beer garden owner's daughter who becomes a toast of Broadway in *The*

Belle of Hoboken. One thing *Sweet Adeline* had that Hollywood couldn't use: Helen Morgan as the heroine. When the show opened in 1929, Morgan was on the brink of a breakdown from assorted ills; by 1934, when Warners made the film, she was a little grainy for heroine parts. Irene Dunne took over the role and she seems out of place. She has a trained soprano, finesse in phrasing, and of course acts rings around her material. But that's the problem—she reads her more importunately melodramatic lines with a flip of emphasis that questions their validity. "Is this for real?" she almost says; *does* say it—watch her eyes. Her colleagues alone must have tried her actress' patience. Wini Shaw as her rival, sappy Donald Woods as her composer boyfriend, wooden Louis Calhern as *his* rival, Ned Sparks as a producer, and dithering Hugh Herbert as a backer are strictly flimsy. What holds *Sweet Adeline* together is Mervyn LeRoy's direction. He keeps everything sweet and dear, as the authors planned, but obviously sympathizes with Dunne. He takes in a touch of Berkeley, small-scaled, in "Lonely Feet" (one of those "through the mirror" numbers), and gets off a Pirandello at the end, when the camera pulls back from what we have thought is the last scene of *Sweet Adeline* but what turns out to be the last scene of *The Belle of Hoboken.* The suggestion that operetta romance is true romance may be hard to take, but it is not debatable that, in the Broadway adaptation, Hollywood felt most comfortable with Broadway's beauty rather than Broadway's sharp perceptions.

Universal attempted to combine the two, and redeem its mistaken part-talkie *Show Boat*, in a 1936 remake. This is by far the best of the three *Show Boat* films, though it emphasizes the sentimentality of the Kern–Hammerstein epic (love lasts a lifetime) rather than its salient idea (human strivings fall away to nothing; the natural world outlasts us all). The casting is superb: Dunne as the heroine, Allan Jones as her gambler love, Helen Morgan as Julie, Charles Winninger as Captain Andy, Helen Westley as his sour wife, Paul Robeson and Hattie McDaniel as family retainers, Queenie Smith and Sammy White as show boaters. Except for Westley and Smith, all had played their roles on stage in the original or revivals—and note that Morgan in the role of an outcast of mixed blood and (we eventually infer) sordid lifestyle is perfectly acceptable. As with *Moonlight and Pretzels*, the director was best known for horror, but James Whale did a fine job in balancing the show's lighter moments with the sorrow and survival that the story mainly features. The film is a quite faithful adaptation—Hammerstein wrote the screenplay himself—so the performers' experiential ease with their characters makes it rich in personal depth. Dunne ages artfully, from frisky teenager to a woman abandoned by her husband to a grande dame of the theatre now coaching her daughter for Broadway. Morgan is at her best, much more attractive than she had been in *Applause* in a similar role, and the chance to see a classic portrayal of Broadway history is no small windfall. Robeson was no actor—McDaniel utterly outclasses him—but his part mainly calls for an easy presence and a rolling basso for "Ol' Man River," and these he has. Jones is useful and the others exactly right, Winninger's jovial Andy well mated with Westley's humorless Parthy.

Show Boat is an atypical operetta in the opportunities it gives strong actors, but all operettas need strong voices; here, too, Universal did the show proud. All the major singers have trained instruments except Morgan, and what she didn't have in technique she doesn't need. Her little voice seldom carried far in a Broadway house, but here on microphone she can reach millions yet retain the intimacy performers like her rely on absolutely. Robeson, who had no problems with volume, nevertheless sang "Ol' Man River" live for the camera, without a playback, bringing it home not as a concert piece but to express it in character as Joe, a lazy and likeable deckhand. Conductor Victor Baravelle keeps the song moving—few conductors do—and at the close, backed by men's chorus, Robeson at last opens up and lets the tune soar.

Because Kern and Hammerstein worked so closely with Whale and producer Carl Laemmle, Jr., where the film *Show Boat* isn't faithful to the original it surpasses it. The authors wrote three new numbers, "Gallivantin' Around," an onstage ditty for Captain Andy's floating theatre; a new love song for Dunne and Jones, "I Have the Room Above"; and a comic duet for McDaniel and Robeson, "I Still Suits Me." All are excellent, though Dunne performs "Gallivantin' Around" in blackface, rolling her eyes and contorting her lips in one of the most objectionable racist jokes in film history. (She also shuffles, rather amusingly, in "Can't Help Lovin' Dat Man.") Though it's seldom thought of as one, *Show Boat* is a backstager, using the changing styles of American pop theatre to play cultural transformation against natural stasis. As the years pass, we get melodrama and minstrel variety, nightclub standup solos, antique story waltzes, and at last modern jive. It was somebody's grand idea to cap all this by letting Dunne's daughter reprise "Gallivantin' Around," updating it with hot Harlem dancing, but the number was cut from the release print—as was "Why Do I Love You?", one of the show's hit tunes—in an effort to clean up the ending. *Show Boat*'s resolution has always been a problem, as Hammerstein never found the way to tie up his theme and his love story contiguously. In the end as we now see it, Jones meets Dunne, after years of separation, in the theatre where their daughter is making her debut. Dunne seems surprised to see Jones, but not much moved. (Their daughter, still on stage with her big moment shattered by the real life going on in the balcony, looks stunned.) In desperation, Whale has the couple sing "You Are Love" again and calls it a wrap. It's a terrible letdown for an epic, but up to that point, Universal really has put itself out nobly—the arrival of the show boat, the drive of the Mississippi in flood and at peace, the midway of the Chicago World's Fair, and the sense of time and space that the story turns on has been experienced as never on stage.

Meanwhile, Hollywood hit on an almost wholly unexploited new form, the musical biography. Pick a subject involved in the music or entertainment world, and there was an instant musical: composers write songs for lavish sopranos, who sing them and the world weeps; impresarios mount spectacular shows and have colorful fetishes; performers hide a wounded heart behind the clown's twinkle. And, as studio chiefs prudently noted, such films are edifying and informative. Also great: *The Great Ziegfeld, The Great Waltz, The Great Victor Herbert.* Twentieth Century-Fox virtually made *The Great Fanny Brice*, calling it *Rose of Washington Square* (1939), and settling out of court with both Brice and Nicky Arnstein for not having said May I?

The credits for MGM's *The Great Ziegfeld* (1936) warn that the film was "suggested by romances and events" in Ziegfeld's life, *very* suggested. The film had a set format: a medley of guest stars, impersonated or in the flesh; specialty numbers of no relevance to plot or characters; little or no attempt to recreate the style of the artists involved; and the "suggested" approach to truth. There are exceptions, but most of these biographies, it turns out, are neither edifying nor informative: they are stories, like all other Hollywood films. They need romance, thrills, rise through fall to recovery or rise and fall mitigated by dream vision. *The Great Ziegfeld* takes the latter approach, both the rise and the fall stemming from Ziegfeld's extravagant showmanship, which could not survive the Depression (the man himself had died as recently as 1932) and the dream vision describing a *Follies* to end all *Follies.* William Anthony McGuire, who knew Ziegfeld well, wrote an episodic script, but the sequences are tied together in that new characters are introduced while characters about to fade out of the chronicle are still prominent. Thus, midway in the segment devoted to Ziegfeld's business and romantic involvement with Anna Held,

Ziegfeld presents Held with a diamond bracelet. She shows it to the chorus girls, and one, a cold blond gold digger, is unimpressed—by other women's jewels. The blonde wants diamonds the easy way. "I'll work," she says. "But I won't suffer" (warning us that of course she will). Seconds later, a dancing stagehand begs Ziegfeld for a chance to perform. Both blonde and stagehand become important later on, when Held has divorced Ziegfeld and falls out of the story. So the very long film never runs out of steam though the story has no suspense—Ziegfeld rises early and stays high till the last few scenes.

MGM went all out on this one and had a huge success, establishing not only a genre but a blue-chip profit history for it. *The Great Ziegfeld* runs three hours, cost two million, earned four, won an Oscar for best picture, and remains a treat, largely for its cast. As Ziegfeld, William Powell embodies the character: spendthrift, unscrupulous, imaginative, impetuous, with superb taste in women and women's clothes. And women find him irresistible. Frank Morgan is his usual excellent self as Ziegfeld's rival and friend, Virginia Bruce as the blonde suffers nicely, Ray Bolger does a fine turn as the stagehand, and Eddie Cantor, Will Rogers, and the muscleman Sandow are authentically duplicated. Best of all is Fanny Brice as herself.* Her sequence is frustratingly brief and director Robert Z. Leonard cuts into her songs with annoying dialogue, but it's the utter Brice as she really was. A kind of *verité* vaudeville sketch in her dressing room in a burlesque house, where she mistakes Ziegfeld for a peddler pushing a mink coat, is the funniest three minutes in film.

As Anna Held, the Austrian Luise Rainer has the second-biggest part. Hers is a controversial performance. She got an Oscar for it, so somebody must have liked her, but modern commentators regularly assault her, especially for the famous Telephone Scene, wherein she realizes she has lost Ziegfeld forever. I think Rainer is pretty special, a gorgeous woman with perhaps too ready a projection of doomed vulnerability. Her accent is right, her figure is right (Held popularized the tiny waist), her pleasantly erratic soprano is right. Her first scene with Powell, in her dressing room in London after a performance, defines the two opposing temperaments that will provision the film's emotional material. Rainer does all the work: she plays the neurotic. Powell is uninvolved, a man who loves woman; Rainer is a one-man doll. Her

---

*Trivium Footnote no. 4: MGM hoped to have Marilyn Miller in it as well, but Miller asked for too much money; Rosina Lawrence impersonates her in a walk-on bit.

inability to hold him substitutes for the lack of dramatic hurdles in his rise to fame as Broadway's spectacular showman.

Naturally, the film is spectacular. There is a balloon number, "You Gotta Pull Strings." There is a tails-spangles-and-ruffles number, "You Never Looked So Beautiful Before," with a few of Ziegfeld's signature walking showgirls. Biggest of all the numbers is Irving Berlin's "A Pretty Girl Is Like a Melody," originally heard in the 1919 *Follies*. This, at least, is historically appropriate and the set designer John Harkrider worked for Ziegfeld, though in this Berkeley age the "stage" is beyond the facilities of any theatre that Ziegfeld used. It begins simply, with Dennis Morgan (dubbed by Allan Jones) alone before a curtain. As he finishes the first chorus, the camera pulls back, the curtain rises, and the stage revolves to show an expanse of winding stairway loaded with dancers, singers, and showgirls. We travel the stairs through changes of decor and sound style to the top of what is now seen to be a gigantic wedding cake with Virginia Bruce grinning at the top.

The ice broken, the spring began to bubble. MGM's *The Great Waltz* (1938), on the rise of Johann Strauss, drew great tunes, what with his concert waltzes, marches, polkas, and operettas providing the score with new lyrics by Hammerstein. The project apparently meant the realization of L. B. Mayer's lifetime dream, and he carefully brought in an unusual number of foreign talents. Fernand Gravet is Strauss, Luise Rainer his wife, and Milizia Korjus the opera diva who almost wrecks their marriage. Gravet is the most direct of the three, intensely caught up in his success as musician and lover, forelock wet and tossing as he scrapes his violin. Rainer embellishes her Anna Held: now she is patient and sensible rather than capricious, though she still sobs hysterically. But even Rainer is not as odd as Korjus, as a lavish diva whose appetite for men and high notes is equally insatiable. With her Mae West looks, lopsided smile, and heavy accent, Korjus was already bucking Americans' sense of the feasible, and when, at their first meeting, Strauss catches his foot in her dress and observes, "I seem to be caught," she whispers, "So soon?" That sort of part.

But Julien Duvivier's direction and Dmitri Tiomkin's musical arrangements are amazing, their collaboration surpassing what Mamoulian and Lubitsch did in urging the pictures on with a musical drive. *The Great Schmaltz*, detractors have dubbed it, but the insult comprehends Duvivier and Tiomkin's achievement—Strauss' tunes have never resounded with such *Schwung*. Even Korjus' incessant bizarre coloratura begins to thrill; this music, the movie tells us, is the spirit behind which all Vienna unites, bourgeois and artists, aristocrats and revolutionaries. It must sound more than charming, more than heady. It must sound obsessively self-absorbed; and it does. The film's highlight shows Gravet and Korjus composing "The Tales of the Vienna Woods" out of a carriage horse's clip-clop waltz rhythm, piping shepherds, birdsong, and a coach horn while a back projection affixes real woods, moistly shining at dawn, to the MGM sound stage. To seal the triumph, Duvivier immediately transports us to a bandstand where Gravet plays and Korjus sings the new piece. Carried away, they waltz around the bandstand in the moonlight, strings running wild and Korjus riding a roller coaster of scales, stalked by one of the most astounding tracking shots ever seen. Duvivier also captures the most eliciting close-ups, making the most of Gravet's wildness, Rainer's pathos, and Korjus' cynicism. The entire movie is a study in techniques none of the various stage *Great Waltz*es could encompass, and its success, along with that of *The Great Ziegfeld*, guaranteed the rise of the musical biography. There were setbacks, such as Paramount's *The Great Victor Herbert* (1939), one of the first attempts to film the life of an American composer. But this wasn't a biography so much as a medley of Herbert hits swirling around a fetid love plot (Mary Martin and Allan Jones).

In this time of consolidation of form, the most gifted directors struggled for freedom. Josef von Sternberg, with his hagiographic approach to the Paramount Dietrich classics, should do wonders for Grace Moore, Columbia thought, and brought the two together for *The King Steps Out* (1936). But this adaptation of a Fritz Kreisler operetta was a disaster. Dietrich in the hands of less exquisite directors was reportedly heard to murmur, "Jo, Jo, where are you?" Moore found him less flattering. "Von Sternberg began," she wrote in her memoirs, "by modestly declaring he was the greatest director in Hollywood. 'I know,' declaimed the Great One, 'exactly what to do with the music . . . I know what to do with you.' " This meant, among other things, having Moore milk a cow during one of her numbers. The quarrels were heated, and despite Sternbergian flashes, the film has no supporters, including von Sternberg; who disowned it and fervently hoped that once closed it would never be seen again.

Rouben Mamoulian had better luck and managed to work outside the genre structure altogether. *The Gay Desperado* (1936), like his *Applause*, is not even precisely a musical. Of its principals, only Nino Martini sings, and the score is a potpourri taking in "The World Is

Mine Tonight" and Spanish folk and pop as well as "Celeste Aida." It's a delightfully ridiculous satire, though it never quite tops out on its premise. Martini, active again in Hollywood as part of the post-*One Night of Love* opera wave, is mainly around to admire Ida Lupino. The bulk of the fun in Wallace Smith's script belongs to a band of Mexican bandits headed by Leo Carillo, who wants to observe procedures laid down by the American underworld as reported—created?—by gangster movies. *The Gay Desperado*, then, is a burlesque of crime *and* of crime films; it is about itself, a funhouse mirror turned inward, as when Mamoulian opens with a typical Chicagoan take-'em-for-a-ride slaughter and then pulls back to show a rapt audience of Mexican filmgoers: film-within-film. Everyone in Mamoulian's world is clued into crime, commits it (not well) or suffers it (with equanimity or impatience). Martini, under Carillo's wing, meets Lupino when he stops her car for his first holdup. She's one of the impatient ones. "Something told me," she says, "this was amateur night."

The Mexican landscape provided Mamoulian with choice compositions, huge cacti guarding desert roads, hacienda walls on which to cast the famous Mamoulian shadows, the moonlit campfire. But his next film, Paramount's *High, Wide and Handsome* (1937), tells a more substantial tale in less consistently exotic scenery. Here, too, is a musical that resists genre. Oscar Hammerstein's screenplay recounts the historical discovery of oil in Pennsylvania just before the Civil War, and follows the farmers' attempt to develop their find despite vicious sabotage from the railroad money bosses. Randolph Scott is the idealistic hero, Irene Dunne the snake-oil salesman's daughter who marries him, Dorothy Lamour the openly sensual woman that small-minded townspeople call "marked," Alan Hale and Akim Tamiroff the railroad magnates, and Elizabeth Patterson Scott's tetchy grandmother; all could have played their roles in a songless melodrama, with thrust jaw from the hero, quiet wisdom from his wife, and sneers from the villains. But Mamoulian rises above traditions of format. Scott is Scott, true. But Dunne is unusual. Whether resenting her husband's preoccupation with his oil battles, or defending Lamour from a mob of the righteous, or coaching her in beer-hall singer's protocol, Dunne reinvents her type. She is more genuine than in *Sweet Adeline* and more interesting than in *Show Boat*. The Dunne–Scott romance and the oil-railroad war form the film's two plot lines, but Dunne implies a third line, that of a gifted woman whose society prizes her wifely gifts and no others. Because she sings the Kern score's big numbers, she dominates the film's emotional poetry, and we constantly see her in performing situations—medicine show, circus, and beer hall. Scott opposes her working, especially as a performer, but we need her on stage to define the film's sentimentality and energy, to reconcile Mamoulian's components of love story and western.

High, Wide and Handsome has been attacked for this collaboration of populist melodrama and nostalgic musical, but because Mamoulian finds the flint in romance and the suave comedy in villainy, he brings it off. His railroad tycoons, thoroughly evil, are no cardboard heavies—some viewers find them almost pleasant—and the use of Lamour as a turncoat who sides with the farmers, against them, and back with them keeps matters humanly ambivalent. Melodrama is all blacks and whites; *High, Wide and Handsome* is grays. Consider the visual environments alone. Mamoulian films the medicine show for shabby, provides splendid vistas of forest and valley (Chino, California, in fact), and shoots a Scott–Dunne orchard as falsely candy as any set ever built. These are extreme stylizations of settings, not accidents. Mamoulian wants his action plot as real as possible so the violence will be believable, but wants the love plot as fanciful as possible to make up for the violence and give us something to root for besides democratic self-reliance.

There is plenty of this. Scott and his comrades speak of their pipeline project as a means to "keep the poor man warm and light up every shack in the country." Dunne, being apolitical, calls the scheme "daffy." But one gets involved. When the railroaders try to smash the farmers with prohibitive rates, Scott calls it "a few men stealing what belongs to all men," and one of the fat cat villains calls *that* a reasonable definition of business. Mamoulian shoots his face tilted back in raucous laughter—not to type evil but to wonder about its insensitivity. Mamoulian keeps things open, wondering. In a western, the essential American good-versus-evil melodrama, the villain must die, or the evil never stops coming at you. But here, once Mamoulian brings out Dunne's circus friends—acrobats, sideshow freaks, and animals—to protect the pipeline (the elephants give it the feel of a Tarzan finale), the villains just shrug and give up. They're not in a western: they're in business. Yet, note that Mamoulian's sense of fantasy is as vital as his naturalism—elephants defending an oil conduit in the Pennsylvania hills! Hammerstein and Kern may have been the era's chieftains of schmaltz, but Mamoulian blends a rich mixture.

Coming out of the silent dream, talkies added new myths to those long established and reorganized Hollywood battles of good and evil.

Yet good is still good, evil the same evil. Under *High, Wide and Handsome*'s visual overlay is a simple story of the salt of the earth inheriting the earth the only way it can be done: by fighting for it. This simplicity, old as film, still had the power in Hollywood, and the film business continued to see its purpose as ratifier of basic truths and instiller of the American virtues, though each studio held different ones to be self-evident. Some films attacked the defects in American democracy; these were not musicals. Still, the musical had a moral system. Its paradigms have already become repetitive—paradigms that suggest the musical's purpose as entertainment based on messages of American self-esteem.

There is, for instance, the egalitarian self-congratulation of *The Hot Heiress, Sunny Side Up, High Society Blues, Love in the Rough,* and *Love Me Tonight,* in each of which a commoner mates with a noble. The men are almost always the commoners: Hollywood sees egalitarianism not as a doctrine of humanist fairness but as a stunt of unstoppable virile initiative. You can't keep a good man down, whether Ben Lyon's construction worker or Robert Montgomery's golfer. *Love Me Tonight*'s castle reverberates with cries of "The son of a gun is nothing but a tailor!"; only dusty aristos would see Maurice Chevalier as "nothing but" his profession. The independent man has something more than a job: good instincts. Or call it charm. In *Happiness Ahead* (1934), one of Warners' tiny musicals, window washer Dick Powell wins blueblooded Josephine Hutchinson without extending himself much. True, he does kiss her—by mistake—on New Year's Eve in a Chinese nightclub where the checks are tallied by abacus. But it is not so much Powell's force of personality as the insuperable male's ease with himself that conquers Hutchinson. Love doesn't disqualify status and money—male self-sufficiency does.

Corollary to democratic (male) self-congratulation is a more universalized paradigm, begot by the work ethic on the Depression fixation with employment. This may be stated as "everybody has the right to succeed if he or she is cute and lucky": the Keeler syndrome. Talent is less important than spunk, or perhaps talent *is* spunk. Get up and *do* it, and they'll cheer; all the world's a Gong Show. But charm conquers.

A third paradigm is an equalizer: little guys outsmart bullies. Eddie Cantor taught in sound what Chaplin had taught in silence: it's how you feel that counts, mainly how you feel about yourself. The little Texas college that beats Yale in *Pigskin Parade* believes in itself; so, more seriously, do the farmer-prospectors who fight the railroad monopoly in *High, Wide and Handsome*. All these types of self-esteem—sex appeal, backstage spunk, and a convinced sense of cause—are really one type, related to such other varieties as Astaire's elegance and Temple's optimism. All stem from a belief in oneself, whether one is one of a kind (like Ziegfeld) or one out of many (like Keeler's youngster).

One other paradigm is that of community; in the musical, friends are terrifically loyal and strangers often supportive. By far, the musical's favorite pattern for teamwork was the threesome. Three sailors on leave, three gold diggers hunting marriage—these trios turn up in all arts, but the screen musical featured them with outlandish frequency. It became a genre, an easy win with its built-in variety of persons, one tender, one peppy, one silly. In 1929, *The Gold Diggers of Broadway* chalked the slate with Nancy Welford, Ann Pennington, and Winnie Lightner, replaced in the remake, *Gold Diggers of 1933*, by Ruby Keeler, Joan Blondell, and Aline MacMahon. The threesome was already a cliché by mid-decade in *Born to Dance*, with James Stewart, Buddy Ebsen, and Sid Silvers as sailors and Eleanor Powell, Frances Langford, and Una Merkel as their girls: a main team, a cute team, a funny team. The threesome didn't even need exactly rationed opposites, as *Sally, Irene, and Mary* (1938) proved. The property had been a stage musical and then a silent, in 1925, with Constance Bennett, Joan Crawford, and Sally O'Neil, and the possibilities in the title so haunted Twentieth Century-Fox that it bought the rights from MGM with no intention of using the original plot. In the new version, Sally (Alice Faye), Irene (Joan Davis), and Mary (Marjorie Weaver) are manicurists who break into show business on a renovated boat. Faye sings the ballad "This Is Where I Came In" in close-up, lips trembling, and romances Tony Martin. Davis performs the big apple in "Who Stole the Jam?" Jimmy Durante clowns. Louise Hovick (June Havoc) menaces Faye. Fred Allen hangs out. For catastasis, the boat snaps its moorings during a performance . . . the usual. The film has nothing in it but fun and the promise that if they hadn't stuck together, the girls might not have made it.

It was genre-oriented studio thinking that made the threesome a regular event, and canny but never bold casting kept the trope alive till the studios collapsed in the early 1950s. If it had bored moviegoers, it wouldn't have lasted: it didn't bore moviegoers. It was the novel that failed, not the familiar, and these post-*42nd Street* years are loaded with a sense of series, of resilient repetition. Hollywood at last had defined the presiding elements of the film musical. Dance, musical style, comedy, and personality were established components, serving various genres in certain proportion. Genre means stagnation—yet the artists seldom complained, for format gave them an identity. Astaire and Rogers didn't lose their vitality playing the same roles in nine RKO films. They flourished. Mae West dined out on formula; MacDonald and Eddy and Abbott and Costello soared on convention. Regard the series format as a sonnet, with fixed rhythm and rhyme: it is a challenge, a frame for concentration.

☆ 7 ☆
The Dance Musical

Dance was sudden, strange, and necessary in 1929. In the scramble to shoot and release musicals, Broadway choreographers were brought in for the kicklines and hoofing that added nothing to character or action. Dance was extra. Only the overhead camera shot, introduced by Maria Gambarelli in *The Cocoanuts* in 1929, distinguished dancing as a function of film.

Anyway, who would film dance in Hollywood? The choreographer? The cameraman? The director? Too often, directors who knew nothing of dance took charge, filming a number from several angles simultaneously and letting an editor paste it together with absurd reaction shots from bystanders. Obviously, dance would work best when an inventive director pulled the motion into his overall conception, or when a smart choreographer took over the camera for the numbers. Two examples: at the end of *The Merry Widow*, Ernst Lubitsch fills the screen with couples waltzing down halls to fill a ballroom in layered swirls of black and white. As the music builds, Lubitsch sharpens the sense of climax by intercutting shots angled from above, shot after shot to tighten the whirl, coil it like a whip. For once, we understand why everyone in Viennese operetta thinks the waltz is so sexy.

The other exemplar is Berkeley. We have already dealt with his trick photography, his expressionism, fantasy, and narrative geometries. But what makes him most influential historically is his discovery that the motion of the camera was as much a part of the dance as the dancers were. Take "Shuffle Off to Buffalo," the opening number in *42nd Street*'s *Pretty Lady*. This is a plot number, opening in the station and taking off for Niagara Falls. Berkeley begins straight on, curtain up and the line kicking on to a rousing strain more Broadway than Broadway itself. Keeler plows onstage—a superb split-second as she cases the house—greets a friend, and dashes on board with her mate as the number begins and the dancing starts—but does it? There is very little dancing in "Shuffle Off to Buffalo," yet so much happens in it that only on repeated viewings does one realize that the camera is doing almost all the work. By the time Berkeley filmed the title number in *Dames*, he hardly needed dancers at all except for some rudimentary tap. Beautiful girls, yes; acrobats, even. Not dancers.

Besides editing and composition, style was discovered, the personal styles of Fred Astaire and Eleanor Powell that outmoded generalized choreography. Dancers had no great public outside of New York in the early sound years—as Marilyn Miller proved—but they started coming west after Astaire did, in 1933. An oft-quoted and almost certainly apocryphal report on his screen test discredits his looks, acting, and voice, and closes, "Can dance a little." Powell, however, seemed a natural. She made her debut in Fox's *George White's 1935 Scandals*, an Alice Faye backstager, but wasn't noticed till her second film, *Broadway Melody of 1936* (1935), for MGM. Noticed? She was seized. MGM made her "the Broadway Melody Girl" in the 1938 and 1940 editions and starred her in two spectaculars, *Born to Dance* (1936) and *Rosalie* (1937). The picture of Powell, thighs bared in black net tights and back bent to forty-five degrees, dancing all over a battleship in the former or hopping on a set of oversized drums in the latter, makes one of the era's great memories. In the end, her musicals were Powell films rather than dance films: she didn't spread dance all over the screen. *She* danced; the other characters sang, joked, and ran the plot. Powell, too, sang, joked, and plotted, but by focusing on *her* dances as the special things in her films, she eliminated the need for dance as expression of person or story. She didn't even have partners. Ray Bolger appears in *Rosalie* in a supporting role, but scarcely dances at all, and while George Murphy, Buddy Ebsen, and Astaire did dance with Powell, she didn't get all that much out of a duet.

This didn't hurt her career, as she was personally engaging and, frankly, the greatest woman dancer in Hollywood's history. *Born to Dance*'s battleship finale, "Swinging the Jinx Away," has been attacked for its too-much production, but it still supplies thrills today, and *Rosalie*'s "I've a Strange New Rhythm in My Heart" discloses a subtle Powell, gliding ornately from room to room of her Vassar dorm as she admits to loving Nelson Eddy. "So you're a princess!" he more or less cries later, when her royalty is revealed. "And I'm a fool." It's a foolish movie, with some peasant ballet that can't hope to compete—but tries to—with Powell.

It was Astaire who created the dance musical, collaborating with first-rate directors, scenarists, composers, and lyricists—and Ginger Rogers—at RKO throughout the 1930s. Alone, he is the statusless dandy, she the shopgirl princess; together, they catholicize class, overthrowing the received wisdom on caste as family and fortune for a new understanding of caste as charm. He gave her class? She has it already, or they could not have taken the ballroom so effortlessly; *she* gave *his* class a shot of energy. She gave him sex? He had it; or what on earth were they dancing about?

They fell into step by chance, as two supporting players still in search of The Break. She had made a swank feature film debut in *Young Man of Manhattan* (1930) as Puff Randoph, uttering the catchphrase "Cigarette me, big boy" and singing "I've Got It (but it don't do me no good)," but was getting nowhere in eighteen films at various studios. Her "Shuffle Off to Buffalo" duet with Una Merkel in *42nd Street* was her best sixty seconds on film till then, an essential Rogers as yet unrevealed: relaxed, a little sloppy but clean, and convinced—for the time being—that romance is the bunk. In mid-1933, they were each a brand X, he walking Joan Crawford through *Dancing Lady* and she getting dubbed (by Etta Moten) in *Professional Sweetheart*, a radio burlesque. Suddenly, they were cast in the "aerial musical picture" *Flying Down to Rio* (1933), RKO's attempt to create genre competition with Warners' Berkeley backstagers: South American tropicana, noble Brazilian beauty loves handsome American bandleader, a woman vocalist and man accordionist-singer for laughs, an aviation motif. It sounds lively.

Messy, too. But this wasn't an Astaire–Rogers film. They were billed fourth and fifth under Delores Del Rio, Gene Raymond, and Raoul Roullien, and make a pair only nominally. We know, from hindsight, that Astaire is recklessly debonair and Rogers wistfully frosty and that they have only to meet to get it on. They don't here. They dance together, but not conclusively. They joke around, but don't get under each other's skin. They don't even meet: they already know each other when the film begins, which cuts them off from the classic Astaire–Rogers "meeting" scene—his ripping her skirt in *The Gay Divorcee*, his ruining her sleep in *Top Hat*, his getting her in trouble with a cop in *Swing Time*, his pretending to be a Russian ballerino in *Shall We Dance*. Not only are they not a duo in *Flying Down to Rio*; they aren't yet themselves. Rogers is more relaxed than we're used to in the later films, less serious about herself but, conversely, lacking her self-spoof. Where are her extremes? Astaire is very second man here, making sardonic huhs about Raymond's scrapes instead of getting into his own. But Astaire, Rogers, and *Flying Down to Rio* are at their best in the big number, the "Carioca."

The origin of a dance craze because of its distinctive head-to-head formation (which must be retained even when a couple goes into a turn), the "Carioca" is florid with South American riffs and doodles, and like just about every other dance lyric, gives the slimmest instructions: "Two heads together, they say, are better than one." Choreographer Dave Gould goes crazy, laying out three separate versions of the number, with Astaire and Rogers (who overdo the head touch and bonk their skulls), then Brazilians, then a black group, then all three casts simultaneously, with Astaire and Rogers on a stage made of seven interlocking, revolving white pianos.

The couple's second film together, *The Gay Divorcee* (1934), sets up the format that was to pull RKO out of its financial troubles and set Astaire and Rogers among the biggest draws in film. *Flying Down to Rio*'s many outdoor scenes were traded in for a distinct sound-stage look emphasizing art deco sets for plot and the huge white Bakelite floor for dancing; Astaire and Rogers were promoted to lead status with eccentric comics in support; the plot kicks into action when he accosts her and she resists; and the courtship is celebrated in a big number and extrapolated in intimate duet. *The Gay Divorcee*'s big one is "The Continental," possibly the longest single number in American film at a little over seventeen minutes; the duet is "Night and Day," a sinuous line riding a dangerously subtle beat. "The Continental" prides itself on its seductive powers, but it is the quiet dance for two on a hotel parquet overlooking the ocean that at last presents the sensual Astaire and Rogers as we know them. "Please don't ask me to stay," she tells him. "All right," he says, adding as she turns to leave, "Don't go." She turns back, smiling. "I've so many things to say to you," he adds, rolling into the importunate song. They continue the tease in the dance that follows, entirely set to the "Night and Day" tune with only a change in meter from fox trot to waltz for emotional expansion. The motion starts as she tries to leave again—he heads her off, pulls her into his arms, and she is suddenly his partner, gliding to his lead yet continuing to resist. He has to force her around, and at one point she repulses him with a slap on the chin, sending him off-balance across the floor. This is momentary, however. The first of their great duets suggests what all the others will confirm, that each is irresistible to the other, as she realizes when the music tapers off and he deposits her on a lush couch. She looks dazed, as if she had just lost her virginity. He looks smug. He gives her class *and* sex.

The Gay Divorcee, the foundation of the Astaire–Rogers style in film, derives from a show that Astaire had done on Broadway in 1932. Called *Gay Divorce*,* it was old-fashioned three-act bedroom farce with an English accent and was written to help Astaire weather the retirement of his sister Adele, who—many thought—carried the team. The show was cut down and cleaned, leaving Astaire and his vis-à-vis, their respective confidants, the hired correspondent in the heroine's divorce case, and in small parts a waiter, a bathing beauty, and the husband. Everyone is reduced to being obstacles for Astaire and Rogers so we can enjoy seeing them surmount them. Also reduced was Cole Porter's Broadway score; only "Night and Day" survives of songs that were either too sophisticated (the confidante's "Mister and Missus Fitch") or trivial (the waiter's "What Will Become of Our England?") for the movie. Some of the Broadway cast came in along with Astaire, though Erik Rhodes' correspondent became sillier than he had been and Eric Blore's silly waiter is cut to bones. A little Blore goes a mile, and with Edward Everett Horton as Astaire's lawyer friend, the comedy minces and dawdles obscenely. Director Mark Sandrich seems to have let Blore and Horton direct their own scenes, and the two—along with their moues and quadruple takes—unfortunately carried over into the whole Astaire–Rogers series.

What is most striking about *Gay Divorce*'s adaptation into *The Gay Divorcee* is how a conventional farce-with-songs became a dance musical, Hollywood's first. The major difference is the difference between an Astaire who has been dancing with his sister all his life and an Astaire who has become a romantic lead. *Gay Divorce* kept reverting to tradition whenever Astaire was not on stage with Claire Luce but *The Gay Divorcee*'s five-song score stresses the dancing lover and dancing in general. "Don't Let It Bother You," the opener, offers showgirls executing a can-can with their fingers; Astaire reprises it dancing for his dinner in the same club. "A Needle in a Haystack" has Astaire literally dancing all over his room: dancing is what he is, so he dances wherever he happens to be—something new in film. "Let's K-nock K-neez" pulls even Horton into the picture with Betty Grable and the

---

*Note the change of title in prudish Hollywood: there's nothing jolly about divorce, but once it has occurred, an ex-wife might as well frolic. By the same principle, death is no joke but everyone appreciates a merry widow.

chorus line; he looks ridiculous but he is dancing. The "Night and Day" duet derives from Astaire's Broadway staging, but "The Continental" is new—the very idea of pulling in spectacular numbers of dancers to gaze down and up at them is not available to Broadway.

It was available to Busby Berkeley, of course, and he might easily have staged something like "The Continental." But in Berkeley's films dancing is not an essential of character. Warner Baxter, Joan Blondell, Dick Powell, and such don't crave to express themselves in dance, and Ruby Keeler could, one believes, do without it. Even Rogers in her two Berkeley films was strictly a chorus dancer, part of the parade in "Young and Healthy" and mainly singing in "We're in the Money." But "The Continental" climaxes the budding Astaire–Rogers affair. It nearly dwarfs them, with its files of black-and-white costumed dancers, several different vocalists, intercut plot scenes, slow pans, long shots, mediums, and close-ups. But Astaire and Rogers start and end it. Locked in Rogers' hotel room by Rhodes, they look down on the dance floor as the music starts and Rogers takes the first chorus. They can't resist the "dangerous rhythm" and dance in the room until Astaire mounts a cutout silhouette of themselves—dancing, of course— on a record turntable. Rhodes fooled, they prance down and join the fun. They *are* The Continental: all the other dancers are mere patterns, smiling and joyless. Sandrich keeps the film moving by bringing in Blore to waddle to the beat as he squires a tray and catching Rhodes on the balcony, singing a chorus to his own accordion accompaniment. Still the dance spreads, as Rhodes discovers the ruse, but the unstoppable Astaire and Rogers claim the number at the close.

The dance musical, then, doesn't just have a lot of dance—it uses dance as an element of narration and character. Anyway, there isn't that much dancing in these Astaire–Rogers films. Their duets, usually three to a picture, last only two or three minutes each. With Astaire's solos (Rogers has few) this yields something like twelve minutes' total dancing in 110-minute films. But the emotional intensity of these numbers builds them big proportionately, anticipating and recalling them during the plot scenes rallies the public, and what a wonderful couple they make. Even when they are shunted into the secondary spots in their third film, *Roberta* (1935), they dominate. Irene Dunne and Randolph Scott are the apparent heroine and hero, she a Russian émigrée dress designer and he an American football hero, with the Paris fashion world the film's gummy setting (hideous clothes) and all the big Kern ballads going to Dunne. Dunne is no dancer and Scott's just a lump, and *The Gay Divorcee* has set a tempo for dance, so every time

Astaire and Rogers appear the film forgets the clothes and the balalaikas and does what we want it to. Astaire's dance band, the Wabash Indianians, extend gloved figures to form an organ keyboard; Astaire plays them. Astaire and Rogers make "I'll Be Hard to Handle" a challenge dance that looks improbably spontaneous. Neither one could do what Dunne does for "Smoke Gets in Your Eyes," but they can dance it into the air, and do, literally: at a climactic, rising line in the melody, they swing themselves high onto a stairway. And whom does *Roberta* fade out on? Astaire and Rogers, in a last gleeful runthrough of "I Won't Dance."

Who exactly choreographed these films? A dance director laid out the ensemble numbers, but Astaire did his own choreography, improvising with pianist Hal Borne and Hermes Pan, who came on the lot as Dave Gould's assistant in *Flying Down to Rio*. For the duets, Pan learned Rogers' part, and then taught it to her. Astaire was a perfectionist, and a three-minute routine took weeks of creation and rehearsal before it was ready to shoot—and then it went up in whole takes until they had a clean one. Nor did Astaire vanish when the editing took place. (He also dubbed in the taps with Pan to keep the sound bright.) These were Astaire's films more than anybody's, which is why he's so admired by film and dance historians as well as by dancers of all kinds. The Astaire–Rogers musical, as form, was synthesized by a number of people—the topnotch songwriters who wrote to fit, the scenarists, the designer Carroll Clark, producer Pandro S. Berman, and supporting comics like Alice Brady, Helen Broderick, and, hell, even Horton and Blore, whose screwball dithering adds another level of fantasy to an already highly textured romance. (Everyone in these films is at least a little crazy; the fun of it is that Astaire knows this and Rogers, each time, has to learn it.) But Astaire created himself and initiated Rogers into his art, and these two acts are central to the formation of Hollywood's dance musical.

Rogers has been unfairly treated by commentators. Because Astaire planned the dances, they say he made her look good. Because women's fashions have changed more than men's have, they reprove her flamboyant ball gowns—that feathered job in *Top Hat*'s "Cheek to Cheek" and the buglebeads in *Follow the Fleet* that cracked Astaire on the jaw in the printed take of "Let's Face the Music and Dance." Because Astaire went on singing and dancing and she almost entirely gave musicals up, they suggest that she can't have been "serious" about style.

This is scummy putdown. Rogers' clothes in these films are smashing in any age, from her tomboy slacks to her backless gowns—and

☆ *THE ELEMENTS OF ASTAIRE AND*
ROGERS: above left, the screwball cohorts
(Horton and Brady in The Gay Divorcee*);*
right, the duet (Shall We Dance); *below,*
Astaire's specialty solo) "Bojangles of Harlem"
in Swing Time); *opposite above, he's wry and*
she's wary (Swing Time); *below, the big number*
("The Continental" *in* The Gay Divorcee*).*

the "Cheek to Cheek" feathers, which Rogers wore over virtually everybody's objection, were a national sensation. As for serious, no one put out harder than Rogers did when working with Astaire; if she hadn't been willing to work she wouldn't have made ten films with him. It is a commonplace to call Rogers Astaire's most effective partner, but I think she was also the best dancer he ever worked with, given his style. Eleanor Powell was technically more proficient, Cyd Charisse more graceful, Rita Hayworth just about the most stunning event in the history of Hollywood's woman dancers. But not even counting personal chemistry, Rogers still did what an equal partner must do with Astaire better than the others did. The quirky hopping turns, the look of surprise when some cranky maneuver is floated off like a soap bubble, the rigidity bent to suppleness and back again, the hand motions, the jests, the grins, the conviction—Rogers isn't just capable: she's *of* it. That's why it works so well.

By the time they made *Top Hat* (1935), it couldn't have worked better. This was the first property conceived entirely for them, with an original screenplay, a great Irving Berlin score, and the usual shenanigans from Broderick, Rhodes, Horton, and Blore. Huge profits assured RKO of the wisdom of the format—in the following year, 1936, Astaire and Rogers placed third in the exhibitors' list of top draws (after Shirley Temple and Clark Gable). *Top Hat* has more of the team's Famous Moments than their other films: Astaire crashing into a tap in a pompous, deadly silent London men's club; Astaire dancing on sand in his hotel room to caress Rogers to sleep in a room below; Astaire, pursuing Rogers, driving the hansom cab in which she hoped to elude him, tapping on the roof to tell her what's what; the two of them dancing "Isn't This a Lovely Day (to be caught in the rain)?" in a gazebo; Astaire shooting down a line of white-tie rivals with his cane in the title song; the startling crane shot that lifts "Cheek to Cheek" just as the music bursts out with a thrill; the view of the famous feet as they step onto the Bakelite Venetian piazza for a brief whirl in "The Piccolino."

The Astaire–Rogers milieu needed a change of air. In *Follow the Fleet* (1936), the pair go proletarian as a sailor and a dance-hall hostess. This time, she does not dislike him on sight: they're old friends, and Rogers has to chase a somewhat reticent Astaire. There is no deluxe Europe, no gala farceurs, no Horton or Blore. It's all shipboard and kitchen in San Francisco. Randolph Scott is back, paired with Harriet Hilliard (later Nelson) as Rogers' ugly duckling sister. Everyone who sees the film dumps on Hilliard, but worse people have played such parts, and she at least gives Lucille Ball something to do as a dance-haller drafted to coach Hilliard in lovemanship. Are there any rules to meeting a sailor? "Yes . . . and no," says Ball. "Yes before . . . and no after."

As in *Roberta*, the Scott romance is the main one, and Astaire is made to contrast with Scott, who is a cinch with girls, a champion rule-obeying sailor, and nonmusical, while Astaire can take or leave them, gets into navy trouble, and not only dances but plays the piano and leads a band. It's a little wearing seeing our stars sharing the terrain with people who don't belong in a dance musical,* and, despite the change of setting, *Follow the Fleet* has a distinct sense of cliché, though the big ballroom duet, "Let's Face the Music and Dance," is Astaire's most ambitious effort in this mode, a tiny one-act dance drama about two losing gamblers who flirt with suicide, then each other.

Berlin wrote the *Follow the Fleet* score, and Jerome Kern and Dorothy Fields wrote *Swing Time* (1936), the masterpiece of the series. With old Broadway hands on the set, there's none of the Hollywood fear of characters singing out wherever they are—another feature of the dance musical: *use* the music. Only two of *Swing Time*'s six numbers are performing spots, "The Waltz in Swing Time" and "Bojangles of Harlem." The others erupt out of the action. Thus, Rogers teaches dance and Astaire pretends he needs a lesson,† takes a few spills, and they're into "Pick Yourself Up," a song about trying, trying again followed by a glorious, breathless exhibition of hot pop stepping capped by the comic duo's attempt to do the same thing. Rogers had been fired for telling Astaire off, and her sidekick Helen Broderick had been fired for insulting Astaire's sidekick Victor Moore. Blore is so impressed with Astaire and Rogers' dancing that he reinstates her, so Moore grabs Broderick to dance her back into her job too. Their parody offers fake ballet, the demolishing of some of the dance-floor furnishings, and an absurd pose for the finish. "You're *still* fired," snaps Blore.

---

*It might be argued that Scott doesn't belong in any kind of musical, but the Hollywood form is more flexible—less fully musical—than the Broadway form, and nonsingers have no problem fitting in between the numbers. It's hard to picture Scott or James Stewart or Clint Eastwood or Jean Harlow in a stage musical, but in Hollywood they waited out the numbers, talked through them, had them dubbed, or depended on mike and mixing techniques.

†Eric Blore runs the dance studio. He offers Astaire a choice of "tap, ballroom, and aesthetic dancing," and Astaire asks for "a little of each"—the neatest description of his style ever observed.

Swing Time reclaims the opulence of the earlier pictures yet keeps one hand in *Follow the Fleet*'s empty decorative till. The Depression is sensed, if not mentioned, and the setting is a rather plain New York, the opulence confined to nightclubs. Director George Stevens even shows us Rogers washing her hair during a love song, "The Way You Look Tonight." So we learn that the glamor of Astaire and Rogers inheres not in fancy duds or continental places but in the offhand manner in which they assert the poetry of musical comedy. What else is the dance musical if not a reordering of the priorities in the musical to stress line, rhythm, image, over other elements? This is why there were so few dance musicals in the 1930s—Eleanor Powell had rhythm, but no image, and Berkeley worked almost exclusively in image. Astaire and Rogers pull the whole style together in a lovely and disturbing number, the most extraordinary seven minutes in the whole series, "Never Gonna Dance."

Never Gonna Dance was the film's title till just before release, and though *Swing Time* says it better—its buoyancy conveys the image most completely—the "Never Gonna Dance" scene proves how deeply feelings run in these movies. It's late in the film, and the couple has reached a parting stage, each to marry another. They're alone on a dance floor dominated by a double stairway, he in tails, she in white, and as she sadly starts up the stairs, he breaks into song. Kern shaped it in rondo form, and Fields filled it with bold puns and references to famous people that sound almost like dada in the context of a pop song. "To Groucho Marx I'll give my cravat," he swears, and "To Harpo goes my shiny silk hat," passing from a sauntering, blue refrain into heartfelt and then rhapsodic strains and back to his blue promise: "Only gonna love you! Never gonna dance." She has come back to join him on the floor, and the dance begins in a walk, their arms waving in despair. The music recalls "The Way You Look Tonight," then changes into something jazzy. He gestures at her: "*Why* must we part?" The "Never Gonna Dance" music pushes in, then cedes to "The Waltz in Swing Time," each shift in melody tightening the vise. They climb separate stairs, meeting at the top in the abandon of utter helplessness, the "Never Gonna Dance" strain full out with a gigantic piano descant as they almost beat each other in their turns. Suddenly, she propels herself out of the scene and he bows alone. It is nothing less than a retrospective of the whole film, and took forty-eight takes to can; somewhere around take number twenty-five, Rogers' feet began to bleed.

Swing Time ends, of course, with the pair in each other's arms, sing-

ing "A Fine Romance" and "The Waltz in Swing Time" in counter-
point high over snow-covered Manhattan, but the sorrow of "Never
Gonna Dance" makes a bigger impression than the happy ending, because it's so different. Actually, all Astaire's dances are different. *The
Gay Divorcee*'s "Night and Day" is ballroom seduction, *Roberta*'s "I'll
Be Hard to Handle" contains spoken comedy, *Top Hat*'s "Cheek to
Cheek" is trick ballroom, *Follow the Fleet*'s "Let Yourself Go" is jitterbug and "I'm Putting All My Eggs in One Basket" is vaudeville
butterfeet put-on, *Swing Time*'s "Bojangles of Harlem" is blackface
with trick photography, and *Shall We Dance* (1937) features a ma-
chine-age rhythm dance in a ship's engine room, ballet burlesqued and
ballet for true, a walking number, and a roller-skating duet. *Shall We
Dance* is the terpsichorean equivalent of Hollywood's legit-pop musical crisis. Astaire is a ballet dancer, Rogers a musical-comedy dancer,
and the climactic number hopes to contrast and blend the two. It
doesn't work. The whole film suffers from dualism, for the ballet business uses an actress (Ketti Gallian) in the plot and a dancer (Harriet
Hoctor) in the big number. Very confusing. Otherwise, *Shall We
Dance* would have been top. Perhaps RKO had evolved the dance musical so well that it no longer worried about the quality of dancing as
long as it had an integrated musical, with its special ability to collect
all sorts of *objets trouvés* into a sort of theme. In *Shall We Dance*, the
theme is recognition of romance, knowing the love of your life at first
sight, seeing him/her through disguises, and so on. The film is full of
thematic jags—Astaire puts on a false front when he meets Rogers, the
pair are falsely believed to be married, they fake a quarrel in "Let's
Call the Whole Thing Off" (the one with "You say either and I say
eyether"), they fake a romance and really do marry to bust the rumor
with a divorce, and we even see iconographic representations of Rogers—in a flip-picture book of her dancing (which director Mark Sandrich then turns into the real thing), in a plastic dummy in a PR stunt,
and in the big number, in which, denied the real Rogers, Astaire
dances with a stage full of girls in Rogers masks.

As a style, Astaire and Rogers never grew tired despite their consistency—same places, same people, same (or nearly) love plot. Every one
of their nine RKO films was a success, and the elated beauty of their
personality that impelled the public to clap at the screen after
their numbers never lost its appeal, but neither of the two stars liked
their interdependence. Rogers demanded more money, more publicity
(to equal Astaire's), and the chance to make diverse nonmusicals on
her own. And their last film for RKO, *The Story of Vernon and Irene*

Castle (1939), turns another change in style, being a bio in which the romance is concluded early and the adventure of making it as newfangled ballroom dancers finds them stranded in Paris and domestic in the United States. And Astaire actually dies at the end. Still, the split was due: the history was already made now, nine times.

Nowadays, many delight to tell of an Astaire–Rogers feud and fondly point out that in their reunion film, *The Barkleys of Broadway* (1949), Astaire tells Rogers: "It took a lot of patience to put you where you are . . . I pulled things out of you! I molded you! Like Svengali did Trilby!" But Astaire needed Rogers more than she needed him, for while she was eager to try anything, his character and talent needed the precisely appropriate partner. Sure, Astaire alone is genius enough. But the public longed to watch him find ultimate completion in a partnership. He himself set this up in the affecting honesty with which he played the love plots and the sensuality that came out in his duets with Rogers. In *Roberta*'s "I Won't Dance," she tells him, "When you dance you're charming and you're gentle," and he is—on the condition that she totally surrenders. This is why they come to blows in "Night and Day": *The Gay Divorcee* only established the seduction. The following films affirmed it.

So Rogers made a flurry of films between those with Astaire, but he (who, remember, spent far more time than she did preparing each one) made only one non-Rogers musical, *A Damsel in Distress* (1937). Fine entertainment, it has its troubles—and lost money.

The plan seems right. The source and co-author is P. G. Wodehouse, the setting London and a country palace. The people are English eccentrics, two American wisecrackers, and a lonely princess locked in a chateau. (It sounds like *Love Me Tonight*, but the atmosphere is entirely different from the Parisian Chevalier–MacDonald idyll. That was operetta with shadows; this is musical comedy in a mist.) Astaire is an American musical-comedy star bedeviled by PR about his love conquests; George Burns and Gracie Allen play the comics, Constance Collier the heroine's dragonlike aunt, Reginald Gardiner a scoundrelly butler (with, however, an irresistible craving to sing Italian opera, to Collier's horror); there are also bandleader Ray Noble as an impeccable noble dope who breaks into swing when he gets near a piano, little Harry Watson as a scrappy page, and a fest of madrigal singers. In other words, very Wodehouse, cut with some American pep. The same old team served brilliantly as always: producer Berman, director Stevens, designer Clark, with a Gershwin score. Fine; but who shall dance with Astaire? RKO considered Ruby

Keeler (too American), Jessie Mathews (too giddy), and at last settled on Joan Fontaine, who could neither sing nor dance. The splendid dance musical suddenly pulled back to the old days when a musical was just a film with some songs and things. *A Damsel in Distress* ingeniously works around Fontaine, giving Astaire, Burns, and Allen a comic dance with whisk brooms in a country inn where they kick each other, get kicked by suits of armor, and kick the armor back; and letting Allen sing "Stiff Upper Lip" outside a funhouse, into which the three then proceed for wild visual-cum-musical effects. The madrigal takeoff, "The Jolly Tar and the Milkmaid," is wonderful: Astaire has sneaked into Totleigh Castle with the singers, and must perform with them to evade detection. It's Wodehouse country weekend snafu made vital. Moreover, Stevens films "A Foggy Day" through a handsome fog as Fontaine, high up in the castle, watches Astaire strolling through the park.

But sooner or later the lovers have to duet, and the agreeably laid-back "Things Are Looking Up" is it. Astaire sings it and they do dance, but we clearly see him extending himself to make his partner look good. At one point, she actually sits down while he glides over her, trying to get a little poetry going. To do her justice, Fontaine is fine doing what she does well. This just isn't her part.

Obviously, Astaire was going to have to find a suitable partner after Rogers: someone who danced. On a larger scale, the musical, dance or otherwise, was going to have to consolidate and replenish the form that made it artistic and peculiarly American—a form that hit its prime in these Astaire–Rogers films because it found character and style through song and dance. It was more musical than the Warners backstager, more fluid and natural than the costume operettas, more integrated than the star vehicles. The dance musical exercised highly evolved musical instincts that most people supposedly can't respond to, and made a fortune. It liked and respected its audience, and taught a self-esteem at once egalitarian (Fred as Mr. Yank) and elite (Fred dances), casual (Fred's self-spoof) and special (Fred's tails), everyday (Ginger) and unique (Ginger). Now, can Hollywood develop this aesthetic with different stars and staff? Or will the integration of musical parts simply disperse as Astaire and Rogers did?

☆ 8 ☆
Opera Versus Croonbelt

THE SOUND FILM'S first purpose was to transmit music, preferably respectable music. But sound turned out to be mainly talking, and the music, to suit the stories, was popular. Still, studio executives longed to find a place for opera—meaning "real" music. William Fox hoped to do well, as well as good, when he brought Irish tenor John McCormack to the screen in *Song O' My Heart* (1930), partly filmed in Ireland on little more than McCormack's charm and art. The film was a public service, for its slight sentimental storyline is a peg on which to hang McCormack's repertory, thus bringing his recital to a national public. Fox even ran ads asking that public to help choose the songs for the film, from such as "When Irish Eyes Are Smiling" and "My Wild Irish Rose." Like the first Vitaphone vaudeville, this was fine musicianship. Like the second Vitaphone, it was popular material, of universal appeal. Immediately successful, *Song O' My Heart* proved film's commercial potential for the real-music voice. McCormack couldn't act and the proceedings were kept dramatically subdued in order not to overextend him, but nobody complained, for *Song O' My Heart* acted like what it was: a chance to hear great singing set off by some romantic and some comic characters. Why didn't Fox just film McCormack in recital? That wouldn't have been a movie; people like a story.

Most opera singers, used to filling huge theatres, tended to a huge dullness or a huge excitement; neither one, we remember from the early musicals, was good for film. But Grace Moore's comeback in *One Night Of Love* reopened the case for the legit singer, and in they came. Baritone Lawrence Tibbett returned for *Metropolitan* (1935) and *Un-*

der Your Spell (1936); tenor James Melton, soprano Lily Pons, and mezzo Gladys Swarthout all followed up debuts with second, third, or fourth films. Now secure about form, Hollywood fit the singers into the framework more gracefully. The studios tried lavish costume operettas or inexpensive modern-dress stories—Mamoulian, always the odd man in, united the two approaches in *The Gay Desperado*.

The modern-dress opera-singer films lacked purpose. Even when Warners put Busby Berkeley in charge of the dances in Melton's debut, *Stars Over Broadway* (1935), the result lacked flash. Melton performs legit and pop ("Carry Me Back to the Lone Prairie") and some Warren–Dubin, and the story—agent Pat O'Brien discovers and manipulates hotel porter Melton, aiming him at a pop radio market until Melton hits the skids and O'Brien gives up and sends him off to Italy—is serviceable. But when Berkeley smelled a production number in "September in the Rain" and planned his usual fiesta in a forest of dancing trees, Warners waxed stingy, and the song had to wait till its reprise in *Melody for Two* (1937), Melton's third and last film, to make its effect.

Melton himself made little effect, but then all of the opera singers had something wrong somewhere. Swarthout's problem was her acting. She wasn't incompetent; she was . . . an opera singer doing film. Paramount's *Rose of the Rancho* (1935), with John Boles, plenty of guitars and mantillas, and a Ralph Rainger–Leo Robin score, is Swarthout's best, with big duet, "Thunder Over the Prairie"; big rouser, "Got a Gal in Californ-i-a"; "If I Should Lose You" for Boles; waltz flirtation title tune ("I could call you a flame or a flower . . ."); and Swarthout's gala set piece, "Where Is My Love?" with swirling strings, flamenco stompings, sneaky waltz theme ("Some night in summer by the moon, my love will come riding"), the usual rhetoric from the chorus ("Why does he hesitate? Why does he linger?"), and a high note on the significant word ("Where is my *love*?").

Pons had less voice than Swarthout but more va-va-voom; she also had a Jerome Kern–Dorothy Fields score to back up the operatic stuff in RKO's *I Dream Too Much* (1935). Detractors have dubbed it *I Scream Too Much*, fans call it *I Cream Just Right*, and Pons does draw heavily on her top register. Henry Fonda, Osgood Perkins, and Eric Blore fill out the cast, but the film is all Pons. She starts at the piano with "Caro Nome," cheers up a child at a fairground with a men's chorus in "The Jockey on the Carrousel," tries swing in "I Got Love" and bares her exquisitely impertinent naval in *Lakmé*'s Bell Song. A drawback was Pons' heavy French accent, impenetrable in the high-flying "Jockey," wherein the choristers have to step in with solo lines so we can follow the lyrics. But what American pop singer could bring off such a number, with its volatile tempo and harmony geared to suggest the abandon of a carousel ride? A sad tale of figurines, a jockey who loves and dies for a dancer, the song lies well beyond the reach of the actors who inhabited the average musical and makes a splendid impression.

The "opera" musical, then, had its advantages. Grace Moore's five Columbia films offer an instance, for while Moore is no actress—she smiles a lot and seems unaware that she's wearing the weirdest clothes in film history—she sure was a singer, and carried her films with vivacious renderings of opera and pop. *One Night of Love* led to *Love Me Forever* (1935); the aforementioned von Sternberg opus *The King Steps Out*; *When You're in Love* (1937), with Cary Grant; and *I'll Take Romance* (1937). The last is typical, small in budget, with Moore as a diva courted by opera company manager Melvyn Douglas. As actor, Douglas is expert, leaving Moore looking foolish until she rehearses or performs opera or accompanies herself on the piano in the title song, a gentle waltz, as Douglas looks on. The opera includes bits of *La Traviata*, *Martha*, *Manon*, and *Madama Butterfly*, the pop "She'll Be Comin' Round the Mountain," and French music hall; Helen Westley plays Moore's tough mother, Margaret Hamilton does a maid, Stuart Irwin is Douglas' sidekick, and the two leads take turns having each other kidnapped. That's the film.

The constant emphasis on pop is no stunt, though it goes a mite haywire when Moore blats her way through "Minnie the Moocher" in *When You're in Love.* It is an attempt to make up for the often scrappy singing of the regular musical-comedy types. Anyone can sing pop, but not everyone has the musicality that penetrates the material to deliver all it has in emotional conception. Fred Astaire had it, and songwriters were crazed to hear Astaire perform their work, though his was neither a golden nor a trained voice. But most of Astaire's colleagues were not great interpreters—which is where the opera people came in, with their cowboy songs and "Shortnin' Bread." They worked pop as well as Astaire, and with a lot more voice, and the drive for musicality became contagious. Kirsten Flagstad, Helen Jepson, Charles Kullman, Lauritz Melchior, Leopold Stokowski, José Iturbi, and others were drummed into the corps; the call went out to ballet people such as George Balanchine; and Jascha Heifitz even undertook a speaking role (as himself, giving a concert to save a slum-area music school) in Samuel Goldwyn's *They Shall Have Music*

(1939). The title reads like a fetish. The odd thing is that Hollywood had already built up a company of extraordinary musical talents, widely enjoyed but uncelebrated. Because they sang pop.

The American singing style had changed remarkably in the decade or so that preceded the implementation of sound in cinema. The parlor ballads, waltzes, and novelty songs largely written and performed by the white Protestant middle class had ceded to black saloon piano and its derivations, the startlingly everyday feeling of the Irish George M. Cohan and the Jewish Irving Berlin and Jerome Kern, who touched base with black ragtime to create an American idiom. New singers appeared to sing the new songs. A more conversational approach to lyrics subdued the "lay 'em in the aisles" bombast. Baritones and belters elbowed aside the clammy tenors and sopranos. Upstart minorities in vaudeville imposed odd jargon and inflections on the midcult. Imaginative "scat" variations on the tune or lyrics made each performance fresh and personal. Bold instrumentalists helped layer the new styles with their explosive accompaniments. And, finally, the rise of radio in the 1920s promoted the new song styles as vaudeville, cabaret, and Broadway could not, sending Fanny Brice and Nick Lucas and Ethel Waters to all corners of the nation.

These three typify the new wave, Brice with her heavy Jewish slant on comedy and—in a wholly different voice—unutterable doomed grandeur in torch songs; Lucas (the "Singing Troubador") with his light presentation, so suitable over a strummed guitar; Waters with her black savvy and sexy repertory. Each got into a few films, and others carried on after them, but the studios never saw these singing talents as exponents of a native art, and continued to look for that touch of opera to "redeem" pop. Yet American art history was made in pop, not in opera. Pop liberated the underdog races, and let women show their guts and men be capricious and tender.

Take Sophie Tucker. In her first film, *Honky Tonk*, in 1930, she delivers "Some of These Days (you're gonna miss me, honey)" in a robust woman's basso, warning a lover of her impending departure and sounding rather pleased about it, and hits a combination of speech, recitative, and all-out singing in her motto tune, "I'm the Last of the Red-Hot Mamas." Tucker's was a sturdy voice, one that puts over rather than dandles a song, but she knew how to build a number, letting it dance out like a lariat to pull it taut at the climax. This she does in "Feathering a Nest (for a little bluebird)," a man's song that she sings without bothering to change the pronouns. This would have been unthinkable for Brice, who acted her songs; Tucker just delivers them.

She even asks her nightclub audience to join in, easing down one aggressive *espontanea* with a "Lovely, darling! Lovely, dear! Lovely!" as Tucker prepares to take over and push home to a big-bang finale. The girl's slender amateur's soprano contrasts vividly with Tucker's husky professionalism: Tucker represents the new mixed culture, up from the tanktown music halls to take the nation, music with an ethnic face, whereas the girl is the old pure culture, a slice of white bread far from her box. An unknown Marilyn Miller or Nancy Carroll might have played the part.

If pop music let women express initiative, it let men relax. Woman belted, men crooned. The word "croon" has been so overused it has no meaning anymore; let's reclaim its definition. The microphone invented crooning. No longer having to send a song into the ozone the hard way, men singers took to using the barest veneer of voice on the radio, giving everything a mellow and intimate air. Many men were crooners, but because Bing Crosby was the best known, his singing style is called crooning. Wrong. Crosby's amazing inventiveness led him into all sorts of riffs and embellishments way beyond crooning. True, his voice rang mellow and he aimed at the intimate. But his rhythmic dexterity, his sly phrasing, his athletic leaps up and down the scale, and his sudden strange distillations of emotional give were not in the crooner's vocabulary. And his immense popularity changed the course of American singing.

Crosby hastened the emergence of the easy-style singer. The dramatic baritone survived in Nelson Eddy and Howard Keel, but they were strictly operetta. Modern-dress musicals needed a more vernacular sound. The tenor who bleated story ballads passed away, though film continued to feature tenors with a lively style, such as Dick Powell—here was another gifted stylist, much underrated now that pop tenors are practically extinct. If the monitors of the Production Code counted any musicians, surely they should have complained about Powell, for beneath the clear-cut look and the paper-route smile lurked a hot lad with a ready kiss. In *42nd Street*, he jumps on stage from the wings to launch "Young and Healthy" with boyish verve, and the lyrics do sound innocent (as in "I'm full of vitamin A"). Powell, however, doesn't. As the number proceeds, he invests the tune with a leer, slipping in a wicked m-m-m just before one line and exploding in a satyr's whinny after "vitamin A." Crosby recorded the song with Guy Lombardo; here is a telling comparison, not between the new and the old but between two types of new. Where Powell is eager, overeager, a little crazed, Crosby is just energetic. Both sound amused at their hunger, but where Powell would like to satisfy it pronto, Crosby enjoys the waiting, with a little scat variation chorus to toy with the tune. (Lombardo and his Royal Canadians assist in setting the tone with an extremely precise arrangement whose only gambol is a pouting guitar solo.) Compared to the old-style tenor who insipidly sings "The Wedding of the Painted Doll" in *The Broadway Melody*, Powell and Crosby are new brooms sweeping into the future.

They made it look too easy to be important, however, and the studios kept on sifting through the legit ranks, trying to find repute and profits in a workable genre. It was MGM that made the breakthrough, not with one star, but a pair. Chevalier and MacDonald, together for the last time in as late as 1934, gave way to MacDonald and Ramon Novarro (in *The Cat and the Fiddle* later that same year), and then to Novarro and Evelyn Laye (in *The Night Is Young* the next year). Neither pairing worked. At last MGM found the solution, as we know: MacDonald and Eddy in *Naughty Marietta*.

Their eight pictures together, from 1935 to 1942, are not as consistent as the Astaire–Rogers series, and not unique. When the King and Queen of Carioca made films without each other, they made different kinds of films, but MacDonald made operettas without Eddy and vice versa, operettas that they might easily have made together. Yet MacDonald and Eddy were, in their way, a true team, mixing the chemistry that permits one to accept disguised princesses, dream melodies, and beautiful doom. Operetta was dying on Broadway by the 1930s, but through mostly careful planning MGM concocted a recipe to produce excellent films of lasting appeal: efficient directors to keep the juice flowing (W. S. Van Dyke II and Robert Z. Leonard), simple stories focused on the central romance rather than plot business, lavish decor, resonant titles from Broadway's past, strong scores of diverse origin excellently conducted (by Herbert Stothart), and lots of singing by the two leads with little help from others. These were less fully equipped vehicles than the RKO dance musical, where assorted folderol helped the principals establish their special world view. Take Astaire and Rogers out of their movies and something would remain: much of the "Carioca," "The Continental," "The Piccolino"; all of "Orchids in the Moonlight," "Yesterdays," "Smoke Gets in Your Eyes," "Get Thee Behind Me, Satan," Eric Blore in a hundred tizzies, Edward Everett Horton in a thousand double-takes, Delores Del Rio, Ralph Bellamy, Edna May Oliver, and so on. But take MacDonald and Eddy out of their films and you'd leave nothing behind except an occasional heavy who gives the love plot suspense.

☆ *MACDONALD AND HER MEN: above, she's worried with Ruggles in*
One Hour With You; *she's startled with Chevalier in* The Merry Widow
(they're locked in jail by royal order: love or rot!); below, she's pensive in The
Cat and the Fiddle *but Novarro's sporty under an umbrella.*

☆ *Above, in* The Firefly, *she's radiant with Jones in a backlot Breughel; she's at war with Eddy in* Sweethearts; *below, she's pathetic with Barrymore in* Maytime. *Who wouldn't be?*

Rose Marie (1936), which followed *Naughty Marietta*, brings in Allan Jones in the opening opera sequence, and James Stewart has a small but important role as MacDonald's outlaw brother, but this is perhaps MacDonald and Eddy's most resonant team effort (if only because "Indian Love Call" is so basic to the camp lampoon). The pair spend much of the action alone together in the wilderness—she is trying to save Stewart from Mountie Eddy and he is tracking him. The antagonistic nature of their respective interests is what makes *Rose Marie* fundamental to an understanding of the MacDonald–Eddy pact. Where Astaire and Rogers fuss a bit and then slip into love, and where Chevalier and MacDonald had only a plot jag to smooth down, MacDonald and Eddy clear the whole social system to get together. She is the aristocrat, he the insurgent (*Naughty Marietta*, *New Moon*, *Bittersweet*); she the star, he the nobody (*Maytime*); she the frontier maid, he the desperado (*The Girl of the Golden West*). Only in *Sweethearts* are they equals, and in *Rose Marie* they are divided by the law code her brother has broken.

Little of the Friml–Stothart–Harbach–Hammerstein stage *Rose-Marie* survived; MGM's plan was to affirm the personalities unveiled in *Naughty Marietta*: the raving coloratura and the arrogant scout who meet on the high notes. Thus, *Rose Marie*'s early scenes revolve around a temperamental MacDonald, the middle scenes bring in Eddy's oppositional steadiness, and the final scenes attempt to conciliate them. We open on a performance of Gounod's *Roméo et Juliette*; curtain down, MacDonald curses out the orchestra and berates Jones for "holding every high A longer than I did": Rose Marie is proud. Wangling some influential help for her brother—Rose Marie is loyal and loves chastely—she entertains the Canadian prime minister with "Pardon Me, Madame." The singing inspires people all over her hotel to join in, even the switchboard operators: Rose Marie has The Gift. And she is gracious, tossing flowers to her admirers in the street. But she learns that Stewart has escaped from prison and killed a Mountie. Rose Marie runs off—cancel her dates!—to the rescue.

Enter Eddy and his Mounties. In the tradition of movie "halfbreeds," Rose Marie's Indian guide has robbed her, and she winds up in a frontier saloon singing for supper. Here is a main chance to trade off pop and legit, as MacDonald stands a honky-tonk belter (Gilda Gray) in a challenge sing on "Dinah" and "Some of These Days." MacDonald flounders, and Eddy sympathizes. "One thing about Belle," he says. "If she ever got lumbago, she'd never sing a note." He looks dandy in his uniform, though he is as stiff on location as on a sound stage. Lake Tahoe provides a stirring setting for an Indian-festival big number, "Totem Tom-Tom," very barbaric with an immense opening long shot and precise closer views of a huge drum (rolled in, played, danced on, and revolved), wild animal costumes, grand totem poles, lake, and mountains.

But we're here for a love duet—if this were RKO, Astaire and Rogers would have danced by now—and MGM attempts to bring the stars together with song and charm. Eddy serenades MacDonald with the title song in a canoe, admitting that he sings it to other women, inserting the appropriate name. "But it didn't work with Maude. Nothing worked with Maude." The line is a dud—neither MacDonald nor Eddy can play corn.

Only a Martian, in 1936, could not have known that "Indian Love Call" is the centerpiece of *Rose Marie*, a mantra of operetta in general and these two in particular. When MacDonald discovers an echo and sings "Three Blind Mice" with herself (Rose Marie has wit), we moderns brace ourselves for the notorious close-up shots. She'll stare grimly at his mouth, right? They'll fight for right of profile, right? Actually, Van Dyke directs straightforwardly, letting out the rope of operetta by inches. First, MacDonald has to shiver in the wild and have mishaps and finally accept Eddy's help. *Now.* She hears distant singing—the Indian love call of Romeo-and-Juliet ghosts! Eddy tells the legend: when a lover gives the call, they answer. Still Van Dyke holds back, giving Eddy the song for a verse and chorus. No Indian echoes, no MacDonald. They separate for sleep. Only later does Van Dyke give in, in a reprise, and this is the one, with MacDonald very into the mime, looking tender, looking away, closing her eyes, and Eddy staring at her transfixed. When they kiss, we hear the Indian spirits' echo.

With *Naughty Marietta* and *Rose Marie* behind them, MacDonald and Eddy set the scene for the standout operetta series, a reference known to millions who have never seen them in action. This is a questionable credit. And it seems that MacDonald had no desire to spend all her career singing love calls with anybody, and she called to MGM's attention a script by Robert Hopkins about a nightclub owner and an opera singer in old San Francisco. MacDonald wanted to play the singer opposite Clark Gable; Gable couldn't see it. But with the script rewritten by Anita Loos and a strong feeling of drama with songs rather than operetta minus one voice, the project showed great possibilities, with lots of Barbary Coast goodtime, a smashing earthquake finale, and a part that screamed for Gable. *San Francisco* (1936)

ended up as one of the year's big films and its lengthy earthquake sequence rivals any recent disaster film for verisimilitude and terror.
Where does it stand as operetta? MacDonald handles most of the music—everything from *Faust* and *La Traviata* to ancient music hall and
"Nearer My God to Thee"—and makes a nifty couple with Gable. "If
there's anything I admire," he tells her when she repulses his first advance, "it's a woman you can trust out of town." (A bit later, he tells
his mirror, "Goodnight, sucker!") Marietta's reticence and Rose Marie's strength are portable. And it's fun to hear the odd number in
what would most likely have been a straight tough guy–demure gal
epic. The fetish for setting pop and legit side by side inspires two versions of the title song: MacDonald sings it and swings it. Her high-
flying descant in "The Battle Hymn of the Republic," a big choral
finale as the San Franciscans march back into their wrecked town, is a
little much, but Van Dyke makes the moment so exhilarating that only
a creep would complain. It may well be that operetta helped to reas-
similate vocal music into dramatic film after the antimusical reaction
of 1930–31. Any movie might contain a song or two, but if a MacDonald could bring presence to melodrama, the sky was the limit.

MGM was eager to get the next operetta going, and MacDonald re-
joined Eddy for *Maytime* (1937), from a Sigmund Romberg show so
successful that two productions ran simultaneously on Broadway in
1917. Irving Thalberg felt the time was right to try Technicolor in its
more natural three-color process,* but his sudden death halted shooting. L. B. Mayer took over, starting from scratch in black-and-white
with a complete change of script, score, staff, and supporting cast. The
result has been called the best of the MacDonald–Eddy films, though
Romberg would have recognized little more than the title, one melody,
and his name in the credits. John Barrymore, so wet that he had to
read his lines off huge cue cards and seems ever about to topple over,
comes between the stars like a beached ham, but with a rich score taking in a large snatch of Act One of Meyerbeer's *Les Huguenots* (a rare
item at the time), Delibes' "Les Filles de Cadiz," special material for
Eddy, and a fake opera, *Tsaritsa*, culled from Chaikofsky's Fifth Symphony, the story hardly matters. The spectacular decor is a relief after
Rose Marie's endless trees, the theme—love matters more than ca-

*Trivium Footnote no. 5: The first three-strip Technicolor musical was *The Dancing Pirate* (1936), a fast failure remembered only by Rodgers–Hart buffs for a superb ballad, "Are You My Love?" Yes, the pirate danced.

reer—consistent with the stars' personae, and the big ball sequence tremendously lavish.

But is *Maytime* a masterpiece? Possibly the best of the MacDonald–Eddy series is *The Firefly* (1937), mainly because Eddy isn't in it. Its male lead is an Eddy role—that of the gallant Napoleonic spy who trails enemy spy MacDonald, loves her, yet must destroy her—but this script called for more comic agility than Eddy had, and Allan Jones stepped in, gentle in comedy, a Zorro in war. As with *Maytime*, the original Broadway libretto was tossed out, but its best songs (by Rudolf Friml and Otto Harbach) were retained and a wonderful new one added, "The Donkey Serenade."

MacDonald had been a dancer on Broadway before she came to Hollywood, and *The Firefly* introduces choreography into the opera musical, with the Albertina Rasch girls twirling during the title credits followed by marching soldiers. This is wartime, France against Spain. MacDonald gets off on an odd foot for a costume operetta, saying, "I can't imagine any man as exciting as service to my country," but the songs are all about love: "When a Maid Comes Knocking at Your Heart," "Love Is Like a Firefly," "The Magic of a Woman's Kiss," "Sympathy," Jones' serenade, "Giannina Mia," MacDonald's "He Who Loves and Runs Away" (performed with a *Tosca* cane), which starts out as a tango and ends as a military march sung by the male chorus while MacDonald throws off coloratura decoration in a Napoleon hat. "The Donkey Serenade" is the gem, set to a clopping beat and accompanied by guitar and a reed pipe as Jones rides along with MacDonald's carriage trying to thrill her. She doesn't thrill easy, but the song's infectious rhythm captures her duenna, the driver, and his boy, who merrily bob to the beat. Friml adapted it from a swinging fox trot, "Chansonette," and it became so popular that revivals of the stage *Firefly* have had to include it, though no one can find a good place for a coach and donkey in a show about an Italian waif taken up by the country club set who becomes an opera singer.

Democratic revolution is touched on in a number of these films, but *The Firefly* gives us a full-scale rebellion when Napoleon's puppet Joseph Bonaparte is plopped onto the Spanish throne and a mob is forced to welcome him to Madrid. A fetid cripple spits, the army shoots at hostile children, and revolt breaks out. Operetta as musical concept and dramatic faerie dissolves into war chronicle—a daring foray out of format, but it is not sustained. In fact, the film falls into inadvertent burlesque that makes "Indian Love Call" look like Edith

Evans and Ralph Richardson reading Magna Charta. We move to the French encampment, where gypsies are entertaining, led by that arch-gypsy, Jeanette MacDonald, who vocalizes a snippet of Rimsky-Korsakof's *Capriccio Espagnol.* "Bring that girl to headquarters," sniffs a French general; how fresh. MacDonald is unmasked and condemned to death. From her prison, she sees Jones wounded and, as the cannons boom, slips into a fraught reprise of "Giannina Mia." After more war montage, a freed people exult and MacDonald finds Jones in a makeshift hospital. A last cut gives us the two plugging "The Donkey Serenade" and "Giannina Mia."

The habit of assigning all song to the two leads is beginning to exhaust our concentration. Is nothing but the love plot worthy of musical elaboration? In expanding the pictorial canvas to include imperialist oppression, MGM had a grand opportunity to expand operetta, too, with choral numbers of populist resistance, with freedom-fighter sidekicks and royalist plotters. MGM didn't take it; and Mayer read *The Firefly*'s relatively low grosses as a sign that Jones lacked Eddy's appeal as MacDonald's partner. Nor did Eddy's film with Eleanor Powell, *Rosalie,* break box-office records. So it was Jeanette and Nelson again in *The Girl of the Golden West* (1938), from David Belasco's play about the tomboy caught between a rogue and a sheriff. There's music in this tale—Puccini made a fine opera of it—but Sigmund Romberg and Gus Kahn's score, original for the film, doesn't dig. Nor was the pair all that well served in a modern-dress backstager in Technicolor, *Sweethearts* (1938). The critics shrugged and the fans reveled, though few supported Eddy's western with a pick-up score, *Let Freedom Ring* (1939), or MacDonald's *Broadway Serenade* (1939), the latter distinguished mainly by a fluffy hat even more spectacular than the one MacDonald wore in *San Francisco.* A better idea was *Balalaika* (1939), which Eddy made with Ilona Massey, a beautiful and gifted actress who got few chances to make her mark. Here she shines as a conspirator in Russia in 1914. Too many writers failed to fulfill the script's premise, an interesting idea for operetta (Cossack loves Bolshevik), and Massey's tense precision shows up Eddy's heavy hand as MacDonald, heavy in an elfin way, never did. But an unforgettable junction of plot and score finds Eddy, a noble disguised as a penniless baritone, singing "The Volga Boatman's Song" for Massey's radical group, disguised as a music school. They test Eddy's cover: is he really a baritone? *Is* he? Does Lenin have a beard? As his voice pours out, the astonished spies/musicians become entranced as musicians, singing and playing along, adding in descants and harmonies, and Massey is stunned. The camera follows Eddy as he moves from man to man, daring them not to succumb; then it closes in on her, capping the scene in her wonder. This is great filming, but for some reason the revolutionary story doesn't pan out and all ends patly in émigré Paris.

Mayer thrust MacDonald and Eddy into a remake of *New Moon* (1940) to retrieve their old glory in *Marietta* costumes and Romberg tunes. This version is more faithful to the original than the Grace Moore–Lawrence Tibbett *New Moon* had been, and the two stars rally us with a potpourri of the hits under the credits; but we have been here before. In the 1940s, Hollywood was to find new ways of bringing Real Music to the people, and MacDonald and Eddy were eased out. *Bitter Sweet* (1940), from Noël Coward's operetta, was a flop *Maytime*, and two solo vehicles—*Smilin' Through* (1941) for MacDonald and *The Chocolate Soldier* (1941) for Eddy—did no better, though the latter gave Eddy his best role as an actor who impersonates a Russian seducer to test his wife (Risë Stevens). Worst of all was *I Married an Angel* (1942), a risqué fantasy that Rodgers and Hart had conceived for the screen some years before and finally turned into a dance musical on Broadway for Vera Zorina. MacDonald and Eddy were wrong for the roles and the score, and they knew it, but Mayer couldn't get Zorina, so in they went. That finished them: came then revue bits and solo outings—Eddy's *The Phantom of the Opera* (1943), with Susanna Foster, *Knickerbocker Holiday* (1944), with Constance Dowling, and *Northwest Outpost* (1947), a Republic western with Ilona Massey; MacDonald's *Cairo* (1942), with Robert Young, *Three Daring Daughters* (1948), with José Iturbi, and *The Sun Comes Up* (1949), with Lassie; the rest was silence. Sadly, MacDonald was passed over for the lead in the film version of *The King and I*, potentially an outstanding meeting of great person and great part.

Operetta's emphasis on fine nonpop music is to be commended, and some of this repertory—MacDonald's "Les Filles de Cadiz" or Grace Moore's *Butterfly* scenes—has not often been bettered anywhere. But operetta seldom used its music as well as the less pretentious musicals did—though pop, on the other hand, suffered guilt for enjoying itself so easily. As early as *The Jazz Singer*, the protagonist endures hideous torment for his love of lowdown performance, and the theme haunted the studios. In *Naughty But Nice* (1939), Dick Powell finished off his Warners contract as a music professor who visits New York to promote his symphony and tangles with Tin Pan Alley. The film manages to respect, need, love, suspect, and ridicule serious music all at once:

Powell wears glasses and has maiden aunts who play violin, 'cello, and harp trios, so he must dance jitterbug; Alley hacks pore through the classics swiping tunes; Ann Sheridan sings a "darky" number (another Alley fetish) called "Corn Pickin'," and Wagner and Mozart vie with Warren–Mercer songs for the ear's pleasure.

Could Hollywood ever accommodate the two styles instead of contrasting them? It did in the 1940s, which is why it no longer needed—or could even bear—MacDonald and Eddy. As an omen, MGM made a short with adolescent contractees Deanna Durbin and Judy Garland in which pop and legit singing stand side by side as allies in the battle for art. Called *Every Sunday* (1936) and based on the screen test that the two girls had just made together, the one-reeler presents "Judy" and "Edna" (Durbin's given name) as boosters of open-air concerts suffering poor attendance. The solution: the girls join the concerts, Durbin singing Arditi's fancy waltz "Il Bacio" for the refined crowd and Garland doing "(Dance to the sweet music of) Americana" for the common folk. No! The point is that everyone enjoys both styles, and the concerts are saved as a huge crowd enjoys the pair sharing an encore of "Americana," Durbin on coloratura.

Ironically, Durbin and Garland went separate ways thereafter, the former to Universal, where Joe Pasternak made her queen of the light classics in modern-dress little miss fix-it comedies.* So Judy sang low and Durbin sang high after all. It's just as well, for mainstream America had already taken its turn into the swing that would eventually lead it to rock, which is as far from legit as music can go (or was, until the Beatles introduced classical technique into the rock sound in such songs as "She's Leaving Home," "Julia," and "Eleanor Rigby"). In the 1940s, the Hollywood musical moved, so to speak, to the left. Or, rather, it created a new center, leaving casquette girls, Mounties, and the whole bittersweet maytime corn dance out on a limb. Early in *New Moon*, MacDonald tells Eddy, "You're very romantic, aren't you?" "Aren't *you*, Madam?" he replies, and she says, "Yes—within reason."

---

*Legend tells that Durbin was let go by accident; Mayer said "Drop the fat one"—meaning Garland—and an underling thought he meant Durbin. But Christopher Finch claims that the MGM music department made the decision, prudently, because two precocious teenagers were too much of a good sing—and perhaps because Garland's pop was going to prove more handy than Durbin's opera.

☆ 9 ☆
The Comedy Musical

Hollywood was expert in comedy in the 1920s; sound smashed all that to pieces. The amoral chaos of Mack Sennett's Keystone Kops, Buster Keaton's unflappable grace under implausible pressures, and Charlie Chaplin's outcast transforming thought into deed against hopeless odds—these and other rules for behavior depended on the same surrealistic naturalism that supported John Gilbert's great loving and Douglas Fairbanks' all-American gallantry. Sound made new plans for comedy, made it verbal and realistic, demoting almost all the experts to has-beens. Harold Lloyd made the transition, as did Chaplin (after his boycott failed to take), but only Stan Laurel and Oliver Hardy stepped out of silence into sound unscathed.

They stepped into a few musicals, too, but made no attempt to assimilate song and dance into comedy or vice versa. They appear in *The Rogue Song*, Lawrence Tibbett's big Russian operetta, as members of Tibbett's bandit gang, but their bits—a shaving routine and an adventure in a cave—have nothing to do with the story. They take more of a part in *Babes in Toyland* (1934), from the 1903 Victor Herbert spectacle, but don't sing in it, an odd way to run a musical. RKO had planned a *Babes* in 1930 as a vehicle for Bert Wheeler and Robert Woolsey, no-fail box office champs since *Rio Rita*, with Irene Dunne, Ned Sparks, Dorothy Lee, Edna May Oliver, and "2,000 others." But this was cancelled and the Laurel–Hardy *Babes*, for MGM, lacks the musical all-aroundness that RKO's blueprint implies, with Dunne's voice, Sparks' gravelly weirdness, Lee's darling charm, and Oliver's fussy pomp. Laurel and Hardy's *Babes* consists entirely of dark settings, infantile horror, and nonentities in every part but the stars'. Moreover, their idea of fun—fighting, panicking, blundering, and cry-ing—adds nothing to the material itself.

It would have been interesting to see what Chaplin or Keaton would have done in an all-out musical. But at least Hollywood could draw from Broadway, vaudeville, and burlesque, where our national comic styles had been evolved over decades of improvisation. All of this transferred easily to the screen. There were standup duos who played games irrelevant to the story (like Wheeler and Woolsey), singles who played the protagonist of their films (like Joe E. Brown), comics who played with the protagonist (like Joe E. Brown's various woman partners), comics who supported (like Horton and Blore in the Astaire–Rogers series), or comics who did specialties (like the Three Stooges, who perform their violent trio in a moment of *Dancing Lady*), some of them singing and dancing and some not. Eddie Cantor was the most complete performer of all, and his vehicles founded the comedy film musical, though they were derived from the stage—*Whoopee!*, direct from Broadway, more or less established Cantor's format. But Cantor's films were too expensive to imitate; only Goldwyn would have poured so much into an idea that could be just as funny without lavish decor, imposing scores, or Goldwyn Girls.

By the mid–1930s, the comedy musical had collapsed. Brown's films suffered poor scores, Cantor was working radio, Bert Lahr and Ed Wynn had not found a place for themselves in film, and other suitable comedians had not tried to. There were to be later attempts, such as the Crosby–Hope *Road* pictures and Goldwyn's Danny Kaye series. But the essentially comic musical—one that exploited comedy through music—remained rare, perhaps because the average musical already had comedy. Some musicals had it organically in the action, or in good lines—the Berkeley backstagers, for instance. Some musicals had it plunked in by improvisational specialists—Fox's Ritz Brothers, say, who would enliven anything with their stupid accents and insulting female impersonations. Because they worked as a unit the Ritzes never individualized themselves like the Marx Brothers, nor were they particularly funny, but they were useful in support of stars who did not play comedy, such as Alice Faye or Sonja Henie. The Warners backstagers are about survival, so their characters joke about working. The RKO dance musicals are about courtship, so their characters joke about love. The Fox musicals aren't really about anything, and had nothing to joke about; enter the Ritz Brothers.

Similarly subsidiary but often the best things in many films were George Burns and Gracie Allen. Both could dance passably and Allen could get through a song, but their speciality was a set of variations on one theme: Allen is daffy and Burns can't believe his ears. Years later, pioneering the TV sitcom, he listened wryly for her crazy comebacks, but in the 1930s he was still playing takes—on a desert island in *We're Not Dressing* or among the English country set in *A Damsel in Distress.* Touring Totleigh Castle, Burns asks the guide, of the present lord, "Does he herd sheep?" Allen corrects him: "One says, 'Does he *hear* sheep' or '*Has* he heard sheep?'"

Most original of the comic stars was Mae West, who kept Paramount afloat during the Depression till mounting resistance to her libertarian ease hunted her from the screen. She was truly subversive; here was one gold digger who meant it, a woman who made no pretense of fearing sex. One of the last of Broadway's actor-managers, her own author and director, West also sang, but she never made a musical. Yet she does truly use the two or three songs that crop up in each film, extending her persona into them, and thought enough of them to hire Xavier Cugat and Duke Ellington and their bands for several of her pictures.

West was one of the country's great humorists. The plots of her films suggest a vanity stunt—1890s-era outfits, pallid competition from the other women, and every man in sight ravening for West's outdated hourglass figure. But she seems to regard the whole thing as a put-on, sociological satire disguised as melodrama in a general air of slang, lawbreaking, and sentimentality. West indulges in the first two and looks on with pleasure while others uphold the third, though she is capable of it herself. But she's no one's fool. She saunters into her first film, *Night After Night* (1932), in a speakeasy. "Who's there?" cries the bouncer at the door. And West's voice comes back, "The fairy princess, ya mug." Or in *She Done Him Wrong* (1933), Salvation Army captain Cary Grant begs her to conform to the Hollywood all-truth of monogamous constancy. "Haven't you ever met a man who could make you happy?" he asks her. "Sure," she tells him. "Lots of times." Or in *I'm No Angel* (1933), a date tells her he's a politician and she replies, "I don't like work, either." These films would have made wonderful musicals. The scene in *Goin' To Town* (1935) in which West attempts to crash society by singing opera—Saint-Saëns' *Samson et Dalila*, naturally—plays a marvelous joke on Hollywood's legit fetish; imagine a whole evening of such spoof.

On the other hand, it takes a sharp talent to set a spoof to music. The films of the Marx Brothers flirt with the notion of going musical, but the brothers' anarchy forbids it. The musical, no matter how loosely structured, has order of a sort; the Marxes are perfect disorder. Because they worked up from vaudeville into the Broadway musical complete with love plot and dances, they figured out how to demolish

☆ *THE COMIC MUSICAL: opposite above, the Goldwyn Girls deliver* "Bend Down, Sister" *in a Cantor vehicle,* Palmy Days *(note fake city through windows); below, final shot of* The Cocoanuts, *the Marx Brothers in their essence—Groucho and Chico assaulting pomposity, Harpo after love, and Zeppo standing there. Margaret Dumont looks on, right; above, Garland parries Brice's Baby Snooks in* Everybody Sing, *not precisely a comedy—but anything with Brice in it was not precisely anything else.*

musical comedy conventions: join them. You want music? Chico plays piano, Harpo, obviously, the harp. (And their playing is characterological: Chico is devilish and Harpo loves beauty.) You want a love song? They have Zeppo, the fourth and youngest of the team and no comedian—he is regularly booed in theatres today when his name comes up in the credits—to sing one. Or Chico will, accent and all. Groucho will attempt a comic song, but if he thinks of something cute to say, he'll stop the band and say it. Thus, the boys raid convention with their pandemonium.

Still, their first films, replicas of their stage hits *The Cocoanuts* and *Animal Crackers* in 1929 and 1930 respectively, cut virtually all the music. Touches of musical here and there seem bizarre; Mae West sings for the fun of it, but the Marx films actually have plot numbers. Like West, the brothers started at Paramount, a studio more director-oriented than the others and therefore less tightly organized for genre. The fourth Marx film, *Horse Feathers* (1932), suggests what a Marx musical might have been like: Groucho, as incoming president of Huxley College, sings "(Whatever it is) I'm Against It" in front of a line of bearded deans. Tailored to Groucho's character by Bert Kalmar and Harry Ruby, the song is a mixture of Gilbertian patter and rhythmic quickstep, with the half-dead deans joining the zaniness with kicks and wiggles like a hypnotized minstrel lineup. Most zany of all is one dean, three-quarters dead, who irritably occupies his chair, immobile, throughout the number. The film also contains a charm song, "Everyone Says I Love You," which Chico sings to the "college widow," Thelma Todd, as part of his piano number. Whenever she looks too charmed, he insults her.

It is *Duck Soup* (1933), the Marxes' last Paramount picture and one of the masterpieces of American film, that most shows the form a comedy musical might take: the few numbers do not undercut but add to the free-for-all as grotesque burlesques of musical comedy styles. A tale of espionage and war in a central European Graustark called Freedonia, *Duck Soup* plunks the Marxes and their florid blueblood stooge Margaret Dumont—in their usual identities—amid diplomats in morning coats, embassy teas, and peasants. The villian (Louis Calhern) is named Trentino, his Mata Hari (Raquel Torres) is Vera Marcal, and Freedonia's enemy Sylvania bears the name of the country that MacDonald ruled in Paramount's *The Love Parade* four years before. But the boys are the boys—Groucho is Rufus T. Firefly, Freedonia's president—and Margaret Dumont is Gloria Teasdale, though she holds merry widow status in Freedonia as the country's main financial hope. Kalmar and Ruby wrote it, score and all; Leo McCarey, a master in comedy, directed, and the thing zooms by so fast that one's first impression is of a heavily plotted musical fantasy. Repeated viewings reveal little plot and only two numbers. It seems fully constructed because each event leads directly to the next—unheard of in Marxian comedy—and its two numbers are *very* number. The first, "His Excellency Is Due," seems to have fallen out of an ancient operetta. It opens the movie, at Groucho's inauguration party; one person is lacking—Groucho, of course. Almost without provocation—certainly no one wants him to sing—Zeppo breaks into something about the clock on the wall striking ten. Dumont and the chorus take this up, and we cut to Groucho in bed. An alarm goes off, he slides down a firehouse pole, and presto! joins the party at the end of a line of flunkies who sing "Hail, Freedonia" over and over. Groucho leans and peers. "Expecting someone?" he asks. Spotted and welcomed, he goes into a patter song, promising to run Freedonia unreasonably, selfishly, tyrannically. The guests take it all in without an opinion, offering deadpan Gilbert-and-Sullivan repetitions of his lines and just standing there while Groucho goes into a screwy dance.

The second number, "The Country's Going to War," is epic, a lampoon of production numbers made up of noncontiguous elements—black spiritual, hillbilly, swing—each with its own performers, costumes, and choreography. And while the Marxes are in the middle of it all, dancing, waving their arms, crawling around, and playing banjos, they are more at the number than in it. They show much greater commitment in the famous *Il Trovatore*-wrecking finale of *A Night At the Opera* (1935), but by then they had moved to MGM and Irving Thalberg was trying to fit them into an "acceptable" musical structure, so lovers Kitty Carlisle and Allan Jones interrupt the mania with inappositely tuneful moodle. *At the Circus* (1939) goes even further, with a Harold Arlen–E. Y. Harburg score in miniature—a love song based on "Three Blind Mice," "Two Blind Loves"; the heroine's center-ring solo, "Step Up"; and a comic novelty for Groucho, "Lydia, the Tattooed Lady," which Bobby Connolly staged in musical-comedy fashion with a prancing chorus, Chico accompanying on the piano, and Harpo almost civilized. This is fun, but it doesn't need the Marxes. Worse yet was *The Big Store* (1941), which features one of the most disliked examples of populist ecumenism, "The Tenement Symphony," sung by Tony Martin; and the unkindest cut of all was *Love Happy* (1949), a conventional backstager with Groucho hardly in it at all and Chico and Harpo horribly tamed.

The screwball comedy never assimilated music, either, though its salient perception—that wit, charm, and nonconformity make an

American romantic elite—might have inspired an intriguing score. RKO's *Joy of Living* (1938), in which madcap Douglas Fairbanks, Jr., teaches Irene Dunne to be wacky, does qualify, but its four Kern–Fields songs have nothing to do with the screwball whirlwind. Indeed, it's stately even for Kern.

There is another possible screwball musical, the Astaire–Rogers *Carefree* (1938). With only three songs (by Berlin) plus one nonvocal dance, a broad range of comic styles from verbal to stunt to slapstick and a cast typical of a Hepburn–Grant romp (Ralph Bellamy as the dull boyfriend, Clarence Kolb as the dull judge, Luella Gear as the funny aunt; when Kolb invites her onto the dance floor she snaps back, "I don't dance at your age"), *Carefree* was no dance musical. The eighth Astaire–Rogers pairing, it was meant to relaunch them after a hiatus of over a year. Thus its novel style. It allowed them their first onscreen kiss and gave Rogers the grander part as a woman who falls in love with psychiatrist Astaire,* goes on a rampage on narcotics, and has to be hypnotized into hating Astaire—only now *he* loves her and has to hypnotize her back. Rogers' binge is great fun, taking in the smashing of a huge pane of glass and peaking in one of Hollywood's most cherished kinds of lark: a scene in which a radio star ruins a show on the air, insulting the sponsor's product and sabotaging the entertainment. Rogers is at her best here, pokey, watery-eyed, and bowing at the orchestra each time it plays radio's habitual ta-da! chord. The film is a screwball feast. But is it a musical?

What's a musical? By the late 1930s, Hollywood had an answer: seventy-five to one hundred minutes of love plot crossed with some instance of personal or communal achievement, using four or five songs and possibly a dance or two, keeping the whole as often as possible in a modern and comic frame; the music is easy to pick up, the lyrics are simple, and the lead personalities are essentially innocent and giving, even valiant, though such minor flaws as sloth or cowardice are okay if they are redeemed by some life-changing act in the final reel. Operetta stretched the definition somewhat, and obviously such early films as *Be Yourself*, *The Smiling Lieutenant*, and *Her Majesty Love* would not have suited the style. But then the performers who inspired those films were no longer active and the performers who replaced them were very different in tone. Not yet ten years old, the musical has already evolved beyond recognition.

---

*It has been said that Astaire always plays dancers, but this was his second role as something else; in *Roberta* he was a bandleader.

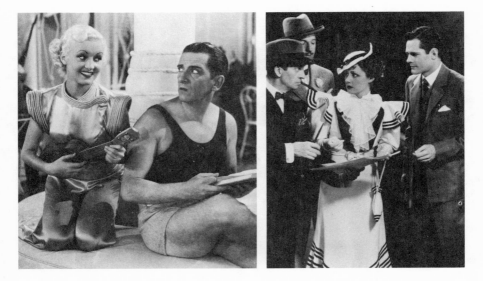

☆ *ADAPTATIONS FROM BROADWAY:* The Gay Divorcee *(Grable, Horton)*, Sweet Adeline *(Sparks, Calhern, Dunne, Woods),* The Firefly *(MacDonald). Porter, Kern, and Friml upgrade the Hollywood tone, though Porter's songs all but vanished and* The Firefly *got a new story.* Sweet Adeline *came off nicely, but Woods is a pill.*

☆ 10 ☆
The Stars of
the Late 1930s

Y OU CAN SEE the change in the people. From the manic Al Jolson and the ebullient Maurice Chevalier we come to the nonchalant Bing Crosby. The various women of the first sound years—Bebe Daniels, Bessie Love, Vivienne Segal, Lilyan Tashman, Dorothy Jordan, Irene Bordoni, and others who could play comedy as well as a love plot, or whose glamor transcended musical comedy frippery—cede to more consistently pretty and pleasant singer-dancers like Alice Faye.

A very few of the old guard were still around. Jeanette MacDonald was now the first lady of operetta, and Jolson hung in there, unreconstructed, in *The Singing Kid* (1936) and *Rose of Washington Square* (1939) and, in the 1940s, was to play himself in *Rhapsody in Blue* and dub his voice in *The Jolson Story*. But their generation had largely dispersed. Ramon Novarro, so big in silent days, should have gone nicely into musicals with his sweet tenor, but somehow or other he didn't fare well, and by 1937 he was attempting a comeback, in *The Sheik Steps Out,* at Republic, not unlike a professional wrestler's making a comeback as the seventh Village Person. Nancy Carroll's last musicals, *After the Dance* (1935) and *That Certain Age* (1938), were obscure addenda. Janet Gaynor gave up on musicals in mid-decade. Lillian Roth vanished as of *Take a Chance* in 1933. Charles King was long departed, Walter Pidgeon was no longer singing, and John Boles, who was, couldn't get a decent role.

Even Chevalier was gone. Plans to follow up *The Merry Widow* at MGM with *The Chocolate Soldier* fell through—it has been said that he requested MacDonald and she said no—and he moved on to Twentieth Century, Darryl Zanuck's new studio which was shortly to merge with Fox. With Merle Oberon and Ann Sothern, Chevalier made *Folies Bergère* (1935), singing all seven songs and playing two roles, a baron and an entertainer hired to impersonate the baron; we get Chevalier in bowtie and boater and Chevalier in tails, Chevalier on stage and Chevalier in the boardroom. It's a wonderful, seldom-seen romp—Roy del Ruth directed in homage to Lubitsch, Dave Gould choreographed in homage to Berkeley, and in one number they have Chevalier and Sothern dancing on a monster version of Chevalier's straw hat. But this was Chevalier's last Hollywood film for two decades. His passing, as much as anything, marks the end of what might be called the First Era of Hollywood musicals.

One might date the Second Era from the emergence of Alice Faye as a top draw in 1937, for Faye, who remained one of the biggest stars till she retired in 1945, set a style that held right up to the collapse of the studio musical in the 1950s. The standard assessment of the style— that Betty Grable precisely replaced Faye and that Marilyn Monroe and Doris Day split the persona's paradoxical halves of sensual woman and tender girl—is a canard: Faye was irreplaceable. She is the nice woman who tries to look tough, a superb singer, a good dancer, and so rich a personality that her success depends not on playing a role but on letting a role play itself while she entertains. The Faye palette dabs anger, pouting, tears; it paints sweet frocks and bad sequins and favors period (usually the wrong one for the film) costumes. She came to Fox in 1934 to replace Lilian Harvey in a backstager, *George White's Scandals*, at the suggestion of Rudy Vallee, back in Hollywood for a second try. The numbers set Faye off nicely. "Nasty Man" shows her lithe and leggy with a pride of showgirls shaking behind her; Vallee sings "Hold My Hand" to a subdued Faye, easily won by the right man but only by him; and the ridiculous "My Dog Loves Your Dog" gives us a pert Faye walking the dog. Fox had the idea of building her up as a Harlow, with bleached platinum hair and pencilled eyebrows, and in her second film, the nonmusical *Now I'll Tell* (1934), she played the third person in Spencer Tracy and Helen Twelvetrees' marriage, sang the lacerating "Fooling With the Other Woman's Man" in a harlot's black satin and feathers—"Headache, headache, nerves you can't control," she cries, "conscience, conscience tugging at your soul!"—and dies in a car crash, Fox's usual method of disposing of homewreckers.

The true Faye, we quickly discover, wants her own home at first hand. In *She Learned About Sailors* (1934), Faye learns only that they—sailor Lew Ayres, anyway—want to get married as much as she does. Yet Faye puts forth such ripe jazz in her flirty-girl production numbers that while her parts become maidenly and the Harlow look fades, her songs remain knowing. So *George White's 1935 Scandals* offers a tintype of "Nasty Man" in Faye's "Oh, I Didn't Know (you'd get that way)," which like its predecessor only pretends to complain about the male's libidinous attack. The lyrics are coy but the music is eager and Faye irresistible. The more she sings, the more she likes it, and after an exuberant dance, she has lost all inhibition; when she hits the line, "My heart is full of joy, oh you naughty boy," she can scarcely go on, and just holds the note on "boy" while the orchestra fills in the tune. This is one of Faye's great qualities, her ability to express the human appetite without making it look smutty. The Production Code encircled the scripts, but it couldn't flatten the spirit.

Faye's spirit was very late thirties, seeing an end to the Depression but having to work to get there. She plays women with talent and initiative who use show biz to pull themselves out of poverty. Faye *was* that part, a New Yorker who moved through Broadway, radio, records, and film, yet somehow never learned to pronounce a final *r*. Faye was always Faye, dressed for the 1930s in films that take place in the nineteenth century and never aging in stories that cover decades. She heads the eternal threesome (completed by Frances Langford and Patsy Kelly) in Paramount's *Every Night at Eight* (1935), trying to land George Raft and singing jobs for her trio and looking into the heart of the rich on a yacht weekend to draw back in disapproval. In *King of Burlesque* (1936), she expresses the age's optimism in "I'm Shooting High," relaxation in "I Love to Ride the Horses (on a Merry-Go-Round)," and informality in courtship in "Whose Baby Are You?" This was another putting-on-the-show musical, and with Warner Baxter as the director (as he had been in *42nd Street*), it seemed twice-told. But the urgency of hard times had blown away. In 1933, "We're in the Money" is irony; *King of Burlesque* plays "I've Got My Fingers Crossed" straight.

By the time Fox and Twentieth Century merged, Faye was ready to star. Even when playing third fiddle to Dick Powell and Madeleine Carroll in *On the Avenue* (1937), it is her contributions to the score that make the film, along with the singing Powell, the fancy sets, the jaunty choreography, the Irving Berlin score, and even the Ritz Brothers, drag and all. Faye, the Ritzes, and chorus open the film with "He Ain't Got Rhythm," telling of a scientist who commits the ultimate sin: he has no music. "He attracted some attention," Faye explains, "when he found the fourth dimension." But he ain't got rhythm; as so often before, Berlin encapsulates a sensual ideology that no one had thought to broach before. It's preposterous—but it's plausible. People don't like intellectuals who can't do what everyone does.

Faye got rhythm. Powell sings "I've Got My Love to Keep Me Warm," but Faye joins him at the end, sashaying onstage in a fluffy white gown embellished with roses to truck to the music beyond all reason. Someone has to keep the energy driving. The musical was getting fat: *On the Avenue* permits Powell to walk out on his own show because Carroll, his love and nemesis, bought a controlling interest—and now no Aline MacMahon lectures him on his obligations to his fellow performers. Only one person remains of the hard luck days: Faye. Berkeley got rural at MGM, Keeler retired, and Powell and Blondell stopped singing. We came out of the tunnel with Faye, watching her strive and win. In *You Can't Have Everything* (1937) she starts out ordering a spaghetti dinner she can't pay for and ends as the author of a Broadway show. In *You're a Sweetheart* (1937), she involves waiter George Murphy in a questionable scheme to keep a show running and ends redeemed, prancing with Murphy in yet another hit.

But she still can't get her mouth around a final *r*. "Drive__! Drive__!" she cries in *In Old Chicago* (1938) when Tyrone Power carries her off in a cab. And "Get out of he__e!" she screams later, when he bursts into her apartment. One of Faye's many costume films, *In Old Chicago* was Fox's reply to MGM's *San Francisco,* with a comparable cast—a woman who sings (MacDonald; Faye), an amoral man (Gable; Power) and a good man (Spencer Tracy; Don Ameche), closing in an exultant disaster finale. But Faye sings no opera; folk, vaudeville, and a rousing Gordon–Revel title tune do for her. Directed by Henry King, *In Old Chicago* was a whopping hit, but not exactly a musical. For the quintessential Faye epic, also directed by King and, like *Chicago,* nominated for a Best Picture Oscar, we turn to *Alexander's Ragtime Band* (1938).

"An American cavalcade!" the ads crowed: from ragtime as a horrid novelty in a San Francisco dive to swing triumphant at Carnegie Hall some twenty-five years later. Faye is caught between Power and Ameche, with Jack Haley as Power's drummer and Ethel Merman as the singer Power hires when Faye marries Ameche. The score is the big thing, a compendium of twenty-one Berlin songs plus the new "Now It Can Be Told" and "My Walking Stick," and if the principals never age, the music does, passing through time from the antique "Ragtime Violin" and "Everybody's Doin' It" to the contemporary "Heat Wave." Appropriately, the title song launches the tale when

Power and his band, auditioning at a club, can't find their music and sight-read the sheets that Faye left lying around. It's tricky stuff, and their first attempts are grotesque. "Swing into it," Power urges, on violin, as Faye indignantly rushes into the picture to take the vocal. And the ragtime band is born.

Comparable to Faye is Bing Crosby. Now recalled primarily as a singer, he, like Faye, was in his time primarily a movie actor: a character who sang. They projected something universally admirable, something the public came to the theatre to recognize and share. It was Faye's moxie; it was Crosby's cool. Two qualities handy in tough times. But where Faye held us through her persistence, Crosby took us along through his extreme lack of it. She is a mover, he an adapter.

With his wingy ears and careless attitude toward his employers, Crosby looked an odd risk for films—he lost a big number to John Boles in *King of Jazz* by getting arrested for drunk driving. But Paramount signed him in 1932 and inaugurated a series of musicals without set format. There is no consistent world view, no musical constants, no regulars. The results are very variable. But they comprise a remarkable document of the American style in pop art, veering without warning from good nature to suspicion and aggressiveness, aware of economic and social relations yet hoping not to face up to them. The Crosby films surprise with their range. If *College Humor* (1933) pictures the usual hurdy-gurdy campus of big games and love-or-die first dates, with Crosby overparted as a drama professor, Richard Arlen a football hero, Mary Carlisle the coed in love with both, and everything happening in no order, suddenly *Going Hollywood* (1933), an MGM loan-out with Marion Davies, presents a more confident Crosby well cast as a film recruit. The hit boosted Davies' flagging and Crosby's as yet unplaced careers, as well as exposing Crosby to MGM's expert manufacturers of film and Davies' famous on-the-set lunch parties.

Crosby was growing. Back at Paramount for *We're Not Dressing* (1934), he played a sailor on heiress Carole Lombard's yacht. She's interested but he's arrogant—i.e., not subservient—which makes things dicey when yacht goes down and Lombard and guests are unable to cope with desert island. Crosby, the free American, copes fine, especially with an unusually serious role that implies a moral judgment on the exploiting class. But Burns and Allen lighten the scene and a charming Revel–Gordon score spells peace on earth. Crosby's soft-colored song style not only made him popular but also helped gentle the hard edges in some of his films—hard and shocking in *We're Not*

Dressing when he and Lombard get into a slapping sequence that looks uncomfortably real.

Crosby's love plot with plutocrat Lombard is significant; a lot of Hollywood's Cinderello trope devolved onto him. In *Here Is My Heart* (1934) he romances a princess (Kitty Carlisle) in Monte Carlo, in *Rhythm on the Range* (1936) an heiress (Frances Farmer) on the loose out west, in *Paris Honeymoon* (1939) a divorced heiress (Shirley Ross)—but lo, he trades her for a peasant (Franciska Gaal). In a costume picture he can commit murder (by accident) and move through the old south with a Reputation, in *Mississippi* (1935), but three Rodgers–Hart ballads define him as a feeling, not an acting, man. Then, in *Double or Nothing* (1937), he begins to take charge. To prove that humankind is honest and bright, a late millionaire has arranged for wallets containing hundred-dollar bills to be found, a cool million to be given to the first stranger to (1) return the wallet and (2) double his or her $5,000 reward. A forgotten classic, the film couples the wish for easy money with a lesson in how to earn it, and presents an intriguing group of wallet finders: Crosby, a penniless singer; William Frawley, a petty hustler; Martha Raye, an ex-stripper who can't control the urge to answer her old calling; and Andy Devine, a bum. The dead man's brother, executor of the will, inherits everything if the quartet fails, and he and his crummy family serve as temptors.

Double or Nothing is rich in music and dance, but some of Crosby's films are scarcely musicals—*Sing, You Sinners* (1938), for example. Yet this film is about music in a way. A widowed mother (Elizabeth Patterson) with three sons (Crosby, Fred MacMurray, and thirteen-year-old Donald O'Connor) had them trained as musicians and expects them to follow through whether they want to or not. They don't. But there they are entertaining in a tavern, O'Connor on accordion, MacMurray on clarinet, and Crosby on guitar, all singing "A Pocketful of Dreams," MacMurray a little stiff but in there. Crosby, as a ne'er-do-well who finds his vocation racing horses, plays a drunk scene, tangles with gangsters, and lets his family down so badly that one dinner scene finds them leaving the table one by one till Crosby is alone staring aghast at the untouched food.

Yet his laziness is his charm: who wouldn't want to be as free a floater as he is? Out dating MacMurray's girl, he sings "Don't Let That Moon Get Away" from his table, and at one point forgets his lyrics, pauses, and recovers the line with a smile. Whether this was staged or an accident of film, it feels so everyday that director Wesley Ruggles let it ride. This is a rare light moment, however. *Sing, You Sinners* deals with struggling more than singing, and when Crosby reluctantly leaves home to find work, his heartbroken mother says, "It'll bring out the fight I know he's got in him." We, too, begin to realize that there's fight in Crosby, and the big blow-up between the family and the gangsters seems to have been filmed without the use of stuntmen. Patterson, too, gives fight, beaning one of the crooks with a chair. At the fadeout, the boys are a singing trio again, like it or not. *We* like it.

It is proof of Crosby's power as an actor that he could get by on a few songs; Faye tended to lose a lot of her personal ethos without a score to put over. But then Faye's style was rhythm and torch; Crosby healed. "Sing a Song of Sunbeams," from *East Side of Heaven* (1939), is classic Crosby, nudging the written melody with vocal bubbles so that it dances about the ear. "People all are softies for a grin," runs Johnny Burke's lyric. "You give out—they're gonna give in."

They gave in most overwhelmingly to a little girl who sings of simple pleasures, dances with Bill Robinson or Buddy Ebsen, chides dad and dollies, defrosts curmudgeons, brings couples together, conquers Depression blues in cities or on the farm with common sense and bottomless idealism, and says, "Oh, my goodness." Those who couldn't see it or who tired of the unchanging format of her films raged powerless at the enthusiasm she generated, but in the late 1930s Shirley Temple became the top-box office star.

In the world.

Doubters persist, but so do her films. There is no legend attached to her, none of the offstage misfortunes common to child stars, and neither her early marriage, early dissolved, nor her political ambitions affected the image of the do-good tyke who was either astonishingly talented or a fluke. She was both—to be able to use one's talent so professionally so young must be fluke. One either likes or hates all her films (the taste cannot be acquired) and as a whole they do not stand up as well as little Shirley herself does. She ran through a not undistinguished aggregate of costars in her prime—Claire Trevor, Gary Cooper, Carole Lombard, Lionel Barrymore, Alice Faye, Frank Morgan, Helen Westley, Robert Young, Victor McLaglen, Jean Hersholt, Randolph Scott, George Murphy, and Jimmy Durante—and John Ford directed her in *Wee Willie Winkie* (1937). But her musicals were whipped out with little ado; they look primitive.

Extraordinarily bright and coached by a no-nonsense mother, Temple got her start in shorts on a minor lot, mainly in Baby Burlesks, kids in diapers and tops spoofing the adult genres. Grotesque. Bits in features at the big lots led to an important spot in the finale of Fox's revue *Stand Up and Cheer* (1934). Temple came on in a high-waisted polka-dot dress to sing "Baby, Take a Bow" with James Dunn, immediately set a fashion for high-waisted polka-dot dresses, and signed with Fox. The studio strategy for launching a personality often jumped off on a crucial loan-out to some other studio at an early stage; the second studio loads the gun and the home studio then fires it, having saved the cost of the first big film. Temple's loan-out, to Paramount, was *Little Miss Marker* (1934), from Damon Runyon's tale of a homeless moppet placed with a bookie. The part is perfect Temple, and Adolphe Menjou as the bookie, Sorrowful Jones, is excellent; with his lank hair, droopy moustache, and flat, wet eyes he looks like a wounded cartoon seal. The script gets a lot of mileage out of Runyonesque lingo, but when Temple delivers lines like "Nix on that" or "Aw, lay off me" when faced with oatmeal, the joke fails: hood jive is not in her catalogue. Worse yet, the film is edited as sloppily as anything that ever crawled out of Gower Gulch. But *Little Miss Marker* was a hit, and Fox reclaimed its prize with a raise of from $150 to $1,250 a week and a careful expansion of her *Stand Up and Cheer* number in *Baby, Take a Bow* (1934), again with Dunn as her gangster father attempting to go straight. Temple is instrumental in the reform, and in keeping Fox in the black. *Bright Eyes* (1934), with Dunn yet again, with her first star billing, with "On the Good Ship Lollipop," and with Jane Withers as a brat who plagues Temple, made back its $190,000 production cost three weeks after it was released. Temple was six years old.

Some enthusiasts prefer *Bright Eyes* over other Temple films for the amusing byplay between the heroine and Withers, who cuts down the sugar content. But sugar was what folks wanted. In *The Little Colonel* (1935), Confederate kid Temple melts Lionel Barrymore to the extent that anyone could, and hits the acme of innocent bliss dancing with Bill "Bojangles" Robinson. Those who dislike hokum probably dislike the Temple–Robinson duets more than anything, but these numbers contributed significantly to the morale of American race relations, especially because they promoted a crossover of racial styles in dance. Temple was a natural tapper, but Robinson taught her to truck; their bald cahoots glows like nobody's business.

As with dancing, so with acting: experts polished her, but she had the basics already. She approached roles as games to be played, learning everyone's lines, and drove Barrymore crazy with her prompting; Menjou called her "an Ethel Barrymore at four." By 1935, her contract nabbed her $4,000 a week, and she was still a bargain, dancing atop a white piano while John Boles played and sang the title song to and about her ("You little bundle of joy") in *Curly Top,* a remake of Mary Pickford's *Daddy Long Legs* or an adaptation of Jean Webster's novel, depending on whether you watch or read. In this one Temple had an older sister, Rochelle Hudson, for Boles to romance while protecting orphan Temple, and the dream of being cared for by a rich benefactor must have been some sugar-plum vision for *Curly Top*'s audiences: kids could be Temple, teenagers Hudson. Boles worked so well with Temple that they teamed up again in a Civil War film, *The Littlest Rebel* (1935), with Robinson back in for "Polly Wolly Doodle" and Temple donning blackface and a miniature Mammy outfit that must be seen three or four times before it sinks in. The horror; the horror. Father Boles, captured up north while visiting Temple's dying mother, must be bailed out by Temple's personal appeal to President Lincoln, which she brings off with a merry gravity.

Temple's mothers tend to die if she had them at all; producer Zanuck must have liked her best as an orphan with a strong crush on daddy. In *Captain January* (1936) this was grizzled old Guy Kibbee (with Buddy Ebsen in for Robinson), from whom do-gooders tear Temple ("Cap! Cap! I don't want to go!" is one of her most famous lines) in a scene pathetic even by Temple standards. In *Poor Little Rich Girl* (1936), another Pickford remake, she has a father but *seems* an orphan. She has to get lost, fall in with two vaudevillians, become a radio star, and sing commercials for a soap company to get daddy's attention. At this point the Temple films drift into a backstager framework, using the stage or radio to excuse Temple's numbers, and with Alice Faye and Jack Haley as the vaudevillians and a Revel–Gordon score, we are assured of some real singing and dancing. (Not all of Temple's films are full musicals.) Temple has a lengthy solo with a squad of dolls, suitably entitled "Oh, My Goodness," each verse in a different style to match the different dolls (from German through Russian and Japanese to some American hi-de-ho) and sings "When I'm With You" in her father's lap, with its somewhat extreme line, "Marry me and let me be your wife." Faye has her spots, and joins Haley and Temple in uniform for the tap finale, "I Love a Military Man." Best of all is "You've Got to Eat Your Spinach, Baby," which Faye first addresses to Haley and which the two then turn on Temple, who has been sent "by the kids of the nation" to expostulate in recitative against the vegetable. They are stern, and she gives in.

She has to; everyone is bigger than she is. Crosby, the ideal American man, Faye the ideal woman, and Temple the ideal kid promoted a standard for endurance under stress: the music in them made survival look easy. And they survived at length. Crosby's career is one of the longest, Faye retired at her option when she was on top, and Temple made twenty-seven feature films, sixteen as the central figure, till her popularity began to wane as of *The Blue Bird* (1940), Fox's attempt to duplicate *The Wizard of Oz*. Drawn from Maurice Maeterlinck's symbolic play, *The Blue Bird* was dull and strange, despite the use of Technicolor a barren adventure. Its high cost made it Temple's first flop, and though she was to make films throughout the 1940s, her age had caught up with her already. She was twelve years old.

One didn't have to be an American role model to gather a genre around one, even at Fox, where the Norwegian skating champ Sonja Henie became a star contemporaneously with Faye and Temple. An Olympic winner in 1928, 1932, and 1936, she produced an ice revue in Hollywood, and the story goes that Zanuck showed up one night, throwing Henie's cohort into a thrill. What should they do? they asked her. And she reportedly replied, "Sell him a ticket." Zanuck bought Henie. What, though, did she bring to Hollywood? As a skater in the Olympics, she had dramatic dash, lent personality to the sport. But as an actress, she was just a skater; she took personality out of film. What to do with her? Obviously, she's the heroine. Give her Don Ameche as a romantic foil, a Cinderella tale for a plot—she's an innkeeper's daughter who enters the Olympics—and lots of comedy from Ned Sparks and the Ritz Brothers and eccentric bits from dancer Dixie Dunbar and Borrah Minnevitch and his Harmonica Rascals. And what have we? *One in a Million* (1936) made Fox two million and ratified Operation Henie. For her second film, *Thin Ice* (1937), Fox built a huge outdoor rink, devised special paint to hide the cooling pipes in the ice, and got everybody into overcoats. *Thin Ice*, too, was a Cinderella tale—Henie loves Tyrone Power, a prince. And so on.

Some said the best thing in the eleven Henie films (nine for Fox) was Henie, pert, wise, and fresh. Others liked the extraneous bits. Presumably everyone liked the big ice ballet—on, say, an Alice in Wonderland theme, as in *My Lucky Star* (1938). The pert and fresh was no act, for Henie couldn't. Neither was the wise: here was one of the most acute horsetraders in the business. She demanded $75,000 a film from Zanuck, and this was *very* renegotiated after the second film to include percentage points; in 1939, Henie made over $400,000. The films are alike, but so are Faye's and Temple's. Henie, however, was no singer, and as an ice film seemed to have to be a musical, hers had holes in their centers.

It may be that the forms that the stars created were more important as stories than the stars were as people: lazybones finds his reason to work in a need to help others; city girl makes it in show biz; tyke challenged by doom is saved by nice big people. These seem to be choice titles in our mythology. And all three stories find their essence in music: lazybones eases into a tune; city girl shakes her thing; tyke sings of nice and dances with big. Yet the stars themselves used music only when convenient, losing the momentum for musical narration established by the dance musical. Look at Henie: they had to make a musical *around* her. Even Warner Brothers, the pioneers of sound, could film the Rodgers and Hart Broadway dance musical *On Your Toes* in 1939, throwing out all music and dance except the "Slaughter on Tenth Avenue" ballet.

Was the musical losing its formal identity? One way to recapture it was to deemphasize dance and operatic vocalism to concentrate on story-telling songs. The major pieces to do this in the late 1930s were Hollywood's first genuine musical fantasies.

☆ 11 ☆
Fantasy and the Story Musical

ONE OF THE MOST fully musical films of the 1930s was a cartoon, Walt Disney's *Snow White and the Seven Dwarfs* (1937). Quaint and magical in the first place, the tale was exempt from the old worry about undercutting naturalism with song and dance, and Frank Churchill and Larry Morey's score—simple tunes, simple lyrics— hasn't a note or word that doesn't feed story or character.* Much has been said of this pioneer work, an eighty-three-minute, $1,500,000 fol- ly that became a fast classic. The highly collective creative structure of the Disney studio, the film's inventive juxtaposition of the comic and the grotesque, the subtle illustrative detail in the backgrounds, and the difficulty in animating Snow White and the Prince, the film's two straights, have often been dealt with. But the score is taken for grant- ed. No wonder: it suits the story so well it serves rather than grabs the senses. What other musical of the late 1930s is as individualized as this one? Sure, it has the directness, the Hollywood hit-trope simplicity in the ballads "Some Day My Prince Will Come" and "One Song." But setting to music such situations as housecleaning, washing for dinner for perhaps the first time in years, and marching home from a day in the jewel mine was novel, and "Whistle While You Work," "Bluddle- Uddle-Um-Dum," and "Heigh-ho" stand out as plot movers, bursting

---

*Disney was so particular about having a plot score that the songwriters created some three dozen numbers before he was satisfied with the eight they used. Disney did approve a ninth, an abysmal theme song, but this was only published and is not heard in the film.

with details of action. For once, a musical film doesn't stand there and sing—it keeps on moving through the songs.

Some critics felt that Disney had betrayed the impishness of the Mickey Mouse shorts. J. C. Furnas speaks of *Snow White*'s "greeting-card simper." But many of Disney's shorts dealt in sentimental fantasy, so this was no betrayal. The low-rental economics of short subjects forced him to stick with features, and his second, *Pinocchio* (1940), is his masterpiece, not despite but through the sentimentality. Like *Snow White* European in look and solemn about its good-versus-evil, *Pinocchio* is unlike *Snow White* in its theme, one already basic to Hollywood musicals: believe in yourself and you'll make it. Like the youngsters who earn stardom in a night, like the kids who put on a show Right Here in This Barn, like the radio singer who conquers mike fright, like the tanktown college team that beats Yale, ad infinitum, Pinocchio is another protagonist who comes through a crisis of self-belief through courage. Pinocchio's crisis is an odd one: he isn't a real boy, but an animated puppet—that's one Frank Sinatra and Alice Faye never had to face. *Snow White* is a fairy tale, *Pinocchio* more a parable. A lonely old woodcutter carves a wooden boy who is brought to life by a virginal goddess with admonishments on the straight and narrow. She assigns the boy a cricket as a conscience, and occasionally materializes when the errant puppet needs help, but the big one—rescuing his father from the inside of a whale—he must pull off himself. This he does, and the fairy turns his wood to flesh.

Yes, it's cute beyond recall, with its cat and goldfish pets and array of cuckoo clocks and music boxes. But the film has menace, for it treats some of childhood's most profound traumas (devotees of Oedipal castration motifs have a field day), and one scene in which bad little boys are transformed into donkeys and carted away is notorious for sending whimpering tykes up the aisle at every screening. Furthermore, *Pinocchio* offers one of Disney's most imaginative musical numbers in Pinocchio's debut in a puppet theatre, "I've Got No Strings," and made technical history in the dazzling opening multiplane panning shot of a sleeping village (to "When You Wish Upon a Star"), so costly that even the ambitious Disney never tried it again. *Snow White* won huzzahs for novelty, but *Pinocchio* is the one with the art in it, the experiment perfected. Anyone who finds it only "sentimental"—and doesn't see why its sentiment makes it so moving—is a jerk.

Between *Snow White* and *Pinocchio*, MGM stepped into the picture with the first live-action feature musical to use neverland magic, *The Wizard of Oz* (1939). This, too, fully integrates its score into its narrative: a story musical. Like the dance musicals, it lets the music express what prose can't, and spreads the poetry around, letting any character dance or sing as necessary. The story musical is not new. The Lubitsch and Mamoulian operettas worked this way, as did the early Broadway adaptations. But in an age dominated by one-size-fits-all love and rhythm tunes, it reaffirmed the validity of plot and character songs. Most important, though it was a typical product of the studio assembly line, with all the front-office censorship and spendthrift collaboration* that implies, it stands as one of the most original and distinctive documents of American art. It is unlike all others, yet holds the key to their form and meaning. It stands midway between the eccentric 1930s and the normalized 1940s—it still has the quirks, but now they're polished quirks. Few musicals have been so carefully put together, yet few unfold so spontaneously. More than any Berkeley backstager or Astaire–Rogers romance, *The Wizard of Oz* is the essential Hollywood musical.

It seemed a white elephant at first, complex to plan, expensive to capitalize, and involving a traditionally risky genre, fantasy. The source, L. Frank Baum's *The Wonderful Wizard of Oz*, made in 1900 a first stab at a native fairy tale, one without princesses, family curses, and the rest of the middle-European elfin cupboard. (Horse-sense lies behind the tale, for while traveling through Oz to get brains, a heart, and courage respectively, a scarecrow, tin woodman, and "cowardly" lion all display those very gifts.) Still, Baum's plan takes in a great deal of out-of-the-world magic. Besides working out all the special effects (including a tornado; the smoky materialization, flight, and melting of a wicked witch; and an attack by winged monkeys), finding enough midgets to accommodate the Munchkin scene, wrestling with the improved but still capricious color film technique, and devising costume and makeup for a human scarecrow, tin man, and lion, there was an artistic problem: what tone does an all-American fairy tale take?

The opening and closing sequences, set in Kansas and filmed in sepia, were easily styled, the dull prairie farm creating its own tone. But once Dorothy has reached Oz, with its witches and creatures and weird places, it's anybody's guess. Baum himself had produced a stage

---

*Eleven writers worked on the script alone. For the record: Herman Mankiewicz started it with a synopsis, Noel Langley composed the basic script, Florence Ryerson and Edgar Allan Woolf added some great bits, E. Y. Harburg edited the above, and Jack Mintz, Sid Silvers, John Lee Mahin, Ogden Nash, Herbert Fields, and Samuel Hoffenstein were also hired in a writing capacity.

musical of the tale in 1902 and several Oz silents, but these were no help—the musical in particular lost much of its native flavor, turning Ruritanian rather than magical and assuming the standard poses in its score. So producer Mervyn LeRoy, director Victor Fleming, and their many assistants and specialists pushed in and invented a new tone, one balanced so delicately between magical horror and everyday charm that only on several viewings does one realize how American the MGM Oz is, with its screwball aunt Glinda, busybody spinster witch, Brooklyn clown lion, and midwestern horsetrader wizard. It shouldn't work—it sounds like a college musical with a tornado. But it works precisely because the magical characters are first introduced to us in the Kansas scenes: Dorothy's grotesque pals are farmhands, the witch is the local bully, the wizard a carnival humbug. When we get to the magic, we know how to take it, as distillations of familiar archetypes. Oz is magical—but it's *our* magic.

The original casting plan projected a different sort of film, with Shirley Temple as Dorothy, W. C. Fields as the Wizard, and Gale Sondergaard as the bad witch. Fields might have worked, but Temple would have been too local and Sondergaard too glamorous for the balance of the familiar and the strange; their extremes would have pulled the film apart. With Judy Garland, Frank Morgan, and Margaret Hamilton in these roles the acting tone was secure. Filling out the event with Ray Bolger as the scarecrow, Jack Haley as the tin man (replacing Buddy Ebsen, felled by makeup poisoning), Bert Lahr as the lion, and Billie Burke as Glinda, MGM had an Oz to stimulate the American imagination.

The single most important factor in the film's success, however, is none of the above. Harold Arlen and E. Y. Harburg's songs do what few film scores have been able to so far: set a style that works for one picture and will never work for anything else. No New Dance Sensation or I Love You would do here: Dorothy sings of a happier place to live in than Kansas (thus setting up the Oz dream and giving the film, Judy Garland's career, and the gay subculture a theme song in "Over the Rainbow"); scarecrow, tin man, and lion sing of their special needs; Emerald City dwellers catalogue the wonders of a specific paradise; and a healthy swatch of action is carried forward in an operatic sequence for Dorothy's first ten minutes in Oz. Arlen and Harburg made one miscalculation, actually including a dance sensation for the hideous forest when the witch's offensive magic attacks Dorothy and her chums, "The Jitterbug." It's a wonderful piece in swing style, and was staged to be the film's big number, with the whole forest in rhyth-

☆ *FANTASY: above, Munchkinland in* The Wizard of Oz *(Burke, Garland);
below, black folklore in* Cabin in the Sky *(Waters, Anderson, Bubbles, Horne).*

mic eruption. But the number doesn't fit; it's *too* American, too local to pass in Oz, though Harburg was careful to write the actors' solo lines in character. Thinking that "The Jitterbug" slowed the narrative and might date the film, MGM cut it, though revival houses occasionally screen prints that contain it—*must* viewing for aficionados.

MGM spent twenty-one weeks and $2,777,000 (five weeks and $80,000 on "The Jitterbug" alone) on *The Wizard of Oz*, so it was a white elephant after all—at first. The average big musical tied up two million and two months of studio time at most, and the outsized *Wizard* project lost money on its first release. It was a popular film, though the pretentious critics savaged it. "It has dwarfs, music, Technicolor, freak characters, and Judy Garland," wrote Otis Ferguson in *The New Republic*. "It can't be expected to have a sense of humor as well." This, in the face of Lahr's superb lion, is garbage. Other writers likened *The Wizard* to *Snow White*, but this, too, is wrong. *Snow White* is Brothers Grimm melded with a little off-the-wall vaudeville. It is carefully European. *The Wizard* is more like *Pinocchio*, with its recognizable archons of good and evil battling around a recognizably next-door adolescent protagonist. Jiminy Cricket, like Lahr's lion, roots the fancy in the plain.

This mixture of imagination and folk myth is what makes *The Wizard of Oz* special and what through rerelease and television viewings has made it a classic, one of the few American films that most Americans have seen. It bears little relation to other musicals, as I say—its tornado and broom rides, spectacular color (the Yellow Brick Road and Emerald City glow in shades that will never be seen again), distinctive song subjects, and fantasy set it utterly apart. Yet it is the most basic of musicals in its egalitarian gung-ho that teaches: to fulfill ambition, apply ambition. The wondrous ruby slippers that Dorothy wins when she inadvertently kills the Wicked Witch of the East are like a badge of confidence, and once she learns how to use them, she can, like her friends, get what she wants, a return trip from Oz. Dorothy could have gone home all along: because she always had self-esteem. The shoes did not protect the Witch: because witches have no self-esteem. And the Witch of the West can't obtain the shoes: because evil cannot steal self-esteem.

One of the last musicals* of the decade, *The Wizard of Oz* made the

---

*Many don't consider *The Wizard of Oz* a musical, though it has seven numbers and various bits, more music in all than any of the Astaire–Rogers RKOs or the Berkeley backstagers. Perhaps doubters can't place it because they are conditioned by most complete statement of the theme that the Hollywood musical had been aiming at from the beginning. Looking back, one spots few musicals that didn't strike the note in some way, and the exceptions all fall in the earliest years before the musical had solidified its format—the Lubitsch boudoir was too sultry for the preaching of Horatio Alger, and an experiment like *Hallelujah, I'm a Bum* too nonconformist to preach. But one reads the message pushing up everywhere, in backstagers, in Astaire–Rogers, in Faye and Temple Cinderella tales; and of course by the late 1930s Lubitsch's operetta, *Hallelujah, I'm a Bum*, and everything like them—disorderly art—was suppressed. The coming decades lost a lot of flavor in adhering to the code for form, character, and theme. The code has been attacked as escapism; it is anything but. A true pop-art escapism would advise the disheartened to float or hide. The Hollywood musical urges each person to assert him- or herself, to take a place of choice. Escapism? Say rather moral rearmament. And just in time for war.

---

genre and *The Wizard* resists typing. Also, the deletion of "The Jitterbug" and the "Renovation" scene of welcome when Dorothy and friends return to the Emerald City denudes the film's final third of music.

The Texture
of Swing

Wᴏʀʟᴅ ᴡᴀʀ II affected the musical as it did other types of film, in stories with a service background, in patriotic demonstration, in historical and nostalgic investigations of the American experience. The revue came back into style, with studios again throwing as many contract stars as possible into the arena. This time the vaudevilles were excused by threads of plot. Paramount's *Star-Spangled Rhythm* (1942) has studio guard Victor Moore and switchboard girl Betty Hutton attempting to fool Moore's sailor son Eddie Bracken into thinking that Moore runs the studio. After a lot of running around and yelling (mostly by Hutton), the story ends and a variety show begins with, among others, Paulette Goddard, Mary Martin, Dick Powell, and Alan Ladd, Bing Crosby closing the film with the Arlen–Mercer hymn, "Old Glory," set against Mount Rushmore and featuring oral reports on what America means to a New Hampshire farmer, a Brooklynite, and so on. Most distinctive was United Artists' *Stage Door Canteen* (1943), set on Broadway with the likes of Katharine Cornell, Helen Hayes, Ed Wynn, Ray Bolger, Harpo Marx, Ethel Waters, Ethel Merman, Gypsy Rose Lee, Judith Anderson, the Lunts, Katharine Hepburn, and others, all made ridiculous by a script that resists no temptation to cliché or bad taste. James Agee singled out Gracie Fields' singing of the Lord's Prayer as his favorite bit, and thought the film "a gold mine for those who are willing to go to it in the wrong spirit."

Terrible films—but don't you know there's a war on? MGM threw *Thousands Cheer* (1943) around Gene Kelly's resentment at being drafted and his love for Kathryn Grayson, this one also culminating in

160 ☆

a big show, too affably hosted by Mickey Rooney; and Fox based *Four Jills in a Jeep* (1944) around the USO tour of Kay Francis, Carole Landis, Martha Raye, and Mitzi Mayfair, with more big show: Betty Grable, Alice Faye, and Carmen Miranda, introduced by George Jessel as "that Brazilian flying fortress," singing "I Yi Yi Yi Yi (I like you very much)." Warners' *Thank Your Lucky Stars* was the odd one for its gag of having the lot regulars perform out of habit. Errol Flynn and Bette Davis sing, Alexis Smith dances, John Garfield attempts "Blues in the Night" (an embarrassment). This sort of thing never works, but with Dinah Shore for ballads and Hattie McDaniel superb in a black number, "Ice Cold Katie (won't you marry that soldier?)," *Thank Your Lucky Stars* came out okay. MGM's *Ziegfeld Follies* (1946), launched in 1944 but so big it took two years to finish, is the best remembered of them all, but it's a great rainbow candybox of horrors. Judy Garland, in her first out-and-out taste of camp, is horrendous in "A Great Lady Has an Interview," written for Greer Garson. Fanny Brice, Keenan Wynn, and Victor Moore in comedy routines are not funny, and Fred Astaire and Gene Kelly in their only film duet, the Gershwins' "The Babbitt and the Bromide," are hoke.

The musicals with a war setting ran little better, tending to favor the uniforms-on-leave structure that had been done to death in the 1930s. But the old tales are gold tales: *Anchors Aweigh* was one of the biggest hits of 1945. How often have we had it before: sailors Gene Kelly and Frank Sinatra—the make-out champ and the wallflower—chase girls, serve as role models for kids, and help Kathryn Grayson impress José Iturbi; so-so score peaks in "I Fall in Love Too Easily" and "What Makes the Sunset," which any character in any film could sing as reasonably as Sinatra does here; Grayson sings "Jealousy"; Iturbi conducts and plays "The Donkey Serenade." It's the usual Joe Pasternak special, lifted by one sequence in which Kelly charms some kids with a tale of a kingdom where a cheerless king has outlawed singing and dancing. Director George Sidney shows the tale in mixed live action and animation, Kelly right up there with Tom and Jerry, teaching the king of joys of music—of being open and uninhibited and therefore influential—and in "The Worry Song" warns him, "Don't expect to get much help if you don't help yourself." It's beginning to sound a little militant.

Kelly's parable is a motto for the whole era of the big band and swing. Music in the early 1930s was generally an autotelic ritual, its own means and end. Increasingly in the middle and late 1930s but especially in the 1940s, music serves; it makes friends, expresses feelings, uplifts, and enlightens. Film scores are obsessed with the benefits of music: Alice Faye tells us "Music Is Magic," Kathryn Grayson orders "Let There Be Music," Judy Garland cries "Everybody Sing (everybody start—you can't go wrong with a song in your heart)." Running through these years is a new awareness of pop music, very nearly a cult of swing. One distinguishes styles. Good-neighbor excursions like *Down Argentine Way* (1940), *That Night in Rio* (1941), and *Weekend in Havana* (1941) pulled in Latin American rhythm and orchestration (not to mention Carmen Miranda),* all sorts of films featured noted bandleaders and their groups, and the still useful Broadway adaptation kept the sophistication and pastiche of the best songwriters, though here the studios proved more cavalier than ever. Hugh Martin and Ralph Blane's *Best Foot Forward* (1943) came west in a respectable facsimile, but Cole Porter's songs for *DuBarry Was a Lady* (1943) and *Something for the Boys* (1944) vanished almost completely. When something inventive came along, like Kurt Weill's *Lady in the Dark*, with its operatic dream sequences, its careful design, and legend-making star turn by Gertrude Lawrence, Paramount paid $283,000 for the rights—a new record—and released it in 1944 having slashed the score (including its theme song, "My Ship"), fudged the design, and handed the star part to Ginger Rogers with little part left in which to star.

Perhaps music was the strongest element in the 1940s film musical, as the stories were mostly old hat and the performers too clean cut after that thirties mob. One even begins to miss Jolson. If he typifies the roughhouse early 1930s, Frank Sinatra typifies the 1940s, with his infinitely engaging vocal quality, smooth delivery, and casual self-portrayal. He appears as himself in *Higher and Higher* (1943) from a Rodgers–Hart show (one of their songs survived the adaptation), and does not quite take part in the plot, about some servants' attempt to pass a maid (Michele Morgan) off as an heiress. Yet without Sinatra, *Higher and Higher* would be half a film, for his many song spots were the action: music is magic. No Crosby film had such a full score, and Sinatra's first starring role, in the backstager *Step Lively* (1944), made it clear how strategic was a great singer to the forties musical. *Step Lively* comes from the stage farce *Room Service*, which had provided the Marx Brothers with their first bad film; here, a pleasant Jule Styne–Sammy Cahn score saves the day, aided by a nice second-line

---

*Economics inspired the south-of-the-border series, as the war closed down European distribution and the studios opened up this alternative market.

cast: George Murphy as a slippery producer, Gloria de Haven as his girl, Anne Jeffreys as a haughty star, and Adolphe Menjou and Walter Slezak as, respectively, canny and foolish hoteliers. Like the Warners backstagers *Step Lively* follows the personal lives of show people to conclude with a show. But aside from a few magical effects in the "Ask the Madam (the Madam knows)" number, Tim Whelan directs for straight and simple. We're still supposed to care whether or not Murphy gets his show on, but we care more about how confidently Sinatra spins out his ballads. Let there be music.

Let there be films about music, about what it means to those who make it. Warners exploited its flair for underworld atmosphere in *Blues in the Night* (1941), on the life of a jazz band. Music is not preached; director Anatole Litvak and author Robert Rossen let an Arlen–Mercer score do the talking. Nor is music a panacea, as it is for Temple and Faye: ecstasy and despair are implicit in the dark photography and in Don Siegel's adventurous montage sequences that synopsize travel and rehearsals in blinding flashes. The actors—Richard Whorf, Betty Field, Lloyd Nolan, Priscilla Lane, Jack Carson, Elia Kazan, and Howard da Silva—hardly make a standard musical line-up, and where other films utilized Jimmy Dorsey or Artie Shaw, *Blues in the Night* used the Jimmy Lunceford and Will Osborne bands, perfect for the freaky, down-and-out look of the piece.

Certainly, the main effect of swing in film was no low-key blues but the exuberance of concert, the rhythmic drive, novelty patter, and improvisational fun. Betty Hutton belting out "Arthur Murray Taught Me Dancing in a Hurry" in *The Fleet's In* (1942) occupies the dead center of Hollywood swing. But swing had an important side effect in its use of black talent, for it brought it into the public eye as film had not yet done. In *On With the Show!* Ethel Waters' part consisted entirely of two numbers so peripheral to the plot that southern theatres could snip them and render the film all-white. But now black singers and dancers were being drawn more into the focus; they had to be, for swing was in many ways a black art. Much of its argot, its rhyme schemes, its rhythm patterns (such as the left-hand "boogie" runs), and dance lore had evolved from black styles, and it seems not only amusing but essential that Harry Warren and Mack Gordon's "Chattanooga Choo-Choo," the strongest number in the Henie vehicle *Sun Valley Serenade* (1941), is played by Glenn Miller but sung and danced by Dorothy Dandridge and the Nicholas Brothers.

Nor were all-black musicals as economically risky as when King Vidor made *Hallelujah*. Songwriters, choreographers, and arrangers knew how much they owed to black music, and began to pay off the debt, so the public's new sense of music as a force in the culture was enriched by their sense of blackness as a force in music—*everybody sing*. In *Birth of the Blues* (1941), Bing Crosby, Mary Martin, and bandleader Jack Teagarden promote the new fairness in Johnny Mercer's "The Waiter and the Porter and the Upstairs Maid," lyrically, musically, and conceptually one of the supreme products of race-relating swing. In the film itself, Crosby forms a white band, but in the song he tells how "stuffy and arty" party guests sent him into the kitchen for some real party with the servants. On dishpan and glasses, "you should have heard the music that the combination made"—and the suggestion that black music has more spontaneity and penetration than white-bread mainline pop is persuasive. At one point, Eddie Anderson (Jack Benny's "Rochester") gives Martin a lesson in how to put over an old standard in black style by conjuring up orchestral vamps and licks out of the soundtrack, and even coaches a black doorman in racial identity by referring to Crosby's band's sound as "our music." The doorman is bewildered: "*Our* music?" "Listen, brother," Anderson tells him, "you ain't no Eskimo." And while it is true that Crosby and his crew make the sound without the help of a single black player, by far the most imposing sequence in *Birth of the Blues* is a black number, a mourning scene for Ruby Elzy (who sang "My Man's Gone Now" in the original production of *Porgy and Bess*) and chorus. Herein we learn yet another of music's purposes: healing. Anderson, injured in a brawl with gangsters, lies in a coma, but Elzy's rhapsody pulls him through.

The swing era peaked just as the United States entered World War II, so its ecumenical outlook coincided with a time of intense national unity. *Birth of the Blues* senses this, hinting at the racial integration of American music in a closing montage over the title song, a retrospective of jazz greats that places W. C. Handy and Fats Waller alongside Paul Whiteman and George Gershwin. The new sound shatters social taboo while it shatters artistic conservatism. Crosby, Martin, and Teagarden in their "Waiter" trio retire the old status-quo pop genres— "We hate 'em; we spurn 'em." Rhythm is the thing now: the rhythms of soul. "And we know who to go to when we want to learn 'em," the song concludes: "The waiter and the porter and the upstairs maid!"

☆ 13 ☆
Wartime People

$\mathbf{T}$HE EARLY 1940s saw the heyday of Judy Garland, Mickey Rooney, and Betty Grable: putting on the show. These were amateur benefits, nightclubs, and vaudeville; another America was revealed in these years, remote from the *42nd Street* fleshpots, rural and pure. Garland and Rooney interlocked turns in MGM's *Andy Hardy* series (Garland to Rooney, shyly, in *Love Finds Andy Hardy* (1938): "I . . . sing, you know) with the *Babes* series: *Babes in Arms* (1939), *Strike Up the Band* (1940), and *Babes on Broadway* (1941), good clean fun. Busby Berkeley directed, somewhat down-scale, though he found things to do, as in *Strike Up the Band*'s symphony orchestra of animated fruit and the effervescent "Do the La Conga," shot from a dizzying round of angles. Berkeley at Warners had been dry and cynical; suddenly, he was sentimental for MGM. In *Ziegfeld Girl* (1941), one of the classic threesome sagas, Garland, Hedy Lamarr, and Lana Turner played girls tapped for stardom. But, Paul Kelly warns in an opening-night pep talk in the dressing room, "The Follies is life." The good will make it, the beautiful will bow out for love, and the materialist will fail. Garland is good; she doesn't want to break up her cheesy act with her father Charles Winninger when Ziegfeld calls. Lamarr is beautiful; she marries a musician. Turner is materialistic; she gets spoiled, wrecks her boyfriend James Stewart, and MGM kills her off on a superb stairway, a showgirl to the end. MGM also flogs in a few shots from *The Great Ziegfeld* to cut corners in spectacle.

The most typical of MGM's wartime musicals, *For Me and My Gal* (1942), had Garland and Berkeley but no Rooney. Instead, Gene Kelly was brought in fresh from his Broadway success as the heel-hero of

☆ *HEROES OF SELF-BELIEF:*
Temple (in Little Miss Broadway*) loves*
everyone, Cagney (Yankee Doodle Dandy)
loves fame, Kelly (It's Always Fair
Weather) *loves himself.*

Pal Joey. A film of that sordid, sexy show would have been unworkable in the 1940s, but Kelly brought a little of the hustler to his roles at MGM. More tender than Astaire in a song (yet on less voice) and more aggressive in a dance, Kelly swaggers and grabs. He grins too much; he gets off on the wrong foot. Garland, in *For Me and My Gal*, is not impressed with his "Hello, springtime," and their budding romance and vaudeville act collapses when he deliberately smashes his hand in a trunk to dodge the draft so they can play the Palace—just when she learns that her brother has been killed in action. "You'll never make the bigtime," she tells Kelly, "because you're smalltime in your heart." (It sounds silly, but Garland brings it off.) So Kelly must prove himself in combat; does; happy ending to a last chorus of the title tune.

One couldn't see Astaire or Rooney in the part; their gallantry was unquestioned. But Kelly is a standout for his egoistic intensity, particularly in *Cover Girl* (1944), one of the gems of the era. Columbia had Rita Hayworth under contract, so Columbia was making musicals, even this expensive one, lavish with fashion and Technicolor (though one of the chorus boys spoils a final moment of the title number with the wrong hand motion). Archetypally beautiful and a first-race dancer, Hayworth was a novel goddess, *amiably* gorgeous, the opposite of Dietrich or West. She couldn't sing—all her numbers were dubbed—but she was basic to the wartime musical, suddenly irreplaceable after years of toiling in ghastly programmers on Poverty Row. Some of her fascination was bound up in the "pin-up" syndrome, but her grace in dance with Astaire or Kelly is something else. In *Cover Girl*, directed by Charles Vidor, Hayworth is the star of Kelly's dingy Brooklyn nightclub, rushed by a fashion magazine and the glamor world. Can Kelly hold her—or should he let her go on to fame? His challenged ego erupts on a deserted street at night as he dances with himself in double-exposure, angry and destructive. The Jerome Kern–Ira Gershwin score is gentle and rowdy by turns, but here Kelly gives the picture an element of power wild for expression, for a business to run and a woman to control. (By comparison, Rooney's women are girls who flirt or have crushes and his business is putting on shows in barns or leading a high-school band on to a big broadcast.) Yet Kelly fit as well with Garland as Rooney did—better, for she had the strength to match his. Though we see her die in childbirth in *Little Nellie Kelly* (1940), a dire act redeemed when she promptly continues the film as her daughter, Garland was not to turn woman till she met up with Kelly in *For Me and My Gal* two years later. Then, when she is back with Rooney in *Girl Crazy* (1943), their eighth film together, a western *Babes*, we see her in perspective. Her "Bidin' My Time" and "Embraceable You" carry more weight than her ballads have previously, and suddenly her torchy "I Cried for You" in *Babes in Arms* seems overdrawn for a schoolgirl in a pet over losing Rooney and the lead in his show to Baby Rosalie (June Preisser)—the right delivery for the song but the wrong song for the character. Kelly tempered her, and *Girl Crazy* was the last of the Garland–Rooney films. We didn't need a little Judy anymore.

Betty Grable was a big Judy, the happy Judy that Garland herself seldom projected. Like Hayworth a pin-up and no great singer, Grable had to leave Hollywood for Broadway in the late 1930s to ignite interest. Fox's Zanuck, a specialist in woman-hero musicals, signed her to replace Alice Faye in *Down Argentine Way* (1940): Grable is an heiress, Don Ameche an Argentinian horse breeder, Charlotte Greenwood Grable's mother, Carmen Miranda a lady in a tutti-frutti hat and banana-boat wedgies. Grable shared the Faye roles with Faye and took over when she retired, romancing John Payne, Victor Mature, Robert Young, Dick Haymes, and Dan Dailey. Typical Fox entries, these films reckoned in glitzy settings, all-purpose song and dance rather than character songs, and handsome leading men who were not necessarily singers or dancers. (Dailey, alone in the list, was both.) Zanuck thought the story musical too much bother, but the public was happy—Grable made the top-ten list from 1942 to 1951, number one in 1943. The year is crucial: Grable was essentially the nation's wartime mascot, and Grable knew it. "I'm strictly an enlisted man's girl," she explained, "just like this has got to be an enlisted man's war." Like Faye, Grable was a working-class Cinderella.

Garland, Rooney, Kelly, Hayworth, and Grable do not comprise a vastly different personality squad than we had in the late 1930s for it was not the performers who had changed so much as the forms. Many of the biggest thirties stars were still around. But those who thrived in less ambitious musicals were most comfortable—Crosby, for instance, who could take his three or four easy-street songs into any character, including a priest, which he played in *Going My Way* (1944), winning an Oscar opposite Barry Fitzgerald as the crotchety old pastor Crosby has been assigned to replace. Astaire, who worked best in a story musical where motion is woven into plot, had some trouble.

After the stability of the RKO years, Astaire found himself with neither partner nor studio so he tried MGM to team up with Eleanor Powell for *Broadway Melody of 1940*. It must have seemed like a dream duet on paper, the two greatest dancers side by each for the first time. And their dances are spectacular. They never coalesce as people, but it's a fine film, with a Cole Porter score and a pleasantly familiar backstage tale of two dancers (Astaire and George Murphy) who want the same Broadway part opposite the same starry dancing lady (Powell). We know that Powell's producers will inadvertently hire Murphy when it's Astaire they want, that Murphy's head will swell, that Murphy will date Powell while she and we both want Astaire there. The script manages to act as if it were going over this material afresh, and, when Murphy gets drunk on opening night and Astaire gallantly fills in for him without letting anyone know, we fall in and enjoy the surprise when Murphy pulls the stunt again the second night—deliberately, this time: he is giving up the part to Astaire. Eleven years after the original *Broadway Melody*, Hollywood's Broadway remains a community in which you support your buddies while pursuing glory: Murphy has sinned, and must compensate with a self-sacrifice. As the heel, Murphy is awfully good, and even holds his own with Astaire and Powell at the finale when they resolve their triangle onstage before the public with some friendly stepping.

But what of the dance musical itself? *Broadway Melody of 1940* has lots of dancing, but none of the musicoemotional exuberance that gave us the "Night and Day" and "Cheek to Cheek" numbers. Astaire and Murphy's act routine, "Please Don't Monkey With Broadway," one of Porter's most witless lyrics, tells us nothing about them; Powell's "I Am the Captain" is just another nautical prance. We're in better shape when Astaire plays "I've Got My Eyes on You" and then dances it as an untold valentine for Powell while she watches unseen. Still, it's a bit of a letdown, and Astaire's second release in 1940, *Second Chorus* for Paramount, is a disaster, with Paulette Goddard not to dance with and Astaire and Burgess Meredith unlikely as trumpet-playing college students. Luckily, Astaire moved to Columbia and found an ideal partner in Rita Hayworth.

The format of the dance musical, however, remained elusive; as we shall see, it was losing its dance orientation to a new strategy favoring stronger stories and preferring singers to dancers. (*Cover Girl* was probably the last of the oldtime dance musicals—and note that the flag had passed to Kelly by then.) As proof, the first of Astaire's two films with Hayworth, *You'll Never Get Rich* (1941), was a lifeless look at a drafted choreographer's courtship of a captain's sweetheart. Astaire is convincing in the army setting (you can take him anywhere) but, for the first time, not fun. He hasn't lost his touch—this is the one in which he does the "Bugle Call Rag" (in the guardhouse; he spends a lot of the film there). But the story is drab and silly. It doesn't *deserve* dancing. Hayworth and Astaire were better served in *You Were Never Lovelier* (1942), when director William A. Seiter shot them on a moonlit terrace where Astaire welcomes Hayworth into his element as the essential American hero, the man who incites romance in women. The script tells us that Argentinian heiress Hayworth is cold. Her father Adolphe Menjou hires Astaire to spark a flame, he does, it catches, and Menjou finds an unwanted American suitor on his hands. Cole Porter had helped *You'll Never Get Rich* to fail with a tuneful but irrelevant score; for *You Were Never Lovelier*, Kern–Mercer songs more successfully stress heart, "I'm Old Fashioned," "Dearly Beloved," and the title tune tempering the flame to a glow.

Between the two Hayworth films Astaire made *Holiday Inn* (1942) with Bing Crosby. Something interesting could come of an amalgam of Astaire's tense tap and Crosby's mellow vocals, and for once Astaire is something of a cad and loses out in the love plot; Crosby schemes and sulks. So *Holiday Inn* was different, a little lackluster in its leading women (Marjorie Reynolds and Virginia Dale) but rich in songs— fourteen, all by Irving Berlin and including "White Christmas," the biggest song hit ever written for a film. The story, about two vaudevillians who break up the act and chase the same girl, is no great shake, and it has to stretch to fit nine holiday songs, but Mark Sandrich directed with flair, Astaire thought of yet another weird dance—with firecrackers—and the film was Astaire's biggest hit since he left RKO. Now we want to see Astaire in something special, a sense of aesthetic renewal—something to rival the opulence and imagination of the RKO wonders, something to take a chance, even if it flops. And we get it: *Yolanda and the Thief* (1945), one of the most hotly contested musicals in the canon. Some call it a flawed masterpiece, some a dreary bomb.

It definitely took a chance. A Technicolor fantasy set in a South American land where con men Astaire and Frank Morgan plot to cheat heiress Lucille Bremer, *Yolanda* was produced by the Arthur Freed unit at MGM, known for a certain enthusiasm in letting each property find its own style of musical. Freed, who came to MGM as lyricist (of *The Broadway Melody*, for starters), himself collaborated with Harry Warren on *Yolanda*'s score, not a great one. Nor is Irving Brecher's script all it should be, veering between romance and satire too separately. Bremer is a little stiff, Mildred Natwick as her screwball aunt doesn't come off (one good line, to a servant: "Do my fingernails and bring them to my room"), Astaire's con man gets few chances to flash charm, and the story drags. It was a terrific setback in the careers of all concerned. But visually and choreographically *Yolanda and the Thief* enchants. Director Vincente Minnelli turns his camera on the deliberately artificial land of Patria, as if playing a fantasy within fantasy, and Eugene Loring staged a gorgeous nightmare ballet of Daliesque expressionism. A second big number, "Coffee Time," worked into a street carnival, admirably complements the dream by pushing outward the bounds of realism, which street fairs often do, anyway. Loring hailed from ballet, and had an unfailing eye for the patterns of things—groups still and in motion, doubles and triples, silhouettes, sheets, hats, rocks, trees, and dancers ever gliding toward or away from them. The surrealism of these two numbers aligns with the plot in that the heroine has a guardian angel. Astaire pretends to be one, but she really has one (Leon Ames), interceding on her and then Astaire's behalf in the name of love. In the film's last moment, Ames leaves a photograph with the couple, of them and their children, taken five years in the future.

Nearing fifty and tiring of The Life, Astaire decided to retire and went out with a sure thing: *Blue Skies* (1946), with Crosby and another Berlin score. Most of the songs were oldies like "Always" and "Heat Wave," and there was an air of encore about the whole thing after *Holiday Inn.* In the earlier film Crosby ran a hotel; here he runs nightclubs. Before, Crosby and Astaire were old show biz pals who love the same girl; same game here. And Crosby sings "White Christmas" again. But after the stately *Yolanda*, *Blue Skies* was dynamite, with Astaire and Crosby pranking through ancient shtick in "A Couple of Song and Dance Men," Astaire leaping off a precipice in "Heat Wave," Crosby smoothly digging into "How Deep Is the Ocean (how blue is the sky)?", and Astaire pulling off the novelty of his life in "Puttin' on the Ritz" through trick photography that presents an entire stage of Astaires, each dancing a solo. Paramount dropped three million dollars into the adventure for spectacular numbers and spent perhaps two dollars on supporting talent. Joan Caulfield and Olga San Juan are only acceptable, the fag so-called comedy of Billy de Wolfe is almost as regrettable as the work of El Brendel, and the other parts consist mainly of lines like "Five minutes, Mr. Adams." *Blue Skies* was all Astaire and Crosby, a kind of party in honor of America's coming through the war with its ambition and relaxation intact: with Astaire and Crosby as they were. If they hadn't changed, then we hadn't. Astaire as *Blue Skies'* Jed Potter remains Astaire; the character's name, like Pete Peters, Jerry Travers, Robert Davis, Tony Hunter, and all the halfhearted aliases Astaire played under, is like a printless ticket into life. Only when he danced did he defeat the illusion of putting the everyday into a style. Similarly, Crosby in his many duplications was artlessly restating the obvious—that charm, a sense of humor, a nice feeling about oneself, and stupendous musicianship will send one right to the top.

An odd note: the early 1940s are as well remembered for secondary comic performers as for stars—Carmen Miranda, Eve Arden, Martha Raye (who was for a while mistyped as a romantic heroine), Betty Hutton (who was graduated to heroine parts but played them the way she played her second-banana roles: loud and busy). The comic musical had settled down as comedy plus irrelevant music, as in the Abbott and Costello vehicles. This duo, extremely popular in the war years, revived a failing Universal with *Buck Privates* (1941), filmed for $180,000 in twenty days and quickly grossing millions. The Andrews Sisters were Universal contractees, so they sang at intervals, but this was no musical. Nor was *Ride 'Em Cowboy* (1942), though prime black talent was pasted in, including Ella Fitzgerald for "A-Tisket, A-Tasket." Even *Rio Rita* (1942), on loan at MGM, turned into an Abbott-and-Costello joke fest, though Pandro S. Berman produced and Kathryn Grayson and John Carroll were hired, presumably to sing.

In Paramount's *Road* series with Crosby, Bob Hope, and Dorothy Lamour, the comedy musical almost happened. These films baffle some, but they do stand as a rare case of Hollywood's admitting that personality is the art. The *Road* pictures depend on Hope as Hope—cowardly but devious—and Crosby as Crosby—disloyal but lovable—and a dangerous exotic place with Lamour as local beauty. Constant ad libs and asides to the audience shatter any sense of story. In *Road to Morocco* a camel announces, "This is the screwiest picture I was ever in," and for a reprise of "Moonlight Becomes You" the three stars lip sync to each other's voices, Hope pushing out his ears to look like Crosby when he gets Crosby's voice. Paramount originally offered the series to Jack Oakie and Fred MacMurray, but *Road* spunk calls for the zany on-and-off camaraderie that only Crosby and Hope could put together. *Road to Singapore* (1940) led off, to critics' quibbles; Roads to *Zanzibar* (1941), *Morocco* (1942), and *Utopia* (1946)—actually goldrushing Alaska—led at length to *Rio* (1947), the most musical of all. What with Crosby's big ballads, the Crosby–Hope patter duets, Lamour's spot, and native specialties, the *Road* pictures kept trying musical flight, but *Road to Rio* even pulled in the Andrews Sisters, the

Carioca Boys, and a puppet troupe and let Hope attempt the worst Carmen Miranda imitation in history. By then, critics were grudgingly raving, not unlike icing a cake that has already been eaten.

What of the Hollywood opera lobby? Swing had largely dispersed it—this is the time when the universally popular MacDonald and Eddy evaporated. But Joe Pasternak, who launched Deanna Durbin at Universal, had moved to MGM to oversee the film careers of Kathryn Grayson, Lauritz Melchior, and José Iturbi. In a sense, Pasternak's *Anchors Aweigh* is the most typical mid-1940s musical. It has everything: classical, pop, uniforms, kids, aggressiveness, shyness, coldness, warmth, California, and a cartoon. But it lacked swing, and that was the salient of the day, so perhaps Fox's *The Gang's All Here* (1943) takes the prize. With Berkeley directing, music by Harry Warren, and Alice Faye in the lead, this was thirties musical reconstructing itself, though Faye sings "No Love, No Nothing" in her traditional trembly close-up and Berkeley took a last chance to build his numbers geometrically around a theme, multiplying Carmen Miranda's bananas in a shot so rich in taboo that it was supposedly banned in Brazil. Benny Goodman's band and such numbers as "Paducah" and "Minnie's in the Money," however, emphasized the whimsey of swing. More than that, while *Anchors Aweigh* is a story musical, *The Gang's All Here* stressed the personality musical, made of incidental capers and star persona. Hollywood was running loose these years; loose fun defines it.

☆ 14 ☆

Americana

B ESIDES STAGING all-star revues and stressing the morale of swing, the musical's war effort comprised recalling an older and less embattled America, even a fantastic-folkloric one. The easiest approach was through biography—oldtime composers, oldtime tunes and costumes. Don Ameche played Stephen Foster in *Swanee River* (1940); Alice Faye played *Lillian Russell* (1940) with an enacted Diamond Jim Brady, Tony Pastor, Grover Cleveland, and Gilbert and Sullivan, and the real Weber and Fields; Bing Crosby played Dan Emmett in *Dixie* (1943), minstrel blackface and all; Ann Sheridan, utterly miscast, played vaudevillian Nora Bayes in *Shine On, Harvest Moon* (1944), the title song shot in Technicolor. Suddenly, after the war, bios came faster and bigger. Nineteen forty-five was a bonanza, with *The Dolly Sisters*, *Incendiary Blonde* (Betty Hutton as Texas Guinan), Robert Alda as George Gershwin in *Rhapsody in Blue*, and Columbia's contribution to classical uplift, *A Song to Remember*, the life of Chopin.

No one held these films accountable to fact; as with *The Great Ziegfeld*, they were primarily excursions into nostalgia. But Warners' *Yankee Doodle Dandy* (1942) was reliable as chronicle, with James Cagney a great George M. Cohan, a load of great Cohan songs staged in style, and perhaps the only instance in all the Hollywood bio film wherein a scene from a stage musical is brought off *exactly* as it was—the "Off the Record" number from *I'd Rather Be Right*, Rodgers and Hart's spoof of Franklin Roosevelt. *Yankee Doodle Dandy* succumbed to the usual You Are There approach in showing Cagney alone at a piano on a darkened stage, slowly picking out the notes to what will become

"Over There," but its patriotism felt more sensibly invigorating than that in other films.

Cliché and ludicrous misrepresentation, however, were the norm. *A Song to Remember* cast Cornel Wilde as a fullback Chopin (he got an Oscar nomination, perhaps for being such a good sport) and Paul Muni in the worst performance of the decade as Chopin's teacher. It contains a textbook of classic camp lines, such as the warning to delicate Chopin that "to make this tour is literally and actually suicide." *The Jolson Story* (1946) at least used Jolson's voice (dubbing Larry Parks), and MGM's *Song of Love*, directed by Clarence Brown, successfully investigated the musician's intensity about music. Paul Henreid is Schumann, Katharine Hepburn Clara, Robert Walker Brahms—don't laugh; wait—and when Brahms first plays one of his pieces for Clara, she impulsively kisses him and he says, "Thank you." Audiences scream. But that is what these people are like. Moreover, Brown poured a great deal of first-rate music into the film, and, contrary to rumor, Hepburn's pantomime piano playing looks flawlessly authentic.

The pop bios especially got unforgivably bad. Cary Grant as Cole Porter wanders through Warners' *Night and Day* (1946) in a daze that seems to ask "Am I this year's Cornel Wilde?" and Robert Walker as Jerome Kern in MGM's *Till the Clouds Roll By* (1947) has nothing to do but appear between the countless numbers making and losing friends for unclear reasons. There is one good moment, when Walker and Van Heflin play through "Ka-lu-a" at the keyboard planning its orchestration and the instruments they invoke peal out on the soundtrack. But MGM hit the apex of grotesque in *Words and Music* (1948), an extremely popular and utterly worthless version of the career of Rodgers and Hart. It's a version, all right, with a pallid Rodgers (Tom Drake), an irritating Hart (Mickey Rooney), and no hint that anyone at MGM had the slightest understanding of the subjects' style. Frank Sinatra's "Ol' Man River" at the climax of *Till the Clouds Roll By* is very, very wrong, and the Cary Grant–Alexis Smith romance in *Night and Day* is unacceptably ersatz, but *Words and Music* is foul and stupid from Perry Como's lazy debauch of "Mountain Greenery" to Gene Kelly's uncomfortable spoken tribute to Hart.

The historical story musicals were much more worthwhile. Deanna Durbin went forty-niner in *Can't Help Singing* (1944), her first outing in color, with a Kern score; Kern also worked on *Centennial Summer* (1946), set in 1876 and perhaps the only musical of the decade to cast seven lead roles with nonsingers: Jeanne Crain, the ever-popular Cornel Wilde, William Eythe, Linda Darnell, Constance Bennett, Walter Brennan, and Dorothy Gish. Yet Kern wrote a strong score, characterful in melody (Louanne Hogan sings most of it, dubbing Crain) and smart in pastiche (patriotic hymn, railroad song, and black specialty, "Cinderella Sue"), though its big tune, "All Through the Day," is an everyone song, sung to a lantern-slide show by the whole cast. Better recalled than these two is Rodgers and Hammerstein's *State Fair* (1945), timeless rural midwest where *Centennial Summer* was old Philadelphia. Parents Charles Winninger and Fay Bainter take his prize pig and her mincemeat to the fair along with their kids Dick Haymes and Jeanne Crain (her mouth always full of Louanne Hogan; a great team there), who pair off with slickers Vivian Blaine and Dana Andrews. With *Oklahoma!* under their belts and *Carousel* in the works, the authors integrated their songs to a fare-thee-well, vocal sections slipping in and out of dialogue as if singing were the most casual thing in the world and the story musical the only way to go.

Most ambitious was Fox's *Where Do We Go From Here?* (1945), a fantasy about where we came from. Fred MacMurray, classified 4-F, uncorks a genie in a lamp and wishes . . . to join the army. The genie accidentally places him among Washington's troops at Valley Forge, and MacMurray hops from age into age, each time caught between gentle Joan Leslie and tricky June Haver. What makes the film special is its score, by Kurt Weill and Ira Gershwin, witty and bizarre. Hollywood regularly slashed Weill's Broadway scores (as did G. W. Pabst in his film of *Die Dreigroschenoper*), but Fox released *Where Do We Go From Here?* with, among other artistic advancements, a twelve-minute opera for the Columbus sequence.

Another fantasy, *Cabin in the Sky* (1943), was the second all-black film since *Hallelujah* to be released by a major studio, but swing had so accustomed the public to black performers that another all-black musical came out the same year, *Stormy Weather*. This purported to be the saga of Bill Robinson, but it comes off as a backstager hung loose to provide lots of room for specialties. Many of the greats got into it (Lena Horne, Cab Calloway, Fats Waller) and black standards—"Ain't Misbehavin'," "Diga-Diga-Doo," "I Can't Give You Anything but Love, Baby," and the title song—provide the score. But the film fears being too black, and controls the ad libs even as it encourages them, though Waller managed to slip in, "I've been ballin' all my life and I'll *be* ballin' as long as I live."

Cabin in the Sky is an artier effort, based on a much-admired show with a Vernon Duke–John Latouche score and a fanciful tale about a good woman who saves a weak man while angels of heaven and hell fight for his soul. Here was another chance for segregated talent to step forward—Ethel Waters, Lena Horne, Eddie Anderson, Rex Ingram, Butterfly McQueen, Duke Ellington and band—but in essentially black art, if written and staged by whites. As the heroine, Waters takes the screen and holds it; the prize number consists of Waters just standing there, handkerchief in hand, singing "Takin' a Chance on Love." Horne, as the bad woman, enjoys her only worthy part in her Hollywood career; MGM didn't know what to do with a black woman who wouldn't play a maid. (Even Waters served Jeanette MacDonald in *Cairo* two years earlier.) Everyone in the film seems touched with something extraordinary, and though MGM felt it necessary to make friends for the piece with a little swing that the folk tale doesn't need, it is to be credited with having done it at all.*

Cabin in the Sky's director, Vincente Minnelli, has entered the buff's hall of fame for his flagrant sense of color (useful now that MGM was turning out most of its big musicals in Technicolor), and he had the luck to work with Garland (whom he married), Kelly, and Astaire. He has been identified with a "golden age" of post-Depression MGM musicals, mainly by people who think *Yolanda and the Thief* superb, *Ziegfeld Follies* bearable, and Judy Garland the hooly blisful martir of solemn art-myth. Some of his films are mediocre or terrible, including the two most overrated musicals in history, *The Band Wagon* and *An American in Paris*. But one of Minnelli's films counts among the four or five greatest: *Meet Me in St. Louis* (1944). As folkloric as a nonethnic, nonregional realistic white domestic comedy could be, *Meet Me in St. Louis* was the most nostalgic of the forties costume musicals, as it looked back to a time (1903–04) when cities were suburbs and families stuck together; it made that old, cleaner, immobile America infinitely appealing. Like most of Arthur Freed's productions, this was a story musical, strong in character songs—but this one believes in itself almost devoutly. Minnelli cuts the sentiment with comedy, informality, and adolescent trauma, however, and the result is so well-rounded that we accept its scale as life-size and fall in, rooting for the love plot, doting on the parents, impatiently awaiting the impending world's fair

---

*It has been suggested that all-black musicals comprised an easy way out: racially integrated musicals would have made a more impressive breakthrough. This is so, but clearly the country wasn't ready for that. Hollywood itself wasn't. *Cabin in the Sky*'s cast reportedly had to take their lunches in L. B. Mayer's private dining room to avoid challenging the color bar in the MGM commissary.

and, like the Smith family, viewing a threatened move to New York as high tragedy.

An excellent script (by seven writers) from Sally Benson's *New Yorker* stories, a charming Hugh Martin–Ralph Blane score (including "The Boy Next Door" and "The Trolley Song"), and a fine cast are the film's most immediate benison. The Smiths are routine: father Leon Ames is stern but likeable, mother Mary Astor is wise, older daughters Lucille Bremer and Judy Garland are flirts, younger daughters Joan Carroll and Margaret O'Brien are cutups, son Henry Daniels, Jr., is one big smile, grandpa Henry Davenport is foxy, maid Marjorie Main is testy; even Tom Drake, the boy next door, is just another preppy heartthrob. The Smiths' street, the 5100 block of Kensington Avenue, is so ordinary that MGM could recycle it for countless period films thereafter. But routine is what this film is driving at: a safe place to be. Indeed, most MGM musicals from *The Wizard of Oz* on are obsessed with finding a safe place. Back in the dinosaur days of 1929, Paramount's backstager *Glorifying the American Girl* understood form so little that it gave its heroine no reason for succeeding as a Ziegfeld girl, let her love plot fall apart pointlessly, and gave her a selfish and exploitive mother. A closing shot of the heroine staring into the auditorium in confusion at the height of a big number on Ziegfeld's Broadway tells us there is no safe place, for she has got there and it isn't. Conversely, the formally confident Jolson film *Hallelujah, I'm a Bum* a few years later dared propose a complex naturalism in its Central Park setting, taking for granted mixed-race friendship, political radicalism, and sexual appetites, showing the mayor of New York handing his girlfriend a thousand-dollar bill, letting the love plot end unhappily for the protagonist, and condoning the workless ethic of the Park idlers' lives. Most distinctive is a moment in which the bums suddenly crouch on the ground as mounted police ride by, photographed and scored for real terror.

Now, by 1944, musicals could not make such "mistakes" in plotting and personality, MGM musicals least of all. No MGM forties musical showed an exploitive mother, or looked at police power from the angle of the culturally disinherited, or failed to follow through with romance. A forties musical could be dull, but it had to be nice, had to locate the safe place. Too much nice dulls *The Harvey Girls* (1945), another of Freed's costumers with Garland, set in the old west and directed by George Sidney. *The Harvey Girls* has a sort of family (the Harvey House waitresses, who live in a dormitory supervised by a matron), a more raffish street and boy-next-door (John Hodiak; his pencil moustache tells us he's sly), and a bigger number than anything in *Meet Me in St. Louis*, "On the Atchison, Topeka and the Santa Fe." To emphasize the nice by contrast, *The Harvey Girls* also has a tough saloon girl (Angela Lansbury) to love Hodiak, hate Garland, and—because it's MGM; forget the contrast—bring them together at the end. But *St. Louis* has a secret weapon: Margaret O'Brien.

The kid makes the film. Her portrayal, uncannily detailed, gives the story needed energy at several points—in a wonderfully sloppy cake-walk during a party, in a wrenching Hallowe'en sequence, in her climactic rampage among snowmen after "Have Yourself a Merry Little Christmas," when father Ames realizes that his family will lose too much by pulling up their roots. And at the start, when a ketchup-making scene clouds the atmosphere in sampler gush, Minnelli cuts in the macabre of the truly innocent as O'Brien rides home with the iceman:

TOOTIE (feeling her doll's forehead): Poor Margaretta. Never seen her look so pale.
MR. NEELY: Sun'll do her good.
TOOTIE: I expect she won't live through the night. She has four fatal diseases.
MR. NEELY: And it only takes one.
TOOTIE (beaming): But she's going to have a beautiful funeral. In a cigar box my poppa gave me, wrapped in silver paper.
MR. NEELY: That's the way to go, if you have to go.
TOOTIE: Oh, she *has* to go!

☆ 15 ☆
The Inertia
of Genre

With Judy Garland, Gene Kelly, and Frank Sinatra on the lot and the Freed unit strong in creative imagination (from Roger Edens, Kay Thompson, Stanley Donen, Betty Comden, and Adolph Green), MGM by 1945 was putting out the best musicals. Warner Brothers, the former prophets of sound, maintained little more than a series of backstagers built around Doris Day, unveiled in a supporting part in *Romance on the High Seas* (1948)—"It's Magic," she sang, often; it wasn't; *she* was, but Warners wasted her in the hideous *My Dream Is Yours* (1949) with Jack Carson and the contemptible *It's a Great Feeling* (1949) with Carson, Dennis Morgan, and a studio menagerie. Gary Cooper says "Yup"; Joan Crawford slaps a face; Jane Wyman faints; and Danny Kaye (not a Warners contractee, but what the hey) imitates a train.

Kaye dominates the late 1940s as Eddie Cantor did the early 1930s. Like Cantor, Kaye signed with Goldwyn and got The Treatment—opulent production, Goldwyn Girls, the works. His films were immensely successful, giving Kaye all the room he needed to be hysterical, fearful, and ridiculous, yet somehow to win out—like Cantor. In *Up in Arms* (1944), from the same source as Cantor's *Whoopee!*, he was a drafted hypochondriac; in *Wonder Man* (1945) he was twins, a tough gangster and his bookworm brother (the gangster was shot early in the story and spent much of the film as a ghost, but let's move right along); and in *The Kid From Brooklyn* (1946) he was a reluctant boxer. These were comedy musicals, for the scores were tailored to Kaye's gifts for mouthy paradiddle, allowing him to spoof jive, opera, movie conventions, or Russian folk song. *Up in Arms* seems the strongest today, for if the war motif dates it, it gives Dinah Shore bright chances in the ballad "Now I Know" and in "Tess' Torch Song," white swing blues fresh off the stalk.

The Broadway adaptations did not stand out much. In fact, when Bing Crosby made *A Connecticut Yankee in King Arthur's Court* (1949), the wonderful Rodgers–Hart version was not consulted, and Crosby ended up with an insipid original score. The same year, MGM made *On the Town*, following the story closely but dropping almost all the songs. Okay; but the music is by Leonard Bernstein. Famed for its location shooting, *On the Town* has less of New York than it thinks it does, as when a shot of the three sailor heroes at Rockefeller Center is so badly faked that one can see the background through the men's bodies. At least it was a dance musical, with Gene Kelly in the lead and co-directing with Stanley Donen; the whole cast leans danceward, for Sinatra and Jules Munshin can get away with anything short of a *plié*, as can Betty Garrett, while Ann Miller and Vera-Ellen are dancers in the first place. Note the threesome plan still vital after all these years—Kelly and Vera-Ellen are the heavy lovers with dream pas de deux, Sinatra and Garrett the perky lovers at first antagonistic in a taxi number (Garrett drives it), "Come Up to My Place," and Munshin and Miller the oddballs. (She's an anthropologist who craves prehistoric man. Munshin will do.)

Kelly's influence as the maximum leader of the post-RKO dance musical was felt all over the MGM lot—in *Good News* (1947), for instance, a remake of the 1930 college romp. There is no Kelly or Vera-Ellen to express the romance in motion, but the exuberance of academe is felt in parades, struts, wiggles, and two big numbers, "Pass That Peace Pipe" and "The Varsity Drag," and the cast is very right: Peter Lawford as the football hero, June Allyson as the sweet coed, Pat Marshall as a gold-digging flirt, Joan McCracken and Ray McDonald as the comic duo. Kay Thompson's late swing vocal arrangements pull the 1920s into the 1940s, and the score is well integrated into the whole in MGM story-musical style, with lyrics to the show's original songs changed to suit specific situations, even to suit the performers. In "An Easier Way," an Edens–Comden–Green ditty deleted from the release print, Marshall and Allyson compare methods of attracting men. Marshall plots to win "chinchilla" and "a villa." Allyson retorts, "I'll take vanilla." It's as much Allyson speaking as the character.

The opera musical was dying, though MGM slipped Lauritz Melchior into *Two Sisters from Boston*, a period piece about a Met hopeful

☆ *POSTWAR PEOPLE: opposite above, Warners had Day, rambunctious in* Calamity Jane; *below, Goldwyn had Kaye, unusually sober in* Hans Christian Andersen *(with Joey Walsh); right, MGM had Sinatra and Durante, insecure in* It Happened in Brooklyn; *and, below, Allyson and Lawford leading student bodies in "The Varsity Drag" in the* Good News *remake.*

(Kathryn Grayson) who works as "High-C Susie" in Jimmy Durante's Bowery cabaret. Very Bowery; says Durante, "Starting next week this place is goin' to be run formal—no one gets in here without a shirt." Grayson's sister June Allyson and proper folks come down to New York, Grayson has to impress them by showing up onstage at the opera, and the plot is on. The film works because—unlike the MacDonald–Eddy series—it isn't solemn about opera: when Grayson makes her debut in the chorus of something MGM calls *My Country* (cribbed from Liszt), she keeps pushing forward to sneak in solo cadenzas, infuriating Melchior and bewildering the rest of the cast but delighting us. And Durante is at his best, working in corny material so ingeniously that an ancient running gag about a piano stool that an assistant keeps lowering on him is a scream. "I don't know what I'd do without you," snarls Durante, "but I'd rather." And of course there's the usual MGM "be yourself" motto—the Bowery can appreciate a high C as well as an operagoer can. Maybe more.

Other established sententia held their ground. *Mother Wore Tights* (1948) let showfolk Betty Grable and Dan Dailey teach their daughter not to be ashamed of their profession. (The film did puncture one cliché in that it opens as a threesome, Grable and two friends off to get a job on stage. But when showman William Frawley asks to see their legs, the other two scatter and are never seen again.) *Up in Central Park* (1948) let Deanna Durbin and Dick Haymes conquer corrupt pols in New York with a Romberg score from Broadway. *Three Little Girls in Blue* (1946) proved that gold diggers (June Haver, Vivian Blaine, and Vera-Ellen) are really sweet kids looking for love (George Montgomery, Frank Latimore, Charles Smith); for depth, Celeste Holm turns up as Latimore's sister for a comedy spot, "Always the Lady," that plays waltz time against march time and ends in French. *It Happened in Brooklyn* (1947) taught the rule of self-confidence to Frank Sinatra, Peter Lawford, Kathryn Grayson, and Jimmy Durante, everyone helping everyone else in the community of the shy or defeated. Grayson hits a height of the bizarre at one point when she says, more or less, "I think I'll sing *Lakmé*," and suddenly does—the Bell Song—fully staged in costume. Durante delivers the film's keynote address while rallying Sinatra, a mellow balladeer in an era of hot swing:

DURANTE: What made Crosby the singer of the age?
SINATRA: His voice?
DURANTE: It helped. But what really did it was his *heart.*

The MGM Freed unit led the field, especially in costume pictures. *Easter Parade* (1948) brought Astaire back (replacing an injured Kelly), with Garland, Lawford, Miller, and a great Berlin score. Garland, already going to pieces in life, still had it on screen (and off, at times; when Berlin tried coaching her during a recording session, she said, "Listen, buster. You write 'em. I sing 'em"). Alleged comedy from Jules Munshin as a waiter proud of his salad is unbearable, but there are so many numbers that there's little action, which is exactly how an empty-silly musical like *Easter Parade* should run. And, wonder of wonders, MGM actually reunited Astaire with Rogers (replacing Garland) for *The Barkleys of Broadway* (1949)—though a comparison of this garish backstager with their RKO classics dampens one's belief in progress. Back in costumeland, MGM found something for Esther Williams to do besides swim in *Take Me Out to the Ball Game*, directed by a now shockingly neglected Busby Berkeley with Kelly, Sinatra, and Munshin recalling the great old Tinker to Evers to Chance double-play infield of the Chicago Cubs in "O'Brien to Ryan to Goldberg." But the studio blew a great opportunity in its musical remake of *The Shop Around the Corner*, Lubitsch's 1939 comedy with Margaret Sullavan and James Stewart as the bickering shopclerks who don't know they're lonely-hearts pen pals. As *In the Good Old Summertime* (1949) with Garland and Van Johnson, under Robert Z. Leonard's direction, Lubitsch's precise charm dribbled and wobbled. The score is zilch, the support poor, and a scene with a drooling baby clears the house. Not till Bock and Harnick's stage show *She Loves Me* did the tale come off as a musical.

But *In the Good Old Summertime* made money while ambitious MGM musicals lost fortunes—Rouben Mamoulian's *Summer Holiday* (1948) for example, in the red to the tune of $1,500,000. Based on O'Neill's *Ah, Wilderness!*, it shattered the ersatz peace of MGM's own *Andy Hardy* series with O'Neill's sharp eye for the details of Growing Up in Smalltown. Here, too, was a safe place, but Mamoulian captures its profound idealism; he shows us what kind of Americans make a place safe. Mickey Rooney as *Summer Holiday*'s protagonist remained Andy Hardy, but around him Mamoulian spins a wonderful tour: through the Miller home in the opening, "Our Home Town," passed from one member of the family to another (as "Isn't It Romantic?" was in *Love Me Tonight*), in a Fourth of July picnic, in young lovers bursting into dance across a green lawn, in the local saloon where Rooney's hard-hearted pickup turns shades of red as Rooney gets progressively more drunk and nervous, and in a last long crane shot of the

Miller porch and street as Rooney cheerfully wanders out into the next commonplace event. Everything in the film is commonplace but, viewed with love and wisdom, seems rare. Mamoulian was hampered by Warren and Blane's dull score, which comes to life only in "The Stanley Steamer"—yet even this appeared to be a reprise of *Meet Me in St. Louis'* "Trolley Song." MGM cut four numbers just before release, though as these were character songs they leave a gap.

An unflawed MGM musical did not fare well, either—Vincente Minnelli's *The Pirate* (1948), now a cult favorite for its blend of dance- and story-musical forms. *The Pirate* lost more money than *Summer Holiday*, even with Garland and Kelly, Cole Porter songs, gorgeous costumes, superb use of Technicolor, and a fine script by Albert Hackett and Frances Goodrich drawn from S. N. Behrman's comedy for the Lunts. In the adaptation, enlivened for youth, an innocent girl in a Caribbean village dreams of loving a brutal pirate, and a vagabond actor who loves her impersonates the pirate; unbeknownst to everyone, the real pirate has been living in retirement as mayor of the village, and is now engaged to the girl. The possibilities for music are uncountable. Porter gave nothing to the villain, Walter Slezak as the former dread Macoco, but set off Garland's dream in the dynamic "Mack the Black" and Kelly's vanity in "Niña" (in which he cascades all over town looking the girls over and suavely rolls a lighted cigarette into his mouth while he kisses one), and celebrates the union of actor and dreamer—for are they not the same?—in "Be a Clown." The dancing is more ambitious, with a savage pirate dance for Garland's vision of her Macoco, and hits a height of style when Kelly goes into a bolero during "Niña" and ends posing before his own poster.

The Pirate tells its tale with wit. Garland has an oft-quoted put-down when Kelly-as-Macoco takes over the town and demands Garland be brought to him. Secretly thrilled, she puts on a doleful face as a shocked citizenry weep for her sacrifice. One girl, overcome, offers to go in Garland's place. Garland peers at her, the prima donna being hustled by a walk-on, and says, "He asked for *me*." Even better is Kelly's advice to Slezak, who, attempting to empty a room, screams and rants to no effect. When Kelly quietly says, "Get out," everyone scrams. "You should try underplaying sometime," Kelly tells Slezak. "Very effective."

Garland's dream motif dominates the film. She thinks Kelly is a pirate; he turns out to be a clever acrobat looking for love. She says of Slezak, "He doesn't drink. He doesn't smoke. He's regular in his church duties." And he's the pirate. At one point, as if she were back in Oz, she cries, "I want to go home!" She does eventually get out of the dream—not by going home, but by leaving it. Garland has grown up. Her Mañuela and Kelly's Serafin make one of the great musical teams, and Minnelli sets them off like jewels in a dream that does at length come true. Yet the film bombed.

A fluke? Or was the story musical losing its hold on the public? The late 1940s saw a time of troubles for Hollywood, from writers and directors eager to treat serious social topics, from federal investigations of moviemakers' politics, and, mainly, from falling grosses. The arrival of television and the courts' demand that the studios dissolve their producing-exhibiting monopolies further eroded Hollywood's economic foundation. More than any other type of film, the musical depended on the studio system: an assembled unit of specialists in musical procedures from arranging to editing. The studios had kept the musical from getting too lively but they kept it alive. If they go down, the musical could easily go down with them.

☆ 16 ☆
The Energy Peters Out

THE STUDIO EMPIRES crumbled in the 1950s, but in the first half of the decade they maintained an active schedule for musicals. MGM stayed top in story and dance, Warners fostered a horrendous series of backstagers with Doris Day, Gene Nelson, Gordon MacRae, and Virginia Mayo, Fox played out the end of its brassy Grable vehicles, and RKO made what is probably the worst backstager since *Glorifying the American Girl* in *Two Tickets to Broadway* (1951), with Tony Martin, Janet Leigh, Ann Miller, Gloria de Haven, the old vaudeville team of Smith and Dale, and a Styne–Robin score. It looks as if it were filmed in someone's living room. Astonishingly, the director was Busby Berkeley. Not a good sign.

The bio did good business, though with Ziegfeld, Gershwin, Porter, Kern, Chopin, Schumann, Texas Guinan, Jolson, and such already done, some of the subjects had to be fetched from afar. Fred Astaire and Red Skelton played Bert Kalmar and Harry Ruby in *Three Little Words* (1950). *Who?* But it turned out that Kalmar and Ruby wrote quite a few songs worth hearing, if not in MGM's strictly fifties arrangements. Mario Lanza was a natural for *The Great Caruso* (1951) and a subdued Danny Kaye played *Hans Christian Andersen* (1952); the Danes fumed at the liberties taken, though the ballet sequences with Jeanmaire were impressive. Eddie Cantor, Glenn Miller, Eddie Foy, and Eva Tanguay were done, well enough, but Kathryn Grayson was hopelessly ill-equipped to play the young Grace Moore teetering between vaudeville and the Met in *So This Is Love* (1953). This was one of Hollywood's last chances to roll out the old "shall I sing it sweet or hot?" rug, but Grayson doesn't sing either the way Moore did. MGM tried another star-studded retrospective of real tunes and fake life in *Deep in My Heart* (1954) with José Ferrer as Sigmund Romberg. This was quite a potpourri, with songs familiar and obscure and Helen Traubel trying her Brünnhilde mouth on ragtime and "Stout-Hearted Men." Her "You Will Remember Vienna," at least, was very winning.

Doris Day appeared in the two best bios of the time, *I'll See You in My Dreams* (1951) and *Love Me or Leave Me* (1955). The latter, centered on Ruth Etting's on-off romance with a racketeer (James Cagney), revived some great songs and was very high-powered CinemaScope entertainment, but the former, one of the most unpretentious musicals ever made, is a neglected gem. The alleged life of lyricist Gus Kahn (Danny Thomas), it derives its rise-fall-rise plot from simple things like marriage, family, and moderate success. The famous flit in and out, but not portentously; this is really a film about a man, his loving, butinsky wife, and his realization, after some tribulation, that she is the greatest thing that happened to him. No scene stands out for description, no big number may be cited. Yet one comes out of it feeling very nicely served.

Hollywood filmed some classic Broadway these days, in faithful renderings. Ethel Merman recreated her ambassador Sally Adams in *Call Me Madam* (1953), Marilyn Monroe took over Carol Channing's Lorelei Lee in *Gentlemen Prefer Blondes* (1953), Gene Kelly, Cyd Charisse, and Van Johnson made a very sound-stage-looking *Brigadoon* (1954), though most of the action occurs outdoors, and Otto Preminger made *Carmen Jones* (1954) with virtually two casts, one seen (Dorothy Dandridge, Harry Belafonte, Diahann Carroll, Joe Adams) and one heard (Marilyn Horne, LeVern Hutcherson, Bernice Peterson, Marvin Hayes), with Pearl Bailey and Olga James switch-hitting. In the vogue for outdrawing television with spectacle, MGM made *Kiss Me, Kate* (1953) in 3-D—the only musical so filmed—but this was so successful a transplant that it needed no visual ruckus. With Cole Porter's best score and a dynamite book by Sam and Bella Spewack set during the Baltimore tryout of a musical version of *The Taming of the Shrew, Kiss Me, Kate* couldn't wait to be a film: a backstager, rich in decor, dance, and comedy. MGM bowdlerized the book but otherwise honored the original. Even the casting worked. Howard Keel outdid himself—for once the swagger really told—and Kathryn Grayson was almost competent. It was the dancing that kept the screen hot—Ann Miller, Tommy Rall, Carol Haney, Bobby Van, and Bob Fosse. With few numbers dropped (and "From

This Moment On," written for but not used in another Porter show, added), the film argued for a more respectful adaptational process, and with *Call Me Madam* and *Brigadoon* might be said to have inaugurated a new era in Hollywood's relationship with Broadway. Adaptations can be too faithful, however. United Artists filmed the Phil Silvers television spoof *Top Banana* (1954) literally on its Broadway stage, complete with audience reaction shots and drab curtain calls. If nothing else, the *Top Banana* film serves as a document of early fifties musical comedy, with its set-changing numbers "in one," blackout lines, and superficial song cues. But it is nothing else.

MGM readied another Broadway hit, *Annie Get Your Gun*, as its big one for 1950 with Judy Garland in Merman's role as Annie Oakley. For her leading man the studio tested and passed up John Raitt, who would have been terrific, and found Howard Keel, who worked out fine. But Garland was uncomfortable with her role, and she wasn't happy with the director, Busby Berkeley. Perhaps both were pulling the story back into the *Babes* world that Garland had outgrown in *The Pirate*. Her recording of the *Annie* songs, extant today, is halfhearted, and the early footage was terrible. Production was closed till George Sidney replaced Berkeley . . . and Betty Hutton replaced Garland. Now the film worked, with Indian festivals and wild-west rodeo the stage show could barely simulate. But something's missing. The film just isn't fun.

At least the original screen musicals couldn't let one down by failing to keep a Broadway piece buoyant. Walt Disney's fairy-tale cartoons had become less adventurous than *Snow White* and *Pinocchio*, but their scores still sought to engage the narrative. *Cinderella* (1950) and *Peter Pan* (1953) had a lot of story music, and while *Alice in Wonderland* (1951) completely fudged Lewis Carroll's tone, it exploited his zany characters in "I'm Late," "The Caucus Race," "The Walrus and the Carpenter," "The Un-Birthday Song," " 'Twas Brillig," and the nonvocal "March of the Cards."

With Fred Astaire and Gene Kelly on the roster, MGM exercised the controlling interest in dance, though the scores were never as fine as those for the RKO Astaire–Rogers set. Dance in the 1950s was less a meeting of hearts and more a nonallusive celebration, often of the self. Astaire once danced solo to show us his loneliness; Kelly danced to show what a neat guy he is. Kelly made *Summer Stock* (1950) with Garland, recovered from her *Annie* mess, in a revival of the show-in-a-barn theme, featuring a "Get Happy" number shot some time after the main production with Garland in a cut-off tuxedo looking considerably lighter than in the rest of the film. Astaire made *Royal Wedding* (1951) with Jane Powell in a revival of an even older trope, Fred as brother of his dancing partner (Powell romanced Peter Lawford). Still, Astaire found something new in dance, defying gravity in "You're All the World to Me" by gliding all over a room, walls and ceiling included. (The room set was fitted into a huge metal package, the furnishings tied down, and the package revolved as Astaire moved.)

Kelly and Astaire each starred in classic entries, but while Kelly's *Singin' in the Rain* (1952) offers endless delight, I can't see why *The Band Wagon* (1953), Astaire notwithstanding, is so admired. A backstager without the slightest taste of the theatre, it was fashioned by Minnelli, Comden, and Green, all stage veterans who should know better, using Schwartz and Dietz standards. The score is great and "The Girl Hunt Ballet," a Mickey Spillane takeoff for Astaire and Cyd Charisse, amusing. But the story is tired, the attempted burlesque of "serious" musicals rude, Oscar Levant atrocious, and Jack Buchanan as uncharming as when he marred *Monte Carlo* back in 1930.

Singin' in the Rain is a surprise backstager: backstage in Hollywood. Set during the first moments of the silent-to-sound time, when a hit musical seemed like a world wonder, the film tells of good versus evil in what appears to be nonstop singing and dancing, from throwaway bits and plot specialties through a time-passage montage of early musicals to a gala set-piece spectacle. All the material is old—old history, mostly old score (Brown–Freed songs culled from MGM's backlist), old gags, old sentimental therapy—yet the picture is fresh. Comden and Green put wit and joy into this one; they seem to know more about old Hollywood than about their own Broadway. Perhaps the important difference lies in the direction, by Stanley Donen and Kelly. This film *looks* like something, from the cooled-down pastel blue of the night scenes to the sunny hillside where Kelly and Debbie Reynolds close the tale with a kiss.

One remembers a huge film, but a second viewing reveals a few principals and a few bit parts except in the one big number. Kelly is a movie star, Donald O'Connor his sidekick, Reynolds an unknown hopeful, and Jean Hagen, Kelly's costar with an ugly voice and wicked soul. Sound comes in and poses its challenge: how does a sound film act? And what to do with Hagen's silly voice? Answer: make a musical and dub Hagen with Reynolds. But how long should Reynolds have to cover the throat of the nasty Hagen? In romance, in plot, in diversions, the film never slackens, keeps unraveling story; and it has a song for everything. An elocution teacher's tongue twister erupts into "Moses

☆ *THE POSTWAR DANCE MUSICAL: above,* Brigadoon *(Charisse, Kelly); below,* Seven Brides for Seven Brothers *(Mattox, Platt, Powell, Tamblyn, D'Amboise, Richards, Rall in "Goin' Co'tin' ").*

☆ *Above,* The Pirate *(Kelly, Garland in "Be a Clown"); below,* Royal Wedding *(Astaire). All from MGM, last archon of studio craftmanship.*

(supposes his toeses are roses)." A walk home from his girl's place when love has struck causes Kelly to prance through the title song, story musical at its best because the singing and dancing is about what's happening. Kelly's plan for "Broadway Rhythm" in the projected film becomes a saga of new-guy-in-town who "gotta dance," getting famous, tasting love, hitting the top. And "Make 'Em Laugh" reviews the old silent comedy. The song itself is insignificant and copies Cole Porter's "Be a Clown" in scan and lyrics. But as O'Connor performs it, it really jumps with pratfalls, attacks, and miscellaneous geeking. The song's purpose is to define a tempo for comedy—O'Connor, repeating the chorus while he runs off a medley of slapstick tropes, doesn't even bother to get all the words out. He is too busy calling up a time when movies did things rather than spoke: he is battered by plywood boards, does a business with a fake door, flirts and fights with a featureless dummy, walks a circle prone on the floor, and then gives an exhibition of the gag, emended by the whammo, exploded by the double-whammo. This routine builds to a climax so corny I almost can't bring myself to cite it—the old "crashing through a paper wall that you thought was solid" bit. But the audience roars. Here is comedy at its most elemental, so the vapid song actually helps the scene. The music puts a face on the comedy, gives it eyes.

So there were still great musicals to make. But there were fewer great performers who specialized in musicals. Except for Kelly and Astaire, the company had altered drastically. Another classic MGM story-dance musical, *Seven Brides for Seven Brothers* (1954), could star Howard Keel and Jane Powell and feature as his six brothers and their six kidnapped brides people of no major oomph. Imagine what the cast might have been like in the 1930s, when, say, Alice Faye's support drew from a talent pool including Ethel Merman, Jack Haley, Bebe Daniels, George Raft, Patsy Kelly, Joan Davis, June Havoc, Lyda Roberti, Jack Oakie, Charles Winninger, and Helen Westley. Alternatively, consider the daffiness, fantasy, cynicism, and satire that Merman, Haley, and the others worked in, and one sees Keel and Powell in perspective. Keel's work in this era took in such events as *Pagan Love Song* (1950) with Esther Williams, the savorless remakes of *Show Boat* (1951) and *Rose Marie* (1954), and a *Kismet* (1955) that drained the sensuality from one of Broadway's steamiest musicals. Powell, last in the Durbin–Grayson line of trained sopranos, starred in *Nancy Goes to Rio* (1950)—"Whee! Musical spree" the ads trilled—and *Rich, Young and Pretty* (1951), two films of such little content that even camp mavens pass them by, despite the presence of parish favorites Carmen

Miranda in the former and Danielle Darrieux and Fernando Lamas in the latter. Both Keel and Powell worked at MGM, the world's capital of musicals by then, yet all these films lack the shirty self-spoof of a *Pigskin Parade* or a *Wake Up and Live.*

Seven Brides suffers this especially. It's wonderful entertainment, even funny in spots, but it takes itself awfully seriously for a musical that ain't, *au fond*, serious. Choreographed by Michael Kidd, *Seven Brides* has some great dance numbers—the "Barn Raising," "Goin' Co'tin'," and "Lonesome Polecat"—and obviously the brothers, who handle them, had to be dancers rather than all-around performers. Still, where's pizzazz? When Warner Brothers remade *The Jazz Singer* in 1953, they could better their original with a full soundtrack, a multi-camera attack, and color. But Danny Thomas can't show us the compulsion of performance that Jolson had to—does not, as Jolson did in *The Singing Fool*, need to break into a razzle-dazzle quickstep while singing "I'm Sitting on Top of the World." Yet that compulsion is what *The Jazz Singer* is based on and what many of the early musicals had, song and dance going off like firecrackers.

In the early 1950s, performers were being controlled by their vehicles. Or, when they cut loose, they overpowered a public conditioned for safe places and tepid comedy. Frank Sinatra, freed from his MGM shy persona, emerged as a gambling, woman-chasing, blues-blown singer in *Meet Danny Wilson* (1952). This is the Sinatra most people know, casual, underplaying, sharing his jokes with the audience as well as with the other characters, and director Joseph Pevney underlines the new natural Sinatra in a dark underworld setting. *Meet Danny Wilson* even touches on *verité* in Sinatra's occasional rudeness or hostility when performing; at one point he calls himself "the King." Is this *Meet Frank Sinatra*? Wilson sings Sinatra's songs: "She's Funny That Way," "That Old Black Magic," "All of Me," "How Deep Is the Ocean?"—a lot realer than the poor-left-out-me ballads he was assigned in his MGM roles.

Also exceptional was *Calamity Jane* (1953), one of Doris Day's few good roles—the rare one, in her early Warners series, in which she doesn't play an actress. This story musical is set in Dakota Territory, where tomboy Day and Wild Bill Hickock (Howard Keel) spar, embrace, spar, and embrace. Unlike *Seven Brides for Seven Brothers*, *Calamity Jane* offers no scenic outdoors (no color, even) and no dancing. It concentrates on narrative, allowing for an unusually full score by Sammy Fain and Paul Francis Webster. "Secret Love," the hit ballad, is dull and dully photographed, but the opening number is a knockout, taking us from Day's ride aboard "The Deadwood Stage" into town, where she introduces a few of the local characters in "A Very Good Friend of Mine," the two songs tied together by a musical refrain, to the words "Whip crack-away" in the first and "Set 'em up, Joe" in the second. Typically, neither *Meet Danny Wilson*'s *film noir* nor *Calamity Jane*'s musical comedy made much of an impression: they were not what Sinatra's and Day's publics wanted from their favorites.

On the other hand, Judy Garland got the vehicle of her career in *A Star Is Born* (1954). Director George Cukor and author Moss Hart must have studied William Wellman's 1937 version with Janet Gaynor and Fredric March, for many of the earlier film's verbal and visual details remain. But in making Esther Blodgett a singer they and songwriters Harold Arlen and Ira Gershwin reinvented the character's impetuosity and frankness. Ironically, Garland had to switch over from MGM, weary of her erratic behavior, to Warners for the role that all those MGM story musicals had been working up to. The film is not a musical so much as a drama with plenty of numbers for Garland, and because her most intense acting always came out in her singing, the performance is a revelation. All the weight problems, comeback concerts, and tabloid snitching notwithstanding, if Garland had not made *A Star Is Born* it is likely she would not have become the legend she did; her first big musical, *The Wizard of Oz*, and her last big one, this one, structure the myth of an innocence so likeable that, grown old and cynical, it still begs for and receives the public's indulgence. Never was Garland so lost as she is at first here, an unknown in a town comprised exclusively of the famous, never so winning as when she gets the parts and the attention, never so alone as when the actor who helped her succeed and whom she helped in more personal ways finally sinks alcoholically into nothing. "It's the true Judy," the fans whisper, awed at the life-art. Hardly. It is an electrifying performance that expands Garland as no MGM role had done.

An immense improvement on the Wellman *A Star Is Born*—Garland wipes Gaynor away and James Mason in March's role is really superb—the musical is apparently a mutilated version of itself. Without Cukor's assistance, Warners added the windy if enjoyable "Born in a Trunk" number, an autobiographical showcase that takes the heroine from vaudeville to bigtown cabaret and Hollywood through a string of old standards. But the completed film now ran three hours. It was a big one, in color and CinemaScope, but not so big that exhibitors would be glad to lose one showing's take a day. "They didn't cut the picture," Garland later reported. "Harry [Warner] gummed it to pieces." Pieces is the word, insiders tell—Cukor's careful development of the Garland–Mason bond is shredded to the point that the audience cannot care about its decline as they should.

Some buffs date the decline of the Hollywood musical from this moment on, marking *A Star Is Born* as the last of a kind: the last big Garland musical, the last original score by golden-age oldtimers, the last of the big remakes when the new version might actually supersede the old. One could as well mark the moment from *There's No Business Like Show Business* (1954) for its gala cast (Ethel Merman, Marilyn Monroe, Mitzi Gaynor, Dan Dailey, Donald O'Connor, Johnnie Ray), gala score (Berlin old and new), and backstager traditions, three elements that faded in the late 1950s. Perhaps the farewell was most succinctly made in *It's Always Fair Weather* (1955), in which Gene Kelly, Dan Dailey, and Michael Kidd, inseparable buddies in the service, meet again ten years later and hate each other, their mutual alienation rendered the more immediate by a masking process that cut the screen into three separate disgusted close-ups. Not to put too fine a point on it, the threesome had dissolved.

☆ 17 ☆
Economics of
a Stereo Era

Big CAME IN in the late 1950s. True, 3-D was retired, but CinemaScope and it variations (VistaVision, Cinerama, Camera 65, and such) held on in larger theatres. (The neighborhood houses made do with reduced prints, which could play hell with composition.) There were few of the technical difficulties that terrorized film when sound came in, few impositions on art—Hitchcock, John Sturges, and others exploited the wide screen like veterans of big—and even some gains for the musical in the expanded use of location shooting. Fred Zinneman shot *Oklahoma!* (1955) in the Todd-AO process in Arizona (Oklahoma looked too modern), showing the corn "risin' clear up to the sky," the "wavin' wheat," and the scurrying chicks and ducks that the score mentions. The film followed the original virtually line by line, cut two songs that no one likes, retained the original orchestrator and conductor, and let Agnes de Mille rework her history-making choreography, so *Oklahoma!* was one of the most exact renderings from Broadway in Hollywood's history.

It was big, but only as big as it needed to be. "It's a pastoral opera now," de Mille noted, citing "the fine skies in the desert" and the animals. "It's different. But I find it very beautiful to look at." It was well cast, too, with Gordon MacRae, Shirley Jones, Gloria Grahame, Gene Nelson, Rod Steiger, and Charlotte Greenwood (as Aunt Eller, written for her in the first place), and James Mitchell and Bambi Linn dancing the dream ballet. If Hollywood was losing its touch in originals, could it concentrate on filming Broadway classics?

But Joseph Mankiewicz's *Guys and Dolls* (1955) suggested that Hollywood looked upon Broadway originals as settings for stars. Frank

194 ☆

Loesser's songs were kept or replaced by Loesser himself, and Michael Kidd restaged his dances, crucial in the show's distillation of the Damon Runyon Tenderloin of gamblers and broads. But producer Samuel Goldwyn planned to hire Gene Kelly, Grace Kelly, and Betty Grable for roles only the first could have played. He ended with Marlon Brando, Jean Simmons, and Vivian Blaine, who made an odd mélange with Frank Sinatra, supposed to be a tense finagler and not half trying. Blaine, who had played her part on Broadway and had logged Hollywood experience in the 1940s, is the worst of the lot, overworking the lines and gestures. Add to this sets that are half real and half stagey and Mankiewicz's labored pace and you have a perfect Broadway show playing the screen like spilled milk.

The problem was that pop music, which as "jazz" and swing had furnished Hollywood with an appropriate sound style and an inextinguishable source of stories in backstagers, had lost its national constituency. In the 1930s and 1940s, most Americans listened to the same music. But the rise of rock and roll in the 1950s splintered the listening audience; and, unfortunately, the studios couldn't figure out how to use the new sound in story films. It was 1929 all over again: which performers to hire, what stories to tell of them, how does a song work, what's a musical? Early tries at rock film, in *Shake, Rattle and Rock* and *Rock Around the Clock*, both in 1956, were loose and silly and, worst of all, square. Wiseass adolescents circulated the rumor that grownups deliberately made them rotten as part of the well-known fiendish conspiracy to silence the new music. Actually, the early rock films did good business. They were cheap to make, as rock had no "production" in this golden age: the musicians stood there and played and sang. These movies look terrible now, with generation-gap plots plus obtruding musical bits—a band plays for a prom—or "big show" tales. And then came Elvis.

Presley's first role, in *Love Me Tender* (1956), was a featured part in a southern post-Civil War romance. Thinking older brother Richard Egan dead in battle, Presley has married Egan's sweetheart Debra Paget. The film was no musical, though Presley does his stuff in four songs, getting rather modern-sounding screams from the Confederate girls standing by. Launched in a hit—Presley made it one—he became a star and made thirty story musicals for various studios from 1957 to 1970. He plays the same fellow in each, with variations—a convict in *Jailhouse Rock* (1957), a quasi-delinquent analyzed by Hope Lange, tempted by Tuesday Weld, and reformed by Millie Perkins in *Wild in the Country* (1961), a boxer in *Kid Galahad* (1962), twins in *Kissin'*

☆ CLASSIC NUMBERS: *above, "Tiptoe Through the Tulips" from the first threesome classic,* The Gold Diggers of Broadway; *below, "You Gotta Have a Gimmick" from* Gypsy *(Wood on trunk); right above, Rooney and Garland in "Do the La Conga" from* Strike Up the Band, *one of Berkeley's most dancey numbers (though the camera still adds much to the motion).*

☆ *Above, Garland's "The Boy Next Store,"* Meet Me in St. Louis; *below, Gingold and Chevalier in* Gigi's *"I Remember It Well."*

Cousins (1964), an heir who trades places with a water-ski instructor in *Clambake* (1967), a hip doctor in love with nun Mary Tyler Moore in *Change of Habit* (1970). Who is he? A country boy, quiet, unselfish, tolerant, not smart but intuitive. Presley couldn't act, but that renders the illusion all the more telling—he *must* be the character because he wouldn't know how to fake it. His was probably the nicest persona in film history, and critics savaged him. "Is it a sausage?" asked *Time.* "It is certainly smooth and damp-looking . . . Is it a Walt Disney gold-fish? . . . Is it a corpse? The face just hangs there, limp and white with its little drop-seat mouth . . . A peculiar sound emerges. A rusty fog-horn? A voice? Words occasionally can be made out: 'Goan . . . git . . . luhv.' " But this was the most successful series of films ever made. To dismiss Presley is New York solipsism.

The films themselves are atrocious. The scores are dull, the supporting casts often amateurish, the productions hasty, and the helter-skelter decor makes Alice Faye's vehicles look like an expert's seminar in the history of costume. *Frankie and Johnny* (1966), with a showboat setting, is typical, with supremely ungifted youngsters (Donna Douglas, Sue Ane Langdon, Anthony Eisley), defeated veterans (Audrey Christie, Harry Morgan, Jerome Cowan), unintelligible plot, a load of songs, extras apparently hired on a come-as-you-are basis, and absolutely no sense of style—a title-song production number imitates boffo staging without suggesting it; and later, when the number is reprised, the original footage is simply run over again.

But Elvis has charm. He's at his best when fighting for the dispossessed, as in *Follow That Dream* (1962), a pleasant argument for populist anarchism. "How many times I got to tell you?" his father Arthur O'Connell says. "The government don't run out of money. *People* run out of money. The government's loaded." Presley takes on both a federal welfare agency and gangsters, politely, naively, but with admirable efficiency. The film manages to suggest not only that authoritarian interference is harmful, but that authoritarians are crummy people who use their power vindictively. The better Presley films are actually rather beguiling, and have only one drawback: by the time he made them, Presley had ceased to sing rock.

Ironic that the very centerpiece of rock-as-rebellion, the popularizer of take-no-prisoners rockabilly sensuality, should have crossed over to midcult white fifties "rhythm," but that's probably why Presley's movies work so well as story musicals. No one knew, then, how to make real rock work for story contexts in film, which is why the major rock mediums are still the concert and the record album. Rock opera?

It's more a rock song cycle, not readily stageable. But then Presley's rock and roll really died (temporarily) when Buddy Holly did and the folkies moved in. Not till the Beatles remixed ragtime, twenties pop, Schubertian *Lied*, and a host of other styles with American rock did the sound open up elastically. Then, we'll shortly see, there were possibilities for rock musicals.

Obviously, Hollywood was going to stick to the Broadway sound with the old regulars as much as possible. Danny Kaye made his best film in *The Court Jester* (1956), a lampoon of the Ivanhoe sort; wiseass kids not clued into the antirock conspiracy went around quoting its "Get it?" "Got it!" "Good" and its dire message, "The pellet with the poison's in the vessel with the pestle." (Don't ask; you had to be there.) Sinatra, Crosby, Grace Kelly, and Louis Armstrong graced *High Society* (1956), *The Philadelphia Story* with a Cole Porter score and all its wit flattened; Porter really went Hollywood in the hit tune, "True Love," a simple-minded waltz he would never have thrust upon Broadway. Gene Kelly squired Mitzi Gaynor, Kay Kendall, and Taina Elg, his club act, in *Les Girls* (1957), better Porter and a *Rashomon*-shaped narrative: three versions of the same past. Astaire was at his best in *Funny Face* (1956), made of old Gershwin songs (and with the title, but nothing else, of an old Gershwin show) and an Americans-in-Paris plot that for location work, zest, and freshness is far superior to *An American in Paris* (1951), a film whose reputation seems to be based entirely on Gene Kelly's intriguing ballet set against a palette of painters' styles. *Funny Face* has no big number, but it has Audrey Hepburn, ravishing in "How Long Has This Been Goin' On?" as a bookworm twirling rhapsodically in a model's chic hat.

The prize of the era is *Gigi* (1958), the capstone of MGM's so-called golden age and one Arthur Freed film that actually exceeds its reputation. Hepburn had played the part (without music) on Broadway, that of a young French girl raised to be a courtesan who chucks the whole thing for love. Leslie Caron, so winning in *An American in Paris*, *Lili* (1953), *The Glass Slipper* (1955), and *Daddy Long Legs* (1955), at last lucked into a champion: Minnelli at his most imaginative, a Loewe–Lerner score, Hermione Gingold and Isabel Jeans as Gigi's mentors, Louis Jourdan as her friend, then protégeur, then suitor, and, best of all, the return of Maurice Chevalier as Jourdan's uncle. A greedy location schedule devoured Paris, including Maxim's, which closed for four days so Minnelli could film an extraordinary sequence wherein *le tout Paris* gossips in song—Loewe, master of pastiche, set it as a cancan—as Jourdan upholds his playboy status with a lavish rendezvous.

Gigi was Freed's last original musical, and the line begun in *The Wizard of Oz* and continued through *Meet Me in St. Louis, On the Town,* and *Singin' in the Rain* came to an end in one of the ritziest films ever—a three-million-dollar production, and it looks it. Here is a musical that uses decor, color, motion, even the juxtaposition of true locale and sound stage, for tone. At Maxim's, in the Bois de Boulogne, in the pages of a Parisian *Tatler,* all over the city as Jourdan berates and surrenders to his love in the title song, or on the beach on holiday, where Minnelli cuts from young love frolicking on the sand with a donkey to Gingold and Chevalier, who style a reminiscence of their old liaison against a painted sky, Minnelli makes a *movie,* as Lubitsch and Mamoulian did when almost no one else knew what a musical was, and as few knew now that musicals were turning into Broadway souvenirs. Even Mamoulian, in *Silk Stockings* (1957), made no history, though with Astaire and Cyd Charisse in an adaptation of the Porter hit. True, this last of Porter's stage scores is dull where *Gigi* sparkles; true also that *Silk Stockings* has nothing to compete with Chevalier, aged, a little pastured, and absolutely in character until the movie can't resist giving him an encore specialty and out comes the old straw boater for "I'm Glad I'm Not Young Anymore." But the Mamoulian film, except for Charisse's frosty commissar (which Garbo brought off so much more incisively in *Ninotchka*), is the same old thing, right down to Peter Lorre's trepak.

If Hollywood had to overstress the Broadway adaptation, at least let it respect the original while turning it out for film. *Pal Joey* (1957) cleaned up John O'Hara's tale, gave Frank Sinatra a spate of songs from other Rodgers–Hart shows, and miscast Rita Hayworth and Kim Novak; *The Pajama Game* (1957), on the contrary, preserved the original score and cast (Doris Day in for Janis Paige). *Damn Yankees* (1958), the tale of a middle-aged baseball fan who sells his soul to the devil to be Tab Hunter and win the pennant for the Washington Senators, was too faithful. Co-directors George Abbott and Stanley Donen threw a camera on a Broadway cast overplaying with Broadway timing and Broadway pauses (for laughs? coughs? latecomers?). What on stage looked game and stylish here looks like a metal-booted cartoon, though Bob Fosse's dances come off well, even "Two Lost Souls," in which Hunter partners Gwen Verdon. She looks better with Fosse in the "Who's Got the Pain?" duet, but the same problem that dogged the Verdons of 1929 and 1930 kept her from making it in film: too expert, too special, too New York (born, however, in Culver City). The cartoon approach could work only on a cartoon—*Li'l Abner* (1959), filmed virtually on stage with one major cast change (Leslie Parrish for Edie Adams), one change of ballad ("Otherwise" for "Love in a Home"), and Michael Kidd's freaky Al Capp plastique intact, is in its bold color the Sunday funnies come to life.

Hollywood in the late 1950s caught up on the Rodgers–Hammerstein classics whose long runs prohibited hasty transformation, and here big began to come into play—had to, with all that reputation to deal with. *The King and I* (1956), with Deborah Kerr and Yul Brynner, upheld the *Oklahoma!* treatment: make it film but keep all its parts in place. A grand event, even if Marni Nixon had to dub Kerr. But *Carousel* (1956) didn't work out well, mostly through ho-hum casting. Sinatra, hired for the lead, ducked out just before shooting—a smart move, as he's completely wrong for the part. But his replacement, Gordon MacRae, was correct, no more. John Raitt, who created the role, would have been perfect; not till *The Pajama Game* did Hollywood give him a tumble. *South Pacific* (1958) was the first really overdone musical, turgidly directed by Joshua Logan and photographed through blurry filters with Rossano Brazzi (dubbed by Giorgio Tozzi), Mitzi Gaynor, John Kerr (dubbed by Bill Lee), and, from the stage, Ray Walston and Juanita Hall (dubbed, for some reason, by Muriel Smith). Not only was the whole score retained, but "My Girl Back Home," dropped from the original, was put back in; Logan treated the property as if it were Scripture. Big, I tell you. The *New York Post* called it "a three-hour ruin of a magnificent musical."

Potentially the biggest event would be *Porgy and Bess* (1959), Gershwin's opera of black life in a Charleston ghetto, originally staged by Rouben Mamoulian with extravagant pictorial intensity in 1935. There were several big considerations here—the filming of a too long underrated American masterpiece, the eliciting stylization of the black idiom in music and dance, and the first American attempt at filming a major opera. Goldwyn controlled the film rights and hired Mamoulian to direct, but after disagreements Goldwyn replaced him with Otto Preminger. Much more of the score than one had hoped to hear was there, and the casting was good—Sidney Poitier, Dorothy Dandridge, Brock Peters, Diahann Carroll, Pearl Bailey, and Sammy Davis, Jr., brilliant as Sportin' Life. But Gershwin's line calls for extremely vital singing, the one thing dubbing can't deliver; and this film was *plenty* dubbed. Opera movies never work. That kind of big—the full-out mutuality of singer-public vocal communication—film cannot raise.

Movies, like popular music an art form that in America never pretended to be anything but a business, had banked nothing against posterity. Except for the rare re-release of a major film, Hollywood's output was product, to amass profits and be forgot. But when television proved unbeatable, the studios joined it, producing series and—most important—selling off the dead backlist for airplay. Television became a museum of film. A wicked museum: with commericals and cutting for time slots. Still, the home screen served to introduce a new generation to films they might otherwise not have seen. Musicals suffered cutting the worst, for since their songs were often subsidiary to plot motion, music and dance were the first things to go when footage was snipped. But it is ironic that while contemporary Hollywood was falling back on the big Broadway transmission, *Million Dollar Movie* was airing Astaire and Rogers, MGM story musicals, and Depression backstagers—all great examples of Hollywood as creator. The film musical, it appears, was here to stay, no matter what Hollywood was doing to it lately.

☆ 18 ☆
The Big Broadway Roadshow

SAPPY AS MOST of them were, Elvis Presley's films were Hollywood's main body of original work in the musical in the 1960s, and among the few that didn't go epic. There were others, but *Let's Make Love* (1960), in which Yves Montand courted Marilyn Monroe with blasé *laissez-faire*, or *Get Yourself a College Girl* (1964), with Chad Everett, Mary Ann Mobley, Nancy Sinatra, and a few rock acts, are not worth more than a mention, and the last of the Crosby–Hope–Lamour vehicles, *The Road to Hong Kong* (1962)—the only *Road* picture with a definite article in its title—was more of the same fun we had had six times before.

The Disney Studio, churning out its family fare, tried its first live-action musical, but *Babes in Toyland* (1961) showed none of Disney's imaginative mythopoeia. This filming of the old Herbert operetta had far more of the score (souped-up, however) than the Laurel–Hardy edition, but the special effects were greasy, the magic heartless, and Ray Bolger as the villain, Annette Funicello and Tommy Sands as the lovers, and nearly everyone else but Ed Wynn as the toymaker were wrong, wrong, wrong. Disney's *Mary Poppins* (1963) was a vast improvement. It lacked the tartness of Pamela Travers' stories, but the magic was true, especially in blends of animation and live action. A runaway hit for its broad appeal, *Mary Poppins* heartened those who felt Julie Andrews was swindled when Jack Warner cast Audrey Hepburn in *My Fair Lady*, and also gave nice opportunities to Dick Van Dyke, Ed Wynn, Glynis Johns, Elsa Lanchester, and Jane Darwell (Ma Joad in John Ford's *The Grapes of Wrath*) as a strange bird woman. Maybe *Mary Poppins* wasn't strange enough, though Travers restrained Disney from bringing Andrews and Van Dyke together romantically and made him honor her downbeat ending: Mary Poppins leaves the Banks family, as she arrived, by flying umbrella. Richard M. and Robert B. Sherman's score is childish, but it does provision a full-scale 140-minute story musical; and, true, if you've got to write songs about the medicine going down and the concept of supercalifragilisticexpialidocious (*-dozisch* in the German dubbing), it's hard to sound sophisticated.

Talk about childish, American-International, the Republic of the 1960s, made a series of story musicals with a surfing theme, starring Frankie Avalon and Annette Funicello supported by oldtimers (Robert Cummings, Buddy Hackett, Buster Keaton, Don Rickles), menaced by a burlesque motorcycle gang led by Eric von Zipper (Harvey Lembeck), and backed up by choruses of California blonds in swimming togs. These films inhabit an amazing innocence; was this the 1960s? In *Beach Party* (1963), Avalon and Funicello arrive for a week at a beach house, but she has secretly invited the whole gang down, to protect her virginity. For plot complications, Funicello takes up with anthropologist Cummings, studying teenage tribalism; for comedy, there is beatnik lampoon and Lembeck's clumsiness. For music, astonishingly, the style is early fifties midcult without a hint of rock. The two leads sing "Beach Party Tonight" at the start, as sweet as two Yodels in cellophane; "Surfin' " provides party entertainment; Funicello gives herself love advice in double-exposure in "Treat Him Nicely," and so on. It's so wholesome that a harmless kiss between Avalon and Luciana Paluzzi in *Muscle Beach Party* (1964) has Funicello calling Paluzzi a nymphomaniac and Paluzzi calling Funicello a professional maiden. Even Rickles, supreme in put-down assaults, is tame.

For musical sophistication, fine star turns, and something bright in story, one had little option but to see the latest Broadway adaptation, bigger and bigger as the decade wore on. Some perpetuate grand performances, such as Judy Holliday's in *Bells Are Ringing* (1960); Robert Preston's in *The Music Man* (1962), delightfully reproduced in toto by the original director, Morton da Costa; or Rex Harrison's and Stanley Holloway's in *My Fair Lady* (1964), though Jack Warner first wanted Cary Grant and James Cagney. In the end, Hepburn was the only major alteration; George Cukor even filmed the show (at a cost of $17,000,000) using Cecil Beaton's costumes and Oliver Smith's sets virtually direct from Broadway. Warner's *Gypsy* pulled the biggest switch of all in replacing Ethel Merman's Mama Rose—one of Broadway's legendary portrayals—with that of Rosalind Russell in a score very dependent on Merman's trumpet. But Russell brings it off, songs and all, talking and whispering through "Small World," forcing "Some People" to work through force of personality, letting warmth ride her through "You'll Never Get Away From Me," and revving up for a wonderfully pushy "Everything's Coming Up Roses" after spilling out her hurt, bitterness, and fury on the last word of the first line: "You'll . . . be . . . *swell!*" A considerable portion of Russell's singing was dubbed by Lisa Kirk, so this analysis feels a little foolish; nonetheless Russell plays a spectacular Rose. The film as a whole has been hated and praised. Mervyn LeRoy's direction is so-so, but the original material comes through, including the brilliant orchestrations, complete with overture. Nothing in the tough story is softened or cosied, and the show's claustrophobic atmosphere of overpopulated rented room and cramped backstage is respected. LeRoy realized that the film needn't look big because it has a big character.

But big paid off, most notably in *The Sound of Music* (1965), one of the two or three most thoroughly viewed films of all time; those attracted by a Cinderella story containing nuns, kids, Nazis, and Julie Andrews were literally overwhelmed (there's a lot of all four) and had to sit through the picture two or three times before they could settle down and go on with life. The Rodgers–Hammerstein show, a vehicle for Mary Martin on Broadway, had been freshened, lightened, and opened wide with a youthful heroine, with "I Have Confidence in Me" to replace the sardonic "No Way to Stop It" and "How Can Love Survive?", with a new premise for "The Lonely Goatherd" incorporating the Baird Marionettes, and with thrilling Austrian topography (the stage show, for all its Franz and Brigitta, could have taken place in the West Bronx), one shot of Andrews whirling alone in the green hills as the camera swoops down and the title song whips in having passed into the nation's memory.

In fact, *The Sound of Music* is neither all that great nor all that horrible. It's not sticky-sweet, despite the kids, for the Nazis have real menace—they didn't in the show—and even the nuns aren't as nice as non-Catholics always think nuns must be. Andrews is fine in a dull part, Christopher Plummer opposite her is a bore, the score is variable, Robert Wise's direction is excellent for this sort of thing, and so on down the line: okay. *The Sound of Music* is less important for what it was than for what it inspired in the industry. Producers determined to clean up ordered more *Sounds of Music*; but there is no menu for art, even pop art, and instead of Broadway-into-film hits, Hollywood produced the biggest squad of bombs in film history. Producers panicked;

☆ *BIG BROADWAY: above,* Camelot, *with real magic and sweaty chivalry; below, the title number in* Mame, *Onna White's stage choreography moved outside (Lucille Ball, center).*

☆ *Above, Streisand recreates Brice's Baby Snooks in* Funny Girl *(in a scene deleted from the release print); center, the notorious parade in* Hello, Dolly!, *irrelevant to the film however thrilling in its detail work (the station is all there, but the building at left is painted flat); below, Chakiris in* West Side Story.

why isn't it working? Do like *The Sound of Music*: big Broadway property, big stars, big score, big money, big hit. The recipe seemed right,
but in movie houses all over the country these *immense* cakes were
falling, and with *such* a noise. Why did no one take notice of Richard
Lester's spry, tight *A Funny Thing Happened on the Way to the Forum*
(1966), the one Broadway transplant that found more in less? Too
much of Stephen Sondheim's score was dropped, but the piece became
a true comedy musical in that only songs that indulged the farce could
pass. Applying the fast-cut wacky style he had developed for the first
two Beatles films, Lester let Zero Mostel, Phil Silvers, Jack Gilford,
and Michael Hordern do their stuff against a sarcastically naturalistic
ancient Rome of brutality, oppression, and buzzing flies. The camera
runs as screwball as the plot to catch the rhythm of farce, as when
hero Michael Crawford, letting go with a love song, hits on a tree and
a lute plops down, or when "Everybody Ought to Have a Maid" creates a mosaic of film fun—quick turns, strange sets, close and far
views (of the four comics, at one point, forming a kickline way atop an
aqueduct), overhead Berkeley spoofs, funny poses, and other craziness.

Mostel, for one, thought the film too busy. "The great thing about
the piece on stage," he said, "was that it was one set, sixteen characters, three houses, and you did it very simply. You go to the movie and
there's horses, zebras, peacocks shitting all over the place, your father's moustache, orphans, winos, donkeys with hard-ons . . ." Lester
almost alone among directors observed a sharp style in filming Broadway. But Lester is a satirist, and in Hollywood a big investment is a
solemn event. Prototypal, then, was *Camelot* (1967), grimly festive, a
big show with big stars and score in the first place. Jack Warner envi-
sioned a faithful rendering with the epic made manifest—real castle,
jousts, and round table, Excalibur resplendent, the sweat of the Middle
Ages and the poetry of chivalry. Alan Jay Lerner adapted his Broadway libretto, finding the spots for twelve of his and Frederick Loewe's
songs (including "Then You May Take Me to the Fair," dropped from
the show early in its run). So far, so good, if you enjoy the original's
ham-handed reduction of T. H. White's highly textured burlesque-ro-
mantic pageant of political-psychological self-hatred. The casting followed the new trend favoring personalities not always musically
talented or, if musical, not right for their parts. In *Can-Can* (1960),
calling in Frank Sinatra, Louis Jourdan, Shirley MacLaine, and Maurice Chevalier necessitated a ruthless overhauling of the original for
the fit, and no attempt was made to reconcile Chevalier's and Jour-

dan's Gallic suavity with Sinatra's and MacLaine's flat American informality. In *West Side Story* (1961), Jerome Robbins' choreography called for dancers for the bulk of the cast, and they cut striking figures against real New York streets. But of the leads, Natalie Wood can neither act nor sing, Richard Beymer seems like something scraped out of a pie, and only Rita Moreno can do what her role calls for. She and the dancing carry the film, in fact. Yet *West Side Story*, if not *Can-Can*, intended to film the stage show with utmost fidelity.

As did *Camelot*. And much of it does look right, in the callous gung-ho of the jousting tournament or in castle eyries by the hearth. But Richard Harris as Arthur, ranting his songs and lines, makes a tricky part impossible and Franco Nero as Lancelot had to be dubbed (by Gene Merlino) in a role expressly designed for the Broadway baritone. The man who sings "C'est Moi," "If Ever I Would Leave You," and "I Loved You Once in Silence" is supposed to know why those songs are there; Nero clearly doesn't. Granted that the naturalism of film acting is vastly better than the mechanical caricatures that Broadway musicals depend so much on (as in Carol Channing, Ethel Merman before and after *Gypsy*, everyone in Gower Champion's *42nd Street* staging, and even Richard Burton in the grungy 1980 *Camelot* revival), aren't there any real actors who really sing? Vanessa Redgrave, as Guinevere, almost is one, for she learned how to weave her thread of voice into something adroitly musical. It's all mike, but it works. Logan pulls an occasional film trick, as in a montage of adulterous rendezvous that creeps in on "If Ever I Would Leave You," but all directors of musicals have at some point to come to terms with the performance of character songs; how can they do so with nonsinging actors or with revamped properties whose scores no longer suit the actors singing them?

Not all the big films were antimusical or antistyle. A Hollywood original, *Thoroughly Modern Millie* (1967) had the right idea in putting Julie Andrews and Mary Tyler Moore into a mystery plot with a twenties setting, with Beatrice Lillie as the villain (she sells girls into slavery), John Gavin and James Fox as stalwart and comic boyfriends, and Carol Channing for a Broadway turn. But the period was flubbed, Lillie given no chance to *do*, and a "Jewish Wedding Song" shoved into the action at what must have been gunpoint. Another good idea, on paper, was the building of a musical around Rex Harrison, based on Hugh Lofting's Dr. Doolittle character, with crazy animals (like the two-headed pushmi-pullyu and a giant lunar moth), circus joys, and Anthony Newley to carry the ballads. But Leslie Bricusse's dead score (a prize of the soundtrack album to anyone who can explain why "Talk to the Animals" won the Oscar as Best Song) and a sluggish determination to wow with size and color sent the picture to the deep six in short order. An even faster flop was *Star!* (1968), a bio with Julie Andrews carefully indicating the elements of zaniness, hysteria, pathos, and selfishness in the character of Gertrude Lawrence and never being anything but a weird Julie Andrews. The woman has supreme talent; this wasn't her part. Nor was the damn thing about anything, despite its strict adherence to the rules: rise-and-fall career, emotional turmoil behind the façade of success, old standards, famous people. *Star!*'s director Robert Wise had become a specialist in the $15,000,000 musical, and at least he did try to recreate something of old theatre styles (and Daniel Massey made an impeccable Noël Coward), though he blew the big number from *Lady in the Dark* out of sync with Kurt Weill's percussive manner. Wise, Logan, and their colleagues were in the process of murdering the film musical by their failure to make decent movies. Not all of these blockblusters went bust, but an investment of $15,000,000, tied up for a minimum of two years, is supposed to return two or three times that amount, not break even or yield pin money.

The blockbuster syndrome might have collapsed by the late 1960s if some of the big musicals hadn't done so well. *Oliver!* and *Funny Girl* in 1968 proved that there were more *Sounds of Music* to be heard after all, and *Funny Girl* promised fresh gala for the form in the successful launching of Barbra Streisand in cinema. Director William Wyler wrapped the newcomer in a prize package, shooting her from the air as she sped out to Omar Sharif's departing ocean liner by tugboat while singing "Don't Rain on My Parade", adding in a roller-skating number that Streisand hilariously ruins and a ballet takeoff (trimmed to seconds in release) to explain Brice as comic and closing, shockingly, with Streisand singing "My Man" in close-up, Brice as person. Francis Ford Coppola might have done better with *Finian's Rainbow* that year had he similarly found film in it. Coppola played it straight, so this classic satire on capitalist-consumerism and racism, daring on Broadway in 1947, seemed commonplace in 1968. The cast, at least, was fine: Astaire as Finian, Tommy Steele as his leprechaun nemesis, Petula Clark and Don Francks as the lovers, and Keenan Wynn as a southern senator. Now that Coppola has become Coppola, film buffs screen *Finian's Rainbow* to place it in the canon, and to be sure it is craftsman's work, "Old Devil Moon" especially—few love scenes in musicals have felt so hot. But the film just doesn't fizz, perhaps because much of the original's charm lay in Michael Kidd's choreography. The film has very little dancing, even from Astaire and Steele.

Kidd, however, pumped a great deal of dancing into *Hello, Dolly!* (1969), directed by Gene Kelly and the first of the huge disappointments that finally closed the era of blockbuster musicals. A meticulous reconstruction of little old New York's Fourteenth Street for a parade sequence was cited as the dead center of overproduction and Streisand, in the name role, was jeered. But the film was at least partly a victim of the escalating expectations that the blockbuster syndrome aroused: *West Side Story* is the greatest, *The Sound of Music* more tremendous, *Camelot* shatters the world; what's left? Kelly did mount a spectacle, true, and Streisand's Dolly is made of ill-assimilated parts of Jewish wiseguy, crypto-glamor girl, and Mae West. Still, other than in the parade the movie fills its space, and Streisand is so gifted that she's still superb. Isn't the character supposed to be chaotic, flamboyant, and a mixture of identities in the first place?

"She's too young for Dolly!" they screamed. In her big number she *returns* to the night life after an absence. When was she last there, at age three? Actually, Kelly is at pains, in a dandy opening, to establish that Streisand is not unknown in town. A still of New York in the '90s comes alive in a period strut as Streisand, face unseen, passes out business cards. The chorus takes up a "Call on Dolly" refrain, the camera pulls around her feathered hat to show us who, and the first song begins. She may be young, but a station porter and ticket man know her well—so she *has* been around. As her train steams up to Yonkers, the credits come on and tempo is set: a farce with time for detail. Sure enough, every song is a Number. When "Dancing"—on Broadway a quintet—becomes an epic with tennis players, bicycles, a park setting with character vignettes and Dolly's waltz with a sanitation man, one has to admit that the proportions are majestic. But everyone in it is good and it's a real musical, unlike so many of its fellows: the story needs the music, the performers know what singing and dancing is for, and everyone gets a chance to utilize his or her talent. The kids are delightful, Walter Matthau elegant, and Louis Armstrong unlooked-for benison. What's wrong with *Hello, Dolly!*? Nothing. The press was gunning for Streisand and big musicals, and the public for such events was limited. In the event, it didn't do that badly.

Paint Your Wagon and *Sweet Charity*, the same year, did very badly; the clink of the money they dropped rings yet. *Paint Your Wagon*, the first all-talking, no-singing, no-dancing musical, directed by Joshua Logan, has Lee Marvin, Clint Eastwood, Jean Seberg, little story, weak comedy, and lots of songs with no lead to sing them. Based on a Loewe–Lerner western with a grand score and three splendid Agnes de Mille ballets, *Paint Your Wagon* became a film embarrassed to be a musical. When Seberg, holding Marvin at bay with a pistol, likens him to her father, "born under a . . . wanderin' star," an allusion to one of the songs, she blushes at the musical-comedy silliness. No; you have to believe in it or not do it. Or: when Harve Presnell's baritone rips into "They Call the Wind Maria," a drugged audience stirs in confusion— what's *he* doing here? *Sweet Charity*, directed by Bob Fosse and starring Shirley MacLaine in Gwen Verdon's role, had no problem of identity—on the contrary, its musical portions are stunning. But the stage show was a slick piece of goods that borrowed the plot but none of the spirit of Fellini's *Nights of Cabiria*, and Fosse carried over the faults in the original. Who besides a New Yorker or a Woody Allen fan wants to see a musical about crummy New Yorkers using each other? *Sweet Charity*'s first bookings did such poor business that the film virtually went into release in revival houses.

This was not the end. Big Broadway musicals continued to roll out in the 1970s, though they were fewer and no longer hoped to equal *The Sound of Music*. Luckily, something new had come along in the meanwhile: rock film.

☆ 19 ☆
The Texture of Rock

Bye Bye Birdie (1963) was the first film to use rock effectively. The Broadway original parodied rock and roll to tease its sweet middle American setting, which erupts in comically innocuous confusion on the appearance of the Presleyesque Conrad Birdie (cf. Conway Twitty) as a PR stunt before he enters the army. Here was rock viewed from the outside with mild contempt, but it was a second start now that the real Presley was doing truly innocuous musicals antithetical to rock's spirit, and the continuation was provided by two Beatles movies, *A Hard Day's Night* (1964) and *Help!* (1965), directed by Richard Lester in the jumpy style that was to work so well in *A Funny Thing*.

A Hard Day's Night follows the Beatles at work and play with irrelevant song breaks and a zany script. (When the quartet amusingly subverts the efficiency of a television station, manager Victor Spinetti foresees his demotion with a sigh: "The news in Welsh for life.") Most writers prefer *A Hard Day's Night* to *Help!* for the absurd atmosphere of *cinema verité*—it's so disorganized that it must be real—but the better-knitted *Help!* boasts a storyline of inspired lunacy involving the sacred ring of the eastern deity Kaili, which Ringo wears. Cultists engaged in human sacrifice need the ring, fail to steal it, and then decide to sacrifice Ringo. The bulk of the action comprises the quartet's flight from the fanatics, with assistance from Scotland Yard, the army, and Spinetti again as a mad scientist ("M.I.T. was after me, you know—wanted me to rule the world for them"). The songs offer puns on the action ("I Need You" sung over shots of military preparations) or heedless of it, as the action is heedless of itself, but the title song effectively expands a wild closing melee. The nuttiness is all-pervasive and irresistible: a Yard detective does a poor imitation of Ringo (George: "Not a bit like Cagney"), a man-eating tiger named Roger responds docilely (in homage to *Bringing Up Baby*) to the finale of Beethoven's Ninth, the story never does end, and the closing credits unroll to Rossini.

Lester had found a successful format for rock, if one that could hardly become common property. An easy way out for others was the concert film—no story, no casting, just a visual record of a rock event, sometimes with a documentary frame of interview or news footage. In 1970, *Woodstock* and *Gimme Shelter* recorded two crucial happenings in the quickly gathered and dispersed rock nation, bigger as history than as music. *Woodstock* captures itself with tactless ease, but *Gimme Shelter*, Albert and David Maysles' film of the Rolling Stones' free show at Altamont, is meant to exculpate the Stones—Mick Jagger, especially—from any responsibility in the several deaths that occurred at the concert, one not only on camera but run through in slow motion and stop-action. Those who feared rock's Dionysian incitement found *Woodstock* palliative, *Gimme Shelter* disquieting. But then rock, unlike twenties jazz, swing, opera, Broadway, theme song, and Hollywood's other musical approaches, admits of interior contradictions that defy all attempts to manipulate it for genre. Rock is larger than story, more riotous than dance, and it carries its character wherever it goes. *What* character? *Woodstock* preached community and transcendence; *Gimme Shelter* might have been set in hell. When Presley was young, rock and roll was already complex in derivation but chartable: controllable. By the late 1960s rock had been so reconstructed as to be pluralistic, ungraspably independent. From group to group, person to person, the art varied instrumentation, performance practice, verbal structure, and world view. It varied from film to film as well. *200 Motels* (1971), composed by Frank Zappa, takes in electric rave-up, atonal symphony (played by London's Royal Philharmonic Orchestra), country put-on, chorale, piano blues, and song titles like "Magic Fingers" and "Dew on the Newts We Got," and parades a freak of incoherent hallucinations concerning the Fifth Dimension's concert tour. *Tommy* (1975), Ken Russell's realization of the Who's song cycle, comprehends post-sixties rock's elastic use of pastiche and the intimacy of *Lied* and *chanson* in a linear narrative about a pinball-playing messiah that touches on adultery, sadism, homosexual rape, and apocalyptic show-biz mysticism, all magnified into Russell's characteristic nightmare realism. *Lady Sings the Blues* (1972) deals in black song in a straight bio (of Billie Holliday). Three completely different movies: yet all are rock films.

So what's a rock musical? Any number of things—with the catch that most rock and roll, heavy metal, and acid, three of rock's most basic styles, do not express character or plot very well and thus resist dramatic motion. Rock is, somewhat, autotelic, intense but narrow, too complete in itself to adapt to the needs of a larger form that would have to contain it. Rock inevitably carries certain cultural associations in its very sound, whatever its lyrics say. In the heyday of the Hollywood musical, in the 1930s, 1940s, and early 1950s, we took for granted that musical characters were sexually monogamous, patriotic, and like "most people" in their perceptions, whereas singers of rock are wired into a subculture that is sexually promiscuous, anarchic, and countercultural. "Sex, drugs, rock and roll!" runs a cheer heard in *The Rose*. True, the fifties sound epitomized by Buddy Holly is sweet and quaint by comparison to new wave groups, and much of rock fits within a folkie blues frame that can encompass almost any cultural outlook. Rock is tricky: because it's so rich. It isn't even definable anymore, so without trying to define it let's consider the four forms that most rock film observes. First there's the story musical, with the songs worked into the action; in *Tommy*, they attempt to carry it entirely. A second type separates story and score, letting the songs comment on the action from outside. *American Graffiti* (1973) is the most famous example, but notice that it merely spliced together old recordings and tracked them over the action, much as a car radio might underscore a conversation; this is hardly a musical. More open use of music is heard in the other two types of rock film, the concert and the bio.

Nineteen seventy-eight is a good year to compare these four forms; it was a big year for rock musicals. The notable concert film, *The Last Waltz*, is the biggest disappointment, though the concert itself proved to be one of the most glorious occasions in American popular music. The Band celebrated its retirement at San Francisco's Winterland with a vaudeville of the great in every rock class from blues to cabaret narrative, culminating in a reunion with Bob Dylan, for whom the Band formerly played backup. Dylan and the Band are steeped in legend together, especially for the "Basement tapes," so popular as a bootleg item that they came out on a commercial label as an afterthought, and the Winterland concert also offered such outstanding numbers as Dr. John's "Saturday Night (If I don't do it, somebody else will)," Joni Mitchell's "Coyote," and the whole gang (Eric Clapton, Muddy Wa-

ters, Ronnie Hawkins) together again for the first time on Dylan's "I
Shall Be Released." Instead of filming the event whole and letting the
music speak for itself—it tells volumes about what rock is—Martin
Scorsese captured it clumsily in segments interrupted by superficial in-
terviews with the Band and doesn't even include the single most electrifying moment, Dylan's entrance.

The commentary approach worked well for *FM*, as this picture of
an embattled radio station trying to retain its selfhood in a commerce
whose name is conformity ran loose enough to permit just about any
rock selection the audience might care to hear. Radio's subject matter
is rock, so let it roll, any way at all; the participation of Linda Ron-
stadt alone gives the silly story presence. But perhaps *FM*'s main purpose was to provide a two-record soundtrack album, which through
Saturday Night Fever the year before had become the record industry's
hotcake.

Three story musicals, *Grease*, *The Wiz*, and *Sgt. Pepper's Lonely
Hearts Club Band*, flooded stores with two-disc albums in 1978, but
only *Grease* repeated *Saturday Night Fever*'s success—a joke had it
that *Sgt. Pepper*, with its cover of bas-relief cardboard, was shipped
platinum and returned double-platinum. If there's a remainder bin for
cinema, *Sgt. Pepper* should fill it. An opera made of Beatles songs
(mainly from *Sgt. Pepper* and *Abbey Road*) placed end to end, the film
told how Peter Frampton and the Bee Gees, from Heartland, U.S.A.,
conquer corporate villainy and bring music *back to the people!* A number of actors played parts suggested by the songs—George Burns as
("Being for the Benefit of") Mr. Kite, Dianne Steinberg as Lucy ("in
the Sky with Diamonds"), Steve Martin as Maxwell (of the silver ham-
mer)—and a host of the famous turned up, unbilled, in the finale. A
big deal and a terrible film, especially in the stars' nowhere performance of the songs. The arrangements are careful copies of the originals (produced by George Martin, the Beatles' producer), but the
closeness exposes the stylistic gap. In "With a Little Help From My
Friends," Frampton is effete where Ringo was charmingly neutral;
Sandy Farina, on hand for what romance comic books call "kiss panels," makes "Here Comes the Sun" sound like a Vegas lounge act; and
Aerosmith (playing villains) in "Come Together" completely miss the
original's slinky grotesque. Most objectionable of all was the film's
false naiveté, its picture of rock as a weapon against The Corporation.
The pop music world is the big oil of American art, after all; how far
can you characterize as innocence the sound of a business run by bil-
lion-dollar grubbers?

The Wiz, drawn from Charlie Smalls and William F. Brown's black version of Baum's book, did better business than *Sgt. Pepper*, but its terrific expense did not pay off. Word of mouth reported that the film was failing because Diana Ross was too old to play Dorothy (whose age was upped to twenty-four), the choreography was confusingly filmed, and the whole thing, like *Hello, Dolly!*, was too big. All wrong. Ross is fine, if insistently doelike, the dancing is fine, a raw Motown party, and the story calls for spectacle in the first place. What killed *The Wiz* was too many songs and Sidney Lumet's sluggish pacing. The cast, particularly Nipsey Russell as the tin man, works hard and knows what to do, but in the grindingly slow motion one comes to resent everyone's sense of detail and wishes they'd stop acting and make the scene. It could have been a nifty film, for, while respecting the stage show's free use of blackness as style for fantasy, it went a step further and turned Oz into a dream vision of New York City. Tony Walton's design makes the Munchkins' playground graffiti come to life; fits the scarecrow's cornfield between burned-out tenements; turns the poppy field into a drug-and-sex tenderloin; places the Emerald City in midtown, obsessed with fashion; and Dorothy can't get a cab. The plot perspective is upended: the original book, the Garland film, and *The Wiz* on Broadway featured a little girl who wants to get home, but the new film gives us an older Dorothy who needs to get out in the world. All the versions advise on the wisdom of achieving self-confidence, proving that rock, for all its contrary ideology, can work for the old-line musical—most beautifully at the end when Lena Horne as Glinda breaks into a gospel rocker and the joint finally starts jumping.

The hugely successful *Grease* was also a Broadway adaptation, this from Jim Jacobs and Warren Casey's spoof of fifties high-school mores. In contrast to *Sgt. Pepper*'s Beatles diversity and *The Wiz*'s rhythm and blues, *Grease* hearkens back to primitive rock and roll, some numbers deliberately recalling certain oldies. "Mooning" and "Beauty School Drop-Out" revive the triplet bass of the stroll, "Magic Changes" reconstructs the elementary chord patterns of one's first guitar lessons, "Born to Hand-Jive" resurrects rock's version of the dance sensation, and so on. The show was still running when the film came out, but there could be no sense of the work's competing with itself, because the film threw away the spoof and turned romantic. The show *Grease* opened with a performance of Rydell High's Alma Mater, immediately reprised by the kids with their own nasty lyrics; the film opens with a shot of John Travolta and Olivia Newton-John kissing on a wave-smoothed beach. Where was this? California, of course—the show took place in something like Detroit. The best number, "There Are Worse Things I Could Do," was sung in the show by Adrienne Barbeau as a proud smash at the nice-nice heroine. In the film, Stockard Channing played it as a sentimentalized torch song directed, from a distance, at her boyfriend Jeff Conaway. *When* was this?—early middle Alice Faye, without Faye's morality of ambition. The film had incredible impact; kids returned to it so often they performed Travolta's hand motions in "Summer Nights" right along with the number on screen. But did they buy all this heartfelt love stuff? At least the romanticism was easier to take than the comedy, largely assigned to oldtimers who couldn't ruin the illusion of growing up taut and tanned near the surf. Frankie Avalon and Edd Byrnes returned from the 1960s (note wrong decade) to do what they did; but Sid Caesar, Eve Arden, and Dody Goodman disgraced their reputations and, as the local hash waitress, the once formidable Joan Blondell acted and sounded like hamburger helper. Only one thing the movie *Grease* had of value: a new theme song that set mood and viewpoint. Written by Barry Gibb and sung by Frankie Valli over cartoon credits, "Grease" the song revived the old "love thyself" message—"We start believing now that we can be who we are"—while the film was too busy making money to contain any message at all.

Of these rock films of 1978, only the bio, *The Buddy Holly Story*, came through well, and that mainly because the star, Gary Busey, carefully revived classic Holly in precise recreation of the sound. (Busey moves around more than Holly did and makes the act outrightly sensual, but it's hard to go back to the straight days after all we've seen.) The storyline takes in the usual simplifications and distortions: Holly's minister denounces his music in church, his parents tell him to give it up, his band the Crickets is reduced by one, Holly plays on tour with a string orchestra; all false. But it's thrilling to hear "That'll Be the Day," "Peggy Sue," and "True Love Ways" virtually as they were first heard.

The question of where rock fits into film was not yet answered. Has it replaced other styles as the correct sound for the American musical? Is it suffering the general incompetence that afflicts the musical today? Or is it wrong for the American musical? Does it carry connotations that militate against the form of the threesome, the go-getters, the romancers, the egalitarian conquerors? What if rock not only connotes but actively deals in the nonideological revolution of the violent energy level that never subsides? Sex, drugs, rock and roll: how do you fit a

☆ *A TOUCH OF ROCK: Above,* Frankie and Johnny *(note sloppy decor), vastly lacking in beat; below,* Jesus Christ Superstar—*note careful blend of ancient and modern in decor.*

story to that? An intriguing possibility was unveiled in a British release of 1979, *Quadrophenia*, in the commentary form—rock soundtrack enhancing an otherwise nonmusical narrative. The track is based
on the Who's 1973 album, like their *Tommy* a cycle that didn't pan
out except musically. Something seemed to be happening *between* the
songs, and the film, directed by Franc Rodam to find the compulsion
and/or exuberance in British teenage riots of the 1960s, filled in without drawing anything away from the music. On the contrary, the
songs feed the film. The Who do not appear, except momentarily on a
television screen. Rather, Rodam follows the fortunes of a young proletarian Mod in his home, club, and love lives, battles with the Rock-
ers, and climactic suicide. What happens to Jimmy? Rodam asks;
what happens to rock? ask the Who. If it can find itself a niche in films
as absorbing as this one, rock needn't worry.

On the other hand, how many films can be made about joyful bed-
lam? How silly and unworldly the earlier musicals were compared to
these—but what ideals they proposed. Heavy rock of the Who's sort is
bold realism and terrific art but in the end it is negative art and cannot
sustain a musical, which is not a realistic form. Rock tragedy—now
you're talking. But how many tragedies do people want to see? They
can see *Grease*, you say? *Grease* isn't a tragedy? Right. But *Grease* isn't
rock, either. It's a doo-wop sitcom with kiss panels.

☆ 20 ☆
Interesting Times

ONCE, the Hollywood studios were where films were planned, written, shot, and edited, and studio theatres played everything made. By 1970, the studios were mainly financiers and distributors and had no "where." It's all freelance now, but while the philistine totalitarianism of the money bosses survives, the craftsmanship is gone. The lack of industry organization does at least permit unusual subject matter—*The Little Prince* (1974), say, based on a dear little French fantasy about an extraterrestrial child's metaphysical adventures. But the lack of organization has dispersed the experts who knew how musicals were made, and in such a world even Stanley Donen, trained at MGM in the gala years, could not bring *The Little Prince* off.

Amid the confusion, straight adaptations of Broadway successes promised to be no-fail properties. *Fiddler on the Roof* (1971) and *1776* (1972), opened up but not changed, worked well, the latter with most of its Broadway cast. *Man of la Mancha* (1972), on the other hand, suffered lack of voice in its cast—Peter O'Toole, Sophia Loren, and James Coco—and *Mame* (1974) gave the decade's choice oomph role to Lucille Ball, suddenly turned grande dame, painfully dry in the songs, and not even clearly seen through a mass of Ponce de Leon filters.

Typical of the post-studio confusion was the film of Stephen Sondheim's *A Little Night Music*, drawn from Ingmar Bergman's *Smiles of a Summer Night* and written to coordinate with a production concept too stageworthy to transfer to the screen. Still, director Harold Prince tried a transfer, opening in an antique theatre with the stage dressed as the Broadway one had been, then pulling back into a real world out-side. Sondheim replaced the expressly theatrical "The Glamorous Life" with a new song to cover the same ground in cinematic proce-dure, the elegant but antinaturalistic Brahmsian quintet chorus was dropped, and Elizabeth Taylor and Diana Rigg joined some of the stage leads to promote the project with celebrity glister. Yet the com-pleted movie had trouble finding a distributor and was released like a convict, in sullen spot appearances in a few cities.

If the 1970s had been the 1930s, Barbra Streisand would have made twenty musicals and every one would have been worth seeing. But filmmaking is slow now and musicals are risky; Streisand made three, worth seeing mainly for her. *On a Clear Day You Can See Forever* (1970), from the Lane–Lerner show, cast Streisand as a modern girl who relives a former life in Regency England under hypnosis, and let director Vincente Minnelli exploit his eye for decor in the preincarna-tion scenes, but a sleepwalking Yves Montand so taxed the action that the picture was slashed into chaos, losing some of Minnelli's best work and leaving—because he shares the romance with Streisand—mainly Montand. Disaster.

Funny Lady (1973), *Funny Girl*'s sequel, also had problems. Sup-porting characters fall in and out of the scene precipitously, "Let's Hear It for Me" looks and sounds like a copy of "Don't Rain on My Parade" with a plane instead of a boat, and Streisand's last scenes, played in a grotesque double-bun hairdo, appear to promise a third in-stallment, *Funny Crone.* The film won a following if only because Streisand is the greatest thing to happen to the musical in some time; and James Caan's easy style as Billy Rose didn't hurt.

Both *On a Clear Day* and *Funny Lady* drew on the Broadway sound, even in *Funny Lady*'s new songs (by John Kander and Fred Ebb), but *A Star is Born* (1976) is contemporary. The two lead roles now depict rising and falling rock singers. Like Garland in her ver-sion, Streisand had to carry the score singlehanded, for Kris Kristof-ferson's noteless voice and lazy diction are as unpleasant as the famous Scavullo photograph of the two clutched in nude embrace that served as the film's logo and aptly sums up its *vanitas vanitatum* air. "A Bore Is Starred" crowed the *Village Voice.* No way; Streisand is top. But the film is a putrid mess and a vanity production from first to last. The one thing that makes it go is the score. These are good songs, mostly by Paul Williams, Kenny Ascher, and Rupert Holmes (Streisand col-laborated on two of them), but the kind that throw around a lot of cynical verbal ideas without finishing a thought, or the kind that float on love lines. They don't fit the story as well as Garland's did hers, but then there's little story to fit here and the best of them, "Queen Bee," "Woman in the Moon," and "I Believe in Love," are Streisand vehicles to the nth, perhaps defining the actress's personal aggressiveness more than the character's.

This might alternatively have been the decade of Julie Andrews musicals, but *Darling Lili* (1970), in which she played a spy for the Germans in World War I opposite American air ace Rock Hudson, finished her off. It might have been a Liza Minnelli decade, except like Streisand and Andrews she made more nonmusicals than musicals, and has also fallen victim to the ignorance of contemporary moviemakers, most notably in *New York, New York* (1977), Martin Scorsese's big-band romance with Robert de Niro as a saxophonist (Georgie Auld dubbed his axe) and the look of the 1940s constantly outfitted in attitudes of the 1970s. Look, if you want to do an oldie, do it; what is this "commentative museum" approach supposed to express other than contempt for the old forms?: in which case, why revive them? Even worse than *New York, New York* was Peter Bogdanovich's *At Long Last Love* (1975), an assault on screwball comedy using a load of Cole Porter songs. Bogdanovich doesn't seem to know anything about Porter's style, musicals in general, or screwball comedy, and a good supporting cast (Eileen Brennan, Madeline Kahn, John Hillerman, and Mildred Natwick) look like amateurs and a poor star (Cybill Shepherd) gives the most atrocious performance in musical history. She's supposed to charm; why is she angry and pushy? Only Burt Reynolds has any idea about screwball comedy and musical delivery— and he's the one who should be most at sea.

This was, then, the decade in which people who didn't belong kept turning up in musicals and people who did belong were betrayed by their material and staff. An antique approach pervades—old songs in *Funny Lady, Darling Lili, At Long Last Love*, and *New York, New York*; old genre in Stanley Donen's *Movie Movie* (1978), consisting of a boxing movie, a trailer ("War at its best!"), and a backstager, all neatly spoofed (though one notes that the would-be Berkeleyesque finale of *Baxter's Beauties* is cheap and dull). Charles Jarrott's *Lost Horizon* (1973), a remake of Frank Capra's spectacle, subverted the old with the new in undercutting the wonder of Shangri-la with the highly seventies sound of Bert Bacharach and Hal David. The film is misconceived from its first moments, when a view of ice-capped mountains under the credits suffers Bacharach's suburban jive ("There's a lost horizon . . .") instead of something suggestive of fantasy. Worse yet, our first sight of Shangri-la—an oasis of peace and long-lasting youth in the middle of the Himalayas—is filmed like a motorcade's arrival at a Holiday Inn. Except the Holiday Inn's pool would be bigger. Bad enough that Hollywood's original work was weak; could it not even keep its past whole?

Of all the failed revivals, a British effort most nearly made it, Alan Parker's *Bugsy Malone* (1976), a revival of the Warners Prohibition-era gangster romance with a period-flavored score by Paul Williams. Parker's script lacks the snappy attack of the Warners writers, but his camera tells a story well and the production has the right look. But Parker cast all the parts with kids, and their limp, in some cases abysmally invertebrate performances (except those of Jodie Foster, Martin Lev, and "Humpty" Albin Jenkins) and the inevitable dubbing in the numbers destroy the film. Moreover, rather than bloody the children in their constant shoot-outs, Parker hits them with whipped cream (though they do die, until an apocalyptic finale sprays everyone with candy death and all sing and dance pointlessly). Still, there are some fine things here. The small band heard on the track is dynamite. The club numbers, "Fat Sam's Grand Slam" and "My Name Is Tallulah," are filmed well, and "Tomorrow" ("a resting place for bums, a trap set in the slums"), a black's commentary on the status quo, is one of the best four minutes of song and dance produced in the 1970s. A scene of Broadway auditions, paced by a constant heartless "Next," is funny, as are the ancient acts—but why, when a singer attempts "Brother, Can You Spare a Dime?", not written till 1932, does someone sneer, "That old chestnut"? A surer grasp of pop history, and the decade's most successful samples of retrenching, were found in two MGM collections of old footage, *That's Entertainment!* and *That's Entertainment! II*, in 1974 and 1976.

Interesting attempts to stay young enlivened several Broadway adaptations which reinvented the originals without ruining them. David Green's *Godspell* (1973) spilled its Gospel parables all over Manhattan: kids bathe in Bethesda Fountain and throw away worldly things to become hippie clowns who tour the town while the camera catches them on a rooftop pool, the Bulova Accutron sign, Lincoln Center, or the top of the World Trade towers, then under construction. The stage *Godspell* was static and episodic, the film *Godspell* busy and episodic; that still leaves one less than overwhelmed. Norman Jewison's *Jesus Christ Superstar* (1973) similarly moved a theatrical event outside, in this case to the Holy Land, relating the ancient myth to modern jive by juxtaposing early Christian and contemporary design.

Ken Russell's *The Boy Friend* (1971) did more for its source, and to it. Sandy Wilson's thin twenties charmer remains, but now we see it on two extra levels, from below in the backstage lives of a provincial British troupe playing it to a sparse matinée public, and from above in the dreams of a Berkeley-minded director, called Max de Thrill, who reviews the stage numbers as he would film them. Many felt that Russell had trashed Wilson and noted a lack of regard for his characters, but one must admit that the movie is vastly entertaining and its Berkeley spoofs stylish. Are they vicious? Russell portrays the chorus girls as sly and talentless, the boys as big, dirty dwarfs, and everyone as a ham directing his part at de Thrill in hopes of being discovered. One person retains innocence in all this—Twiggy, the fashion model who came out of retirement at something like twenty-one to play the heroine, a backstage gopher thrust into the star's part after the usual accident. Twiggy is the first genuine Ruby Keeler we have had since Keeler, not an imposing talent but a champ in charm, and when Glenda Jackson as the injured star clumps backstage on her crutches for confrontation as Bebe Daniels had done in *42nd Street*, we realize that Russell has moved the Warners backstager forward in time to prove that the old community is broken. It's everyone for himself now.

No wonder the old forms no longer work: moviemakers don't believe in their morale anymore. The heroine of Bob Fosse's *Cabaret* (1972) gets by living entirely in lies. *Cabaret* derives, like *Godspell*, *Jesus Christ Superstar*, and *The Boy Friend*, from the stage, but more radically, with fewer songs and more character than the original. Its grungily splashy Kit Kat Club contrasting with a plain, almost sepia-toned Berlin rooming house; its acidly commentative numbers cutting vertically into the narrative; its palpable sense of history running wild caught in an elated number, an ironic number, an alienated number, all made it a sensation, and it stands as one of the best musicals of the era. Yet it is not exactly a musical.

On stage, directed by Ronald Field, *Cabaret* was two musicals intertwined, one a tale of foreigners and natives in pre-Nazi Berlin and the other a series of cabaret turns explicating the tale. Fosse realigned the story with Christopher Isherwood's original telling and stripped it of music, limiting all the numbers to the onstage scenes and a Nazi youth's beer-garden performance of "Tomorrow Belongs to Me," which turns into a spontaneous Nazi rally in one of Fosse's best ideas. No question that his camera narrates and describes insightfully, but because only one of the story characters (Liza Minnelli) works in the cabaret, we don't get to know them through their songs—which is what, at base, a musical does best. Minnelli we know, from her frenzy in "Mein Herr," materialism in "The Money Song," momentary honesty in "Maybe This Time," and final passive accommodation of evil in the tumultuous title song. But her friend, writer Michael York, their mutual lover Helmut Griem, York's pupil Marisa Berenson, and the other people have no numbers, in what might be called the Randolph Scott effect: they hear the music but have none themselves. This makes them a little remote, almost imperceptibly at first but increasingly on the repeated viewings that classics like *Cabaret* tend to get.

In all, this was a troubled time, one of talent and creativity but of a depleted or misunderstood form. If 1929–1933 was the experimental era, the rest of the 1930s the time in which genre was defined, the 1940s and 1950s an age of story musicals, and the 1960s one of big Broadway, what were the 1970s? There was a little of everything; it's hard to generalize. Perhaps the 1970s are best thought of as the decade which loved *The Rocky Horror Picture Show* (1975) and *The Slipper and the Rose* (1976), the two most unlike musicals ever made. *Rocky* derives from a British show, a spoof of monster movies painted with kinky isms and assorted punk boogie. *Slipper* is Cinderella, with fairy godmother, wicked stepmother, and the whole Perrault peruke. Both films are story musicals, *Rocky*'s score tending to rock and the Sherman brothers' *Slipper* songs upholding the simplistic sweetness of tradition. But where *Slipper* was lavish family fare, the low-budget ($1,000,000) *Rocky* plays midnight shows to costumed kids who smoke dope, throw things at the screen, call out set responses to lines, and, at the more hip centers, stage their own *Rocky Horror* in the aisles synchronously with the action on screen. In *Slipper*, a lovely waltz theme characterizes the ball, dancers pair off, the audience coos in pleasure, and Cinderella and the Prince later sing lyrics to the theme ("He Danced With Me/She Danced With Me"), wistful and winning. As *Rocky* begins, Barry Bostwick and Susan Sarandon get a flat while driving through a storm in a forest. Bostwick must go for help. "Try the castle!" the kids scream, squirting each other with water pistols.*

Yet both films teach the advantages of personal liberation; one could argue that most art does, except tragedy. Cinderella has to get out from under her stepmother's rule; Bostwick and Sarandon discov-

---

*The ritual responses are witless, but one trembles to think what these kids might be doing if they didn't have their weekly *Rocky* habit to busy them. Outsiders can view the proceedings without risk in a segment of *Fame*.

er sexual openness. Perhaps *Rocky*, written by Richard O'Brien, really teaches nothing but the joy of spoof. It's very seventies: nihilist, exhibitionistic, and contemptuous of outsiders. When it is finished, nothing is left; even the straitlaced narrator is drawn into the proceedings during a dance number called "The Time Warp," which has the gentleman first holding up a ludicrously precise footmap of the steps and then, repeating the words, jumping around on a table with his hands on his hips. *The Slipper and the Rose* ends with Cinderella in the Prince's arms, but *The Rocky Horror Picture Show*, in a way, doesn't finish, though the story is somewhat wrapped away in a few pointless murders and the return of some characters to their planet. One could go on endlessly comparing the two, but it is in casting that they seem most apart. *Slipper* draws on front-line talent, with Gemma Craven a wonderfully taut heroine, Richard Chamberlain possibly the only Hamlet who played the Prince in a Cinderella musical, and Edith Evans and Michael Hordern as the royal ancients. It's creamy and condign. *Rocky*, on the other hand, puts forth unknowns and director Jim Sharman shows them at their worst; one presumes he's supposed to, given the campy nature of the material. Tim Curry in the central role of the transsexualizing Dr. Frank N. Furter, who makes the Rocky monster, manages to suggest that he's crossed five or six rather than a mere two genders, Meat Loaf in a small part (he gets eaten) is if possible more unappetizing than usual, and author O'Brien as Curry's henchthing is a pictorial history of sinister. It's the pits, all of it, and glad to be.

Slipper was extra traditional, *Rocky* extra novel, and maybe the 1970s was the era that didn't know what it wanted. As many big Broadway musicals flopped as succeeded, neither contemporary nor traditional music could necessarily save a film, old formulas both bubbled and fizzled, and even the biggest stars could suffer enormous popular failures. What were the 1970s, then? Who can say? The success of *The Muppet Movie* (1979) suggests incoming innocence, but don't those little Muppet fans grow into *Rocky* freaks? Or will the Muppets' whimsy bless them with a thirst for faerie that can only be slaked by *The Slipper and the Rose*?

☆ *21* ☆

Rest in Peace

No MATTER HOW the musical's confused present develops, it is undebatable that the form has been running down since the 1950s. We know the reasons—inflation has made the middle-budget musical unworkable; rock doesn't work well for most stories; the current generation of moviemakers doesn't know how to make a musical; and the intense naturalism of contemporary American film makes anything but a backstager unthinkably quaint.

Yet they keep coming, often in the old genres. Nineteen seventy-nine and 1980 saw at least one entry in most of the established categories of musical. There was a bio, for instance, *Coal Miner's Daughter*, with Sissy Spacek ably recreating Loretta Lynn's singing style to affirm the nation's growing interest in country music. There was a comedy musical, *The Blues Brothers*, about the reformation of a band but directed by John Landis as a demolition derby with allusions to music-making. The stars, John Belushi and Dan Aykroyd, had exhausted their bop spoof on television's *Saturday Night Live*; unlike the Marx Brothers, they haven't worked up characters tasty enough to fill a screen—even Landis' crashing cars lose the weight of shock and surprise after a while. Worse yet, Belushi and Aykroyd are totally upstaged by the musical help, especially Aretha Franklin, who tears the screen apart in "Think" as the proprietor of a soul-food café. The comedy musical always had more comic action than comic (or other) music, but *The Blues Brothers* isn't rich in comedy.

Many had hoped that Bob Fosse would second *Cabaret* with something special, and in *All That Jazz* he reinstated the dance musical. Unlike those of Astaire, Powell, and Kelly, this one avoided story songs, concentrating on dance and at that giving more to ensembles than to principals. Astaire, Powell, and Kelly distilled themselves in dance; Fosse distills show biz. So *All That Jazz* is special, a piece about the performing industries and the people who inhabit and exploit them, set as a narrative about the last days of . . . well, Bob Fosse. The autobiographical correspondence is uncanny. Fosse's stage shows, films, collaborators, acquaintances, and enemies are not merely depicted; some of them play themselves. We see Fosse's tintype, Joe Gideon (Roy Scheider), planning and rehearsing a musical called *N.Y./L.A.* (i.e., *Chicago*) that stars Scheider's ex-wife Leland Palmer (i.e., Fosse's ex-wife Gwen Verdon), using a model of *Chicago*'s set, referring to a conductor named Stan (played by *Chicago*'s conductor Stanley Lebowsky), reading the script with, among others, Mary McCarty (who was in *Chicago*), suffering heart failure (as Fosse did during *Chicago*'s rehearsals), possibly being replaced by somebody called Lucas Sergeant (as Fosse nearly was by Gower Champion), who is seen planning lighting design on a model of the set for *I Do, I Do* (which Champion directed); and so on, from the film's start to finish.

For some reason, a great many people objected to this, though Fellini is praised for his autobiographical renderings. Fosse's use of Giuseppe Rotunno, Fellini's cinematographer, inspired sympathetic commentary that *All That Jazz* is Fosse's *8½*, his attempt to order in art what has happened to him in life. It is certainly one of the most provocative and imaginative musicals ever made and, to the surprise of the Hollywood smart money, became a hit. It could not have been produced in the age of the studios, for it has no genre, no star Something, no safe place (the protagonist doesn't even dance)—not with its frank sexuality, open-heart surgery, and surges of contempt and horror for the hypocrisy of show biz. In a kind of television eulogy before the fact, Ben Vereen calls Scheider "the *numero uno* game player." *The Girl Most Likely*, "Who's Got the Pain?", *Sweet Charity, Cabaret, Lenny*, the snake number in *The Little Prince, Chicago*: all a game. That's why Fosse is the best, he seems to say: he was the most insincere, more so than raving television hosts, idiot television critics who review themselves, producers who bury their star director at the crucial point, or a fellow director too eager to inherit Fosse's project and who, in a startling Felliniesque pre-death wake, chews out a resentful farewell. Yet it must be worth the game, for Fosse captures the exuberance of the musical no less than Astaire, Powell, and Kelly did. Or, rather, he drags the camera around to show what lies behind "The Continental," "Swingin' the Jinx Away," and "Broadway Rhythm," from the opening cattle-call auditions to a special birthday tribute in top hats by Scheider's girlfriend (Ann Reinking) and daughter (Erzsebet Foldi) in his living room. The death, though heralded by a luscious angel and a last grand dance number, is flat fact; but the life has been full. Most viewers felt lifted.

The backstager was still with us in Alan Parker's *Fame*, observing the new *Chorus Line* vogue for digging into the offstage lives of performers with more intense revelation than *42nd Street* or *Moonlight and Pretzels* did. Of course, nowadays the characters have more to reveal: *Fame* takes in child molestation, porno film, gay shame, abortion (which earlier backstagers couldn't show), and even failure (which earlier musicals didn't believe in). The failure belongs to a minor character, an actor who departs high school in the flush of Hollywood promises and turns up years later waiting table in a hamburger joint. *Fame*'s central figures may suffer, but we're sure they'll make it, and perhaps *Fame* might better have been called *Talent*, since we see the drive of the gifted more than the urgency of coming celebrity. (The title song, however, emphasizes making it—"Baby, remember my name.")

Christopher Gore originally named his script *Hot Lunch*, which is way off. It tells mainly of eight kids at New York's High School of Performing Arts, from auditions to graduation, and tells its story well. A hostilely illiterate black dancer (Gene Anthony Ray), a lively black actress-singer (Irene Cara), a Puerto Rican comic (Barry Miller), a shy actress (Maureen Teefy), a shy actor (Paul McCrane), a blue-book dancer (Antonia Franceschi), a lazy dancer (Laura Dean), and a musician (Lee Curreri) who seems the only one without a major problem engage us deeply because Parker makes their lives as interesting as anything they might do on a stage—and can they do! The hot lunch refers to a number improvised in the cafeteria out of musicians' idle riffs and dancers' exercises; audience and cast at once, the whole crowd gradually joins in, and while Parker centers on Curreri at the piano and Cara next to him singing the lyrics, the camera roves, pulling all the practice, relaxation, and fulfillment of performance into the scene to show us not the desperation but the fun of using one's talent. It's not an obsession, it's what you always do. So why call it *Fame*?

The narrative is inevitably episodic and its pieces don't always tally. The comic's story overpowers the others, for Parker seems to think it's the most interesting; so do we. Franceschi and Dean are made too minor; we want more. And there are sensational or formalistic touches that humiliate the otherwise brilliant naturalism, as when an obvious creep lures Cara into a "screen test" that is immediately revealed to be a porn loop. She sobs, but goes along with it—ridiculous; no one's that dumb. Ray's vulnerability under the hostility is indicated but neither defined nor developed. And Curreri's cab-driver father parks outside the school to play an amplified tape of his son's music, causing a traffic jam so the kids can dance around and on top of the cars. This is an unreal excuse for a number; obviously, in going in for realism Parker can't make a story musical (as he did in *Bugsy Malone*) and thus has to reach a little for his numbers. But we don't buy it. Far more successful is the finale, graduation ceremonies set to Walt Whitman's "I Sing the Body Electric" and involving the whole class—dancers, singers, chorus, and orchestra. Thrilling in itself, the scene complements the cafeteria number narratively: "Hot Lunch Jam" is raw and spontaneous (the amateurs) while the graduation is polished (the ready professionals). When the movie cuts out suddenly at the commencement's climax, one senses the audience's unwillingness to leave. They want the rest, want to learn, now, about the fame. The real High School of Performing Arts thought the script too raunchy to approve and denied Parker permission to film there (the unoccupied Haaren High on Tenth Avenue stood in; some of Performing Arts' teachers appear as themselves, very effectively), but it would be hard to conceive of better PR for the school than this, or a film with more claim on a sequel. What *does* happen next?

Broadway adaptations were as uncommon as story musicals these days; Milos Forman combined both in *Hair*. Unlike recent big Broadway films, *Hair* avoided the box-office but nonmusical stars and the slavish reproduction, using only the stage show's score and spirit. It seemed odd to film one of the keynote works of the 1960s for 1979, but Forman had wanted to do *Hair* since its premiere in 1967 and the project had been on and off for years. At one point Forman visited Gerome Ragni and James Rado, the show's librettists and stars, to discuss it, but the two called in a tarot reader and he advised against it.

The show *Hair* is about as stupid as that story suggests it might be; what carried it was Galt MacDermot's inventive music and Tom O'Horgan's staging. Forman had Michael Weller (author of another prototypal event in the sixties *Zeitgeist, Moonchildren*) write a script to contain the score, handed the dancing over to Twyla Tharp, cast John Savage, Treat Williams, Annie Golden, Don Dacus, Dorsey Wright, Beverly D'Angelo, and Cheryl Barnes for character rather than celebrity, and filmed a splendid picaresque of coming into and then fleeing the 1960s. Forman's Central Park hums with the high color of the freewilling outcast, his middle-class party is sedate, his church a vision of redemptive beauty, his army post a pandemonium of uptight. Savage is the protagonist, heading from middle America to service in Vietnam, but on the way he passes through the hippie kingdom and his life is changed. He never even makes it to Vietnam, for Williams, the hippie ringleader and Savage's social and cultural opposite, takes Savage's place in the barracks while Savage enjoys a final rendezvous with D'Angelo; Williams is dragged off to war in Savage's place, and dies in combat. End of the 1960s.

Rather than invent another Oz, Forman combines his visual attack with MacDermot's music to present a veristic magic, and the first sight of the Park, with the movie theatre virtually flying in a circle around the singer introducing "(the age of) Aquarius," counts as one of the most intoxicating shots in film. Unfortunately, the expensive production was not popular: most adult moviegoers had no intention of celebrating a time they disliked and could not forgive. Those who let bygones be were put off by Forman's sharp re-creation of the destructiveness and selfishness of the time, not to mention the unapologetic sexual promiscuity. Treat Williams' Berger was too familiar a figure, with his self-righteous freeloading and trashing and stealing. Paradoxically, amid all the emotional violence, and in a time of war in which he is supposedly to take part, Savage finds a safe place: it is Berger who dies.

In 1979–1980, then, the genres proved resilient, still functioning, if sparsely. There was no original story musical and no opera musical, and this in itself points up the two most crucial problems in the form today: the music that called for extraordinary personal communication—that elated a narrative to its utmost and burst the limitations of naturalism and fantasy alike—is the least important element in the contemporary musical. The earthiness that kept *The Wizard of Oz* close to home and the romance that floated Astaire and Rogers over the Bakelite are lost arts in American pop music. Rock's special gift is to merge the earthy and the romantic, but this worked well only for surreal farce like that in *Help!*. True, *Hair* floated—but when *The Wiz* needed to, it couldn't. Rock is heavy.

Yet it was a rock film that afforded a most astonishing musical experience, Mark Rydell's *The Rose* (1979). Written by Bill Kerby and Bo Goldman with a score picked up from here and there, the film tells of the last few days of a singer not unlike Janis Joplin. It's not a bio, but some of Joplin is there in the heroine's love for/fear of her southern hometown, voice-shredding vocal style, pronounced sexuality and alcoholism, and death by drug overdose. Mary Rose Foster suffers a messy celebrity, bullied by her manager (Alan Bates), sleepwalking or rampaging through an exhausting, endless schedule, and unable to work things out with the nice, strong, simple man (Frederic Forrest) who might be able to make her happy, burning out of control onstage as in life. Yet the mania that destroys her is what makes her so vital in concert. We begin to feel that you can't have one without the other, or you'd have to be Bing Crosby or Alice Faye, and the kind of music they sang so well is no longer our kind. Rock demands more of a performer: it is the opera of pop, which is why we need Jeanette MacDonald and Deanna Durbin even less than we do a Crosby or Faye today. Throughout the story we see Rose making impossible mistakes, and she doesn't seem to lack perspective so much as flourish, like a trapeze daredevil, without it. She must live on the edge or she couldn't take her music so deep and digging.

The Rose was a huge hit, but critics complained that Rydell and the authors had left holes in the tale, and that Bette Midler, in her film debut, was simply swishing around in her stage persona of the silly, dirty female queen. The first charge is fair. We never do find out about Rose's problem with her parents, why she so badly needs to conquer in her hometown that she insists on singing in the local bar where she got her start despite the customers' contemptuous behavior and her boyfriend's obvious distaste, why she lets everyone push her around. The film appears to think that it has told us, and if this is a tragedy, we have to know. Otherwise, it might be a cheap quickie with an implied rise and grisly fall with no reason for either. *The Rose* was years in the making and looks all it should; moreover, it *is* a tragedy in that Rose, a hero of great impact in her culture, does identify the force that destroys her: she is utterly alone. But what flaw made her alone? Why does rock cost its artists so much—where are they all going? *The Rose* could have told us.

The second charge, that Rose is pure Midler, is unfounded. Much of the score calls for a mean, wailing blues rock that Midler had to master for the film, and the ad libs in the concert scenes paint the character, not the actress. Midler live plays flaky self-spoof in the seventies manner. The Rose is vulnerable and rebellious, with the unpointed hysteria of the 1960s. More to the issue, Midler manages to act around the gaps in the script, making Rose uniquely complete as a principal in a musical; where else have we had a portrayal of this breadth and nuance? Of the film's nine numbers, she carries eight of them alone (the ninth is a drag act at a Manhattan club, where "Barbra," "Carol,"

"Diana," "Judy," and others salute Rose with one of her songs), a feat rivaled only by Garland in *A Star Is Born*; and Midler gets more out of her music because it's more sharply oriented to the character. "Whose Side Are You On? (Are you with me, or am I all alone?)" sets Rose's inability to believe she's worth belief; "Midnight in Memphis" cites the restlessness in being solitary; "Sold My Soul to Rock and Roll" makes the connection between rock and sex; "Love Me With a Feeling" and "When a Man Loves a Woman" show the two sides of romance, the fleshly and the spiritual; "Stay With Me" follows what seems to be the last of many desertions.

It is. Her boyfriend gone in disgust, Rose kills the pain with heroin and phones her parents in sight of the high school football field where she had sex with the whole team one night in her senior year. As she spaces out in the phone booth, a younger team finishes its practice and the field lights go out like a shutter clicking over a corpse. Delivered to her fans by helicopter, Rose barely holds on for "Stay With Me," then attempts "Let Me Call You Sweetheart" *a cappella* but breaks off to ask, in one of the great exit lines in film, "Where you goin'? Where's everybody goin'?" And dies.

Midler has not been given her due for *The Rose*. This is a spectacular performance, one of the few in recent musicals inextricably wired into its musical component. The character structures the rock; the rock defines the character. Few of the great acting-singing parts we have crossed paths with here have been so exclusively portrayed; as with Jolson in *The Jazz Singer*, Garland in *A Star is Born*, and Streisand in *Funny Girl*, without Midler there could have been no *Rose*—indeed, it was originally drafted as the tale of a male singer, precisely because it would have been much easier to cast that way. Given that Midler has made the final breakthrough for rock as a successful medium for the musical, is it too much to ask that she now consider doing as much to revive the great Broadway sound that went quiet when the blockbusters crapped out? Hollywood was once the land where musical talents of many kinds came to find their ultimate place in the American pop mythology—as lovers, loungers, fighters, or crazies—because they were basic to an American vision or so necessary to expand it, from Broadway, vaudeville, radio, and wherever else there is. Yes, Hollywood failed to place such people as Fanny Brice in the parables, but the culture has opened up considerably since then. (Would a Streisand or Midler have made it in film in 1930? Doubtful.) One of the reasons why it has is the participation of such people as Eddie Cantor, Fred Astaire, Mae West, the Marx Brothers, and Deanna

Durbin, none of them standard-cut role models in the received virtues. Yet all worked their altars. Midler and *The Rose* are, in a sense, the latest event in a history of transformation through stasis: Jolson, in steady helpings, broke the ground for West, while Astaire readied a stage for Kelly, while Chevalier's finesse necessitated the clumsiness of Crosby, and then Garland grew up to connect the aggressiveness of Eleanor Powell with the innocence of Alice Faye, and then Streisand claimed Brice's unplayed cards, dealing in Midler, while Minnelli took over for Garland by right of genes. Nobody changed character from role to role: that's stasis. But each role-player enlarges possibilities in the game. Hollywood has lost its tenacity in maintaining the generations, but—who knows?—smash adaptations of *A Chorus Line* and *Annie* could reinvent the film musical all over.

I refuse to end on an up note. Midler and *The Rose* are exceptional; a tour of the state of the art is better taken in the two would-be whizzes of 1980, *Can't Stop the Music* and *Xanadu*. These are the films that the 1980s deserve, though moviegoers rejected both. The two used old genre—putting on the show—and *Xanadu* even used old face, Gene Kelly's. He didn't dance much; who can blame him: to *that* noise? Olivia Newton-John has two expressions. She used the miffed one in *Grease*, so in *Xanadu* she shows the impish one, as a muse who flies off the wall (so to speak) to inspire Michael Beck as she apparently inspired Kelly decades before. The "show" Kelly and Beck want to put on is a disco-jazz club, and, mission accomplished, tutelary Newton-John vanishes in a special effect to leave a mortal copy of herself behind to console Beck (as Ava Gardner did for Robert Walker in *One Touch of Venus*). Disco is impossible in film, even one as foolish as *Xanadu*, because disco is entirely narcissistic. It's made for dancing, partying, and exhibitionism, not for watching or listening, not above the age of eleven. So how can one bring off a disco musical?

Can't Stop the Music tried hard to. The first gay musical, its "show" comprised the assembling and launching of a singing group. To make a disco musical, you must not only employ disco, but think disco in all elements of production. The script must be as stupid as the lyrics. (As in "YMCA": "You can do whatever you feel." Whatever you feel *like doing*? *Whomever* you feel?) The disco sound is combined with the disco "look," which results in a two-hour jeans commercial. The singing stars will be *the* disco group, the Village People, and other lead roles will be filled by those who are to acting what the Village People are to music: Bruce Jenner, Valerie Perrine, and Steve Guttenberg. Because disco aesthetics are set by the gay regime, a certain tone is observed: in the Village People's Christopher Street fantasy costumes, in Village locations, in at least one bared-torso shot from every male principal, and in a production number to "YMCA" for the stars and a horde of teenage brutes that, according to rumor, caused two fatal seizures, three heart attacks, and nineteen cases of aggravated drooling among Hollywood notables at an industry preview. But because gay is still a Secret, cover procedures are observed: the Village People will be assigned girlfriends in the "Magic Night" sequence, Nancy Walker—as opposed to, say, Franklin Pangborn—will direct, and Valerie Perrine will have breasts. The score is a cinch, as the Village People come with their own cockamamie concert written by a Frenchman named Jacques Morali, and for miscellany places are found for a roller-skating number, for veteran pros encouraged to make asses of themselves (June Havoc as Guttenberg's mother did; Russell Nype as a blue-chip lawyer provided the film's sole moments of show biz expertise), and for I-Love-New-York comedy (when Jenner is mugged by what he took to be a lovable granny). Critic Stephen Harvey got this film's number in describing its audience as "those eight-year-old boys whose favorite movies, when they grow up, will be *Auntie Mame* and *All About Eve*" and in predicting that "by the year 2100, it's probably going to be hailed as the *Gang's All Here* of the Eighties." In other words, folks, what you have here is camp that doesn't even bother to *be* before it *turns. Can't Stop the Music* and *Xanadu* are the fast-food trays of the Hollywood musical: little lies in bags.

That's where it stands. Not with *The Rose* and its sense of continuity in art, but in the cynicism of the opportunists of trend. Sure, the musical survives in revival and even on television—where negatives haven't deteriorated and where fade-resistant Technicolor prints were struck—but the form is mainly one of old energies now. Like Fanny Brice's "Rose of Washington Square," the musical "ain't got no future, but oy! what a past." Nice thing to have, a past. Nice to consider who you were, in times when it isn't easy to be what you are.

☆ ☆

A Selective
Discography

THE STUDIOS' INSISTENCE on turning out musicals with every tune a potential hit makes for engaging home-listening, though one would be hard put to reconstruct plot line or characterization from the love, dance, and comedy songs as the action is often carried out *between* the numbers. Also, there is a major problem in the late discovery of the soundtrack album. Not till the 1950s were relatively complete recordings standard practice; earlier, recording-studio-cut hit tunes filled the gap, not necessarily made by the people who sang in the film. Even if they were, it's not the real thing. Luckily, enterprising individuals have taken it upon themselves to issue private (or "underground"; or "pirate") recordings of old musicals. These can be hard to track down, however. Those interested should apply to the nearest serious record store, the kind that stocks imported recordings or elite cabaret artists. Somewhere near Mabel Mercer and Charles Trenet you might find the undergrounds.

Let's take it all chronologically. For the very first sound years, two excellent collections recommend themselves. *Stars of the Silver Screen* (RCA LPV-538) compiles sixteen ten-inch 78 discs by such as George Jessel, Lupe Velez, Maurice Chevalier ("Louise"), Bebe Daniels, and Dennis King. Miles Kreuger's liner notes provide historical perspective and the stars take the ear in a tour of the first musicals, variable in quality but always fascinating. Charles King in "Broadway Melody" is subdued compared to what he does with it on screen, Gloria Swanson full of voice in a tune from *The Trespasser*, the Duncan Sisters astonishing in a jazz obbligato on "I'm Following You" from *It's a Great Life*, Fanny Brice irreplaceable in "Cooking Breakfast for the One I

Love" from *Be Yourself*, Everett Marshall thrilling in a "darky" number from *Dixiana* with some of the strangest lyrics ever heard, and Jeanette MacDonald the living end in "Dream Lover," the big ballad from *The Love Parade*, written as a "hesitation waltz." MacDonald sails right over the hesitation marks, keeping the phrasing symmetrical and winning all hearts. *Legends of the Musical Stage* (Take Two 104) is even more enticing. Though its notes don't say so, these are all sounds off the track, and thus bear a sharper witness than Victor's commercial cuts. *Sally* (Marilyn Miller and Alexander Gray), Ethel Merman's short *Ireno*, *Puttin' on the Ritz* (Harry Richman), and *Honky Tonk* (Sophie Tucker) are among those present, the Tucker cuts alone worth any five MGM albums of the 1940s.

Maurice Chevalier and Jeanette MacDonald may be heard to advantage on, respectively, an import (WRC SH 156) and an American bargain release (VIC 1515). The Chevalier is a treasure, fourteen selections from his first eight Hollywood films (except *The Smiling Lieutenant*), half of them in French. These are studio-made, but Chevalier was one performer who could give as much in the recording booth as on the sound stage. MacDonald is less outgoing here than she had been on screen, as most of the selections were taped when she was past her prime. Still, it's a fine souvenir, and students of Hollywood's pop-legit fetish, so suitable for the academic monograph, will want to contrast MacDonald's sedate and sassy verses of "San Francisco."

The spirit of the Warners backstager has been preserved on two United Artists releases, *The Golden Age of the Hollywood Musical* (LA 215-H) and *Hooray for Hollywood* (LA 361-H), drawn from the soundtracks. Most of these cuts represent big Berkeley numbers, and without the visuals one has not that much more than one tune repeated over and over. Still, consider the titles: "I Only Have Eyes For You," "Remember My Forgotten Man," "42nd Street," and "Lullaby of Broadway," among others, on the first; and "You're Getting to Be a Habit With Me," "The Lady in Red" (from *In Caliente*; terrific), "Dames," and "All's Fair in Love and War" on the second. Not to hear Dick Powell, Ruby Keeler, Wini Shaw, and the rest in this material is never to have heard it—and nothing touches Frances Langford's voice-cracked "Hooray for Hollywood" from *Hollywood Hotel*.

From the private Box Office label come two-disc compilations on Porter, Rodgers and Hart, and Kern. The Porter set contains soundtracks of *Rosalie*, *You'll Never Get Rich*, and *Something to Shout About* among other tidbits (the best being Gertrude Lawrence in two cuts from her 1929 disaster *The Battle of Paris*). The Rodgers and

Hart set is the best: *The Hot Heiress, Love Me Tonight, The Phantom President, Mississippi,* and *Hallelujah, I'm a Bum* (including the "Sleeping Beauty" footage, cut from release prints) under one cover. The Kern has a lot of Irene Dunne—*Roberta, High, Wide and Handsome, Sweet Adeline,* and *Joy of Living,* plus *Music in the Air.* These are the Broadway masters; what of the Hollywood specialists in simplicity? As of this writing, Box Office has just released albums on Richard Whiting and Ralph Rainger, and there is sure delight in an import, *The Great British Dance Bands Play the Music of Nacio Herb Brown* (SH 267), taking the Brown–Freed collaboration from *The Broadway Melody* to *Babes in Arms.* Dance bands can be annoyingly persistent about holding to a beat and the vocalists are vapid, but Brown's transparent chording and direct melody benefit from this approach. "Singin' in the Rain" is especially well done.

In the late 1930s, both Alice Faye and Shirley Temple have their collections. Columbia CL 3068 features Faye's studio recordings; Silver Screen 100/3 carries her—on soundtracks—from *Now I'll Tell* to *Hello, Frisco, Hello,* virtually the whole career. One may invest in both albums without doubling a single title. Temple has had several retrospectives, the best being Fox 3006, one disc's worth of her best stuff hot off the track.

For separate thirties titles, one applies to the pirates. One company that evades identification by issuing each record under a different label has provided some great double features: *The Broadway Melody* with the Tibbett–Moore *New Moon, Whoopee!* with *Puttin' on the Ritz, The Love Parade* and the Lubitsch *Merry Widow,* and *Everybody Sing* with *Pigskin Parade.* The sound is erratic, *Whoopee!* is missing "A Girl Friend of a Boy Friend of Mine" (to be heard on Take Two 104, cited above), and *New Moon* is billed as *Parisian Belle,* but it's the goods, all right, complete with portions of dialogue and the blips and pops of the Vitaphone days. *Whoopee!* in particular is unmatched for punk whimsey. After hearing it you may want to dive back into the 1930s and never come out. It's been done.

Pelican 2019 presents *The Rogue Song,* Tibbett's debut sensation, a lost film (the sound discs survived the negative and prints) and a rather dull score, though Tibbett is wild and bright. Operetta fans may also collect MacDonald and Eddy in *Naughty Marietta* on Hollywood Soundstage 413, to my mind the best of their scores. The 1936 *Show Boat* comes and goes; I have it on Xeno 251. Perhaps the choice operetta disc of the decade is that to *The Great Waltz* (Sountrak 109), though without Duvivier's omnipotent camera one takes but half an

236 ☆ *The Hollywood Musical*

art. Musical comedy fans will prefer Alice Faye, in modern dress no matter what the setting, in *Wake Up and Live* (HS 403), a fine Revel–Gordon score; buffs of the comedy musical will thrill to an Eddie Cantor double feature on CIF 3007, *Kid Millions* and *Roman Scandals*; and Garland fans will cream twice over for *Babes in Arms* coupled with *Babes on Broadway* (Curtain Calls 100/6–7), despite odious cover art. And of course there's Jolson, at his best in two Warren–Dubin scores, *Wonder Bar* and *Go Into Your Dance*. With Helen Morgan and Dick Powell also in evidence, however, you learn to treasure singers who can deliver a tune as the composer set it down.

What about Astaire and Rogers? This part is tricky. Their scores are so popular that the undergrounds go out of and come back into print at some pace. British EMI (EMTC 101) issued a disc of *The Gay Divorcee* and *Swing Time*, and the tautologically named Scarce Rarities Productions (SR 5505) put out *Follow the Fleet* and *A Damsel in Distress*, but these have both vanished and no doubt have been replaced by others. Keep alert—four or five Berlin, Kern, or Gershwin songs performed by these two, twice over (as each film fits on one side) is no mean bargain.

Nineteen thirty-nine brings us to the first commercial soundtrack issue, MGM's of *The Wizard of Oz*, actually published decades after the premiere. In 1939, the only Oz album was Decca's set of four ten-inch 78s made in the studio with Garland and the Ken Darby Singers. MGM's LP (E 3464) includes a great deal of dialogue and omits "The Merry Old Land of Oz"; the Decca set, lately on MCA-521, omits "If I Were King of the Forest" but lo, includes "The Jitterbug." It's listener's choice. The MGM, taken off the reel, is authentic and presents more of Lahr's classic turn as the lion, but one should hear "The Jitterbug." Ideally, get both, and supplement them with the tiny chorus that connects the poppy field sequence to the Emerald City entrance, called "Optimistic Voices," on a Bette Midler recital (Atlantic SD 7270), which also contains Midler's nicely updated "Lullaby of Broadway."

The 1940s. With Decca's discovery of the Broadway original cast album, made with the stars and orchestra and in the performing style of the debut production, Hollywood began to see the light, though at first it continued to make studio albums—one or two stars and a pickup orchestra in "radio" arrangements: Deanna Durbin in *Can't Help Singing*, Nelson Eddy and Risë Stevens in *The Chocolate Soldier*, Garland in *Meet Me in St. Louis* and *The Harvey Girls*, and Crosby and Astaire in no less than twelve tunes from *Holiday Inn*. Toward the end of the decade MGM began to release soundtrack albums but cut the selections to fit the ten-inch disc; the pirate LP remains one's best bet. Sountrak 111 pulls up whole swatches of *Good News*, dances and all, and *The Gang's All Here* (CIF 3003) proves a heyday of swing. The disheartened will need to play Carmen Miranda's "The Lady in the Tutti-Frutti Hat" from the latter for cheer-up purposes, whereas the giddy will come down to earth to Alice Faye's "No Love, No Nothing." CIF also backs the Rodgers–Hammerstein *State Fair* with the Kern–Hammerstein *Centennial Summer*, a veritable Louanne Hogan festival, Hogan being Jeanne Crain's voice in both. Dance buffs should investigate Silver Screen 100/24: *Cover Girl* and *You Were Never Lovelier*, a Nan Wynn sampler, Wynn being Hayworth's voice. Kids, the stars are out tonight. Forbidden material awaits in *Cut!* on DRG (ORTF 1), outtakes from 1938 to 1971 but centering on the 1940s and Judy Garland, in deleted songs from such as *Ziegfeld Girl*, *The Harvey Girls*, and *The Pirate*.

By the 1950s, the commercial soundtrack LP became standard equipment, and at this point we cease to depend on underground productions. A personal selection: in the bio, *Love Me or Leave Me* (Columbia CL 710) holds twelve cuts, all by Doris Day and all worth hearing; Day's background as a band vocalist connects with Ruth Etting's, though Day attempts no imitation. (Those in search of the real Etting should try Columbia ML 5050 or Take Two 203.) *Star!*, shorn of its dumb script, makes pleasant listening and revives quite a few forgotten beauties. (Surprise hit: " 'N' Everything," sung by Garrett Lewis.) In the Broadway adaptation, *The Boy Friend* (MGM 1SE-32 ST) is fun, especially when Twiggy takes two old Brown–Freed hits, "You Are My Lucky Star" and "All I Do Is Dream of You." *A Little Night Music* (Columbia 35333) is a must for Sondheim's following, with one new song and some new lyrics for old ones.

In the original, *Gigi* remains a standout on MGM E 3641, though the wonderful Maxim's "Gossip Chorus" is not included; students of the Broadway-Hollywood interchange might check out the cast album of the more recent stage version (RCA ABL 1-0404), with four new Loewe–Lerner songs. No Chevalier, but plenty of chances for Ph.D. dissertations with endless footnoting. *Bugsy Malone* (RSO RS-1-3501) grows on you, as does *The Slipper and the Rose* (MCA 2097), particularly its chromatic waltz tune, "He Danced With Me." In rock, you can move from the basics through MOR to post-Beatles pastiche by sampling, respectively, *The Buddy Holly Story* (Epic 35412), the Streisand *A Star Is Born* (Columbia 34403), and *200 Motels* (United Artists

S-9956). And while I have reservations about *The Last Waltz* as film, the concert itself (Warner Brothers 3146) is a glorious Baedeker through the great rock past. Perhaps the last note is to be heard in *The Rose* (Atlantic SD 16010), in the final cut when, after two hours of voice-grating blues, Midler eases one down with Amanda McBroom's transcendent title song, a folkish ballad accompanied simply on piano. The song is heard over the credits, but no one leaves the theatre. On the contrary, one listens in amazement.

In the mid–1970s, MGM re-released most of its prize soundtracks on two-disc albums. Best bets are *The Pirate/Pagan Love Song/Hit the Deck* (2-SES-43ST), *Seven Brides for Seven Brothers/Rose Marie* (2-SES-41ST), *Singin' in the Rain/Easter Parade* (2-SES-40ST), with a Jane Powell sale-quake on 2-SES-53ST: *Royal Wedding/Nancy Goes to Rio/Rich, Young and Pretty*. "It's thrilling," MGM's *Rich, Young and Pretty* ads explained, "when Vic Damone sings love songs to Jane!" By a stroke of luck, contract commitments kept Damone off the album, so it's largely Jane; one Powell fan I know suffered a nervous breakdown trying to decide which title to play first. So you see how it is.

The Disney people have smartly kept all their major tracks in print, by separate title in various children's editions or in compilations. The best of the latter is *The Magical Music of Walt Disney* (Ovation-5000), a four-disc set moving from *Steamboat Willie* to *Pete's Dragon*, a live-action fantasy of 1977. Cleverly arranged medleys from the soundtracks give eloquent digests of *Snow White, Pinocchio, Dumbo, Bambi, Cinderella, Peter Pan, Lady and the Tramp, Sleeping Beauty*, and *Mary Poppins*. One complaint: the last side is mainly given over to Muzak used in the two theme parks, which reminds us that democracy will never work.

☆ ☆

A Selective Bibliography

TAKING THE general histories first, I'm sorry to say that they aren't an impressive lot. Douglas McVay's *The Musical Film* (New York: A. S. Barnes, 1967), limited in size by its series format, is superficial (of the 150 Hollywood musicals released in 1929, 1930, and 1931, McVay mentions two, in passing) and ruined by weird opinions. (McVay spends twenty pages on the Garland *A Star Is Born*, "the greatest picture of *any* kind I have ever seen"; I'll take vanilla.) Lee Edward Stern's *The Movie Musical* (New York: Pyramid, 1974), similarly concise, ranges more widely, holds sensible opinions, and is nicely illustrated. But the lack of original analysis and the failure to engage rock are drawbacks. John Kobal's *Gotta Sing, Gotta Dance: A Pictorial History of Film Musicals* (New York: Hamlyn, 1970) is the lavish entry, without color, however, and garishly designed. Kobal relies heavily on the reminiscences of people like Ben Lyon, Joan Blondell, Ann Sheridan, and Vincente Minnelli, which is just as well because Kobal's part of the writing is loaded with errors.

Illustrated studies of individual actors' careers have become popular. Pyramid's small-format, paperbound life-and-work series, well illustrated, offers among others studies by Lee Edward Stern of Jeanette MacDonald, with the same virtues as his history cited above; by Patrick McGilligan of Ginger Rogers, nicely detailed and fair rather than effusive; by Barbara Bauer of Bing Crosby; by James Juneau, refreshingly level-headed, of Judy Garland; by Jeanine Basinger of Shirley Temple and Gene Kelly, both cliché bound; and by George Morris of Doris Day, with a good report on Day's early Warners musicals. Citadel Press has specialized in large-format books opening with a bio-

☆ 239

graphical essay, and then taking each film through a cast-and-credits list, plot summary, and contemporary critics' blurbs, the whole profusely illustrated. I think there's something wrong here—why reprint the idiot comments of journalists when the author, presumably an expert, can tell us so much more about each film? Those I haven't daunted might look into volumes on Maurice Chevalier by Gene Ringgold and DeWitt Bodeen; MacDonald and Eddy by Philip Castanza, who gushes; Shirley Temple by Robert Windeler; and Elvis Presley by Steven Zmijewsky and Boris Zmijewsky. There are many others, though other subjects made fewer musicals. In Citadel's format but more carefully designed and with more complete data and notes is W. Franklyn Moshier's *The Alice Faye Book* (Harrisburg: Stackpole Books, 1974). Faye and her films are basic to the musical, both historically and today on television, and serious students should put some time in here. A good start: turn to page 98 for a still of what Moshier captions as the "distinctive Faye pose." Try striking this pose yourself, if possible in one of Faye's costumes. How do you feel?

Volumes on Fred Astaire and Judy Garland each cover their subjects much better than anything Citadel has published, both verbally and pictorially. Stanley Green and Burt Goldblatt's *Starring Fred Astaire* (New York: Dodd, Mead, 1973) boasts much commentary on the making of the films and the experience of seeing them; with Astaire, most creative of stars, one must have more than data, and this book supplies it. Christopher Finch's *Rainbow: The Story of Judy Garland* (New York: Grosset and Dunlap, 1975) is a biography rather than a career study, but Finch's analysis is so acute and Will Hopkins' design so stylish that one must call it *the* book on a musical star's work. There have been Garland biographies trashy and earnest (a few are both), but only Finch has caught her and the legend; and his pictures, from the cover's frame enlargement* of Dorothy entranced by the magic to the last view of Garland in concert, exhausted by it, are a book in themselves.

Buffs of auteur theory prefer studies of directors, but few of the voguish ones worked in the musical and the pickings are lean. Try

---

*Frame enlargements are photographs made using the film itself as a negative, as opposed to stills, which are snapshots posed on the set. Stills supply perhaps 99.9 percent of all movie illustrations, yet obviously they are not authentic records of what one actually sees in the theatres. You can tell a frame enlargement from a still in that the actors in a frame frequently look a little awkward or off-center and the focus is sometimes a little awry.

Tom Milne's *Mamoulian* (Bloomington: Indiana University Press, 1970), which records *Applause*'s opening sequence and *Love Me To-night*'s finale in frames eloquently depictive of the director's mobile eye. A terrible event is Hugh Fordin's *The World of Entertainment!* (Garden City: Doubleday, 1975), a lengthy chronicle of the Freed unit that records release dates, production grosses, telegrams, and so on, and doesn't say word one about the films themselves. A terrific event, in Citadel's bio-and-films format but comparable to Finch in design, is Tony Thomas and Jim Terry's *The Busby Berkeley Book* (Greenwich, Conn.: The New York Graphic Society, 1973), rich in analysis, reminiscence, and rare photos, including frame series of "Shuffle Off to Buffalo," "Lullaby of Broadway," and "All's Fair in Love and War."

Walt Disney instances a special case, as his studio prudently controls the use of illustrative material; but a Disney study without pictures lacks resonance. Leonard Maltin's *The Disney Films* (New York: Popular Library, sec. ed., 1975) emphasizes the features over the shorts, telling much, but the black-and-white reproduction isn't too nifty. Richard Schickel's biography, *The Disney Version* (New York: Simon and Schuster, 1968), is favored by the cognoscenti, but Schickel's resentment of Disney's wealth and power nags through the text like a soapbox nut's exhortation. Horrors! the genius turned out to be a capitalist. The Disney people withheld permission from Schickel's publisher to use Disney art; I'm with them. On the other hand, the studio put a trove of sketches, storyboards, outlines, and other art at Christopher Finch's disposal for a smashing coffee-table issue, *The Art of Walt Disney* (New York: Abrams, 1973). The studio holds the copyright on the book.

Now, a miscellany. Alexander Walker treats the first sound years with wit in *The Shattered Silents* (New York: Morrow, 1978), and Miles Kreuger has collected all pertinent material that appeared in those years in *Photoplay*, the most adult of the movie magazines, in *The Movie Musical From Vitaphone to 42nd Street* (New York: Dover, 1975): articles, photos, and brief reviews. Alec Wilder's *American Popular Song* (New York: Oxford University Press, 1972) offers somewhat technical analysis of "The Great Innovators" in the first half of the century, and deals with Hollywood specialists like Harry Warren and Richard Whiting as well as the big Broadway names, almost all of whom composed for the screen as well. Publishers are increasingly putting out shooting scripts, including those of a few musicals, but these may be so edited on the set that they serve more as a record of what was planned than of what was filmed. I followed *Gold Diggers of*

1933 (Madison: University of Wisconsin Press, 1980) along with the film and found virtually every other line altered and whole sections missing (some were dropped, others filmed but cut before release). Wisconsin's series is well produced, with juicy frame enlargements and introductory notes; they have also put out *The Jazz Singer* and have promised *42nd Street*, *Footlight Parade*, and *Yankee Doodle Dandy*. For general reference, try Tom Vallance's *The American Musical* (New York: Barnes, 1970), with alphabetical capsule notes on actors, directors, choreographers, and songwriters, as well as a few abstracts on such topics as ballet and "ghosting," and an index by film title so you can work backwards to check a work's credits.

Two books deal with the planning and filming of one production, Aljean Harmetz' *The Making of the Wizard of Oz* (New York: Knopf, 1977) and Doug McClelland's *Down the Yellow Brick Road* (New York: Pyramid, 1976), which affirms my belief that this film is the A-prime Hollywood musical. McClelland's paperback has more pictures but Harmetz has the advantage of Knopf's bibliophile elegance and some stunning color frames. Moreover, she has researched the subject with completeness and affection. Harmetz is heartily recommended— to anyone, film buff or not.

I have saved the best for last: Arlene Croce's *The Fred Astaire and Ginger Rogers Book* (New York: Dutton, 1972). Croce, dance critic for *The New Yorker*, is a brilliant stylist, a perceptive analyst, and grand company. Film by film, she takes one through the nine RKO classics and *The Barkleys of Broadway* with appreciations of every detail of production, an excellent choice of illustrations, and, for dessert, tiny flip-page preservations of a moment each from "Let Yourself Go" and "The Waltz in Swing Time." Croce went to a lot of trouble. When she wants to show something and a still won't do, she has the appropriate frame enlarged: Rogers' *Swing Time* shampoo or "Eric Blore in consternation." Charm and wisdom, unbeatable.

☆ ☆

The Ethan Mordden Hall of Fame and Disrepute

BEST FILMS

The Love Parade
Whoopee!
Love Me Tonight
42nd Street
Gold Diggers of 1933
The Merry Widow [1934]
Top Hat
Swing Time
Show Boat [1936]
The Great Waltz [1938]
The Wizard of Oz
Pinocchio
Meet Me in St. Louis
Singin' in the Rain
Gigi
Cabaret

WORST FILMS

Glorifying the American Girl
Just Imagine
Honey
Variety Girl

Two Tickets to Broadway
Frankie and Johnny
Never Steal Anything Small
Lost Horizon
Paint Your Wagon
At Long Last Love
Sgt. Pepper's Lonely Hearts Club Band

BEST PERFORMANCES

Bessie Love in *The Broadway Melody*
Eddie Cantor in *Whoopee!*
Maurice Chevalier in *One Hour With You* and *The Love Parade*
Jeanette MacDonald in *Love Me Tonight* and *Naughty Marietta*
Helen Morgan in *Show Boat* [1936]
Bert Lahr in *The Wizard of Oz*
Judy Garland in *The Wizard of Oz* and *A Star Is Born* [1954]
Ethel Waters in *Cabin in the Sky*
James Cagney in *Yankee Doodle Dandy*
Margaret O'Brien in *Meet Me in St. Louis*
Jimmy Durante in *It Happened in Brooklyn*
Rita Moreno in *West Side Story*
Zero Mostel in *A Funny Thing Happened on the Way to the Forum*
Rosalind Russell in *Gypsy*
Barbra Streisand in *Funny Girl*
Walter Matthau in *Hello, Dolly!*
Nipsey Russell in *The Wiz*
Gary Busey in *The Buddy Holly Story*
Bette Midler in *The Rose*

WORST PERFORMANCES

The complete works of El Brendel
Jack Buchanan in *Monte Carlo*
Josephine Hutchinson in *Happiness Ahead*
Kathryn Grayson in *So This Is Love*
Lana Turner in *The Merry Widow* [1952]
Oscar Levant in *The Band Wagon*
Pamela Tiffin in *State Fair* [1962]
Natalie Wood in *Gypsy*
Cybill Shepherd in *At Long Last Love*
John Cassisi in *Bugsy Malone*
Peter Frampton and the Bee Gees in *Sgt. Pepper's Lonely Hearts Club Band*

MOST BIZARRE PERFORMANCES

Lillian Roth in *The Love Parade*
Marilyn Miller in *Her Majesty Love*
Baby Leroy in *A Bedtime Story*
Joan Crawford in *Dancing Lady*
Burgess Meredith in *Second Chorus*
Ray Bolger in *Babes in Toyland* [1961]
Carol Channing in *Thoroughly Modern Millie*
Julie Andrews in *Star!*
Lucille Ball in *Mame*
Everyone else in *Sgt. Pepper's Lonely Hearts Club Band*

MOST UNDERRATED PERFORMANCES

Joan Blondell in *Gold Diggers of 1933*
Aline MacMahon in *Gold Diggers of 1933*
Harriet Hilliard in *Follow the Fleet*
Luise Rainer in *The Great Ziegfeld*
Ann Miller in *Easter Parade*
Doris Day in *Calamity Jane*
Barbra Streisand in *Hello, Dolly!*
Lee Marvin in *Paint Your Wagon*
Twiggy in *The Boy Friend*
Burt Reynolds in *At Long Last Love*

BEST DIRECTORS

Rouben Mamoulian for *Applause, Love Me Tonight, The Gay Desperado*, and
    Summer Holiday
Ernst Lubitsch for *The Love Parade, Monte Carlo*, and *The Merry Widow*
Lloyd Bacon for *42nd Street*
Busby Berkeley for *Gold Diggers of 1935*
Julien Duvivier for *The Great Waltz*
Vincente Minnelli for *Meet Me in St. Louis, The Pirate*, and *Gigi*
Richard Lester for *A Funny Thing Happened on the Way to the Forum*
Ken Russell for *The Boy Friend*
Bob Fosse for *Cabaret* and *All That Jazz*
Milos Forman for *Hair*
Alan Parker for *Fame*

BEST ORIGINAL FILM SCORES

The Love Parade
Love Me Tonight
Hallelujah, I'm a Bum
Top Hat
Swing Time
Shall We Dance
The Wizard of Oz

BEST MUSICAL NUMBERS

"The Wedding of the Painted Doll" in *The Broadway Melody*
"Stetson" in *Whoopee!*
"Beyond the Blue Horizon" in *Monte Carlo*
"Sweeping the Clouds Away" in *Paramount on Parade*
"Isn't it Romantic?" in *Love Me Tonight*
"Shuffle Off to Buffalo" in *42nd Street*
"Remember My Forgotten Man" in *Gold Diggers of 1933*
"Don't Say Goodnight" in *Wonder Bar*
"Dames" in *Dames*
"Night and Day" in *The Gay Divorcee*
"Cheek to Cheek" in *Top Hat*
"Lullaby of Broadway" in *Gold Diggers of 1935*
"The Waltz in Swing Time" in *Swing Time*
"Bojangles of Harlem" in *Swing Time*
"Never Gonna Dance" in *Swing Time*
"All's Fair in Love and War" in *Gold Diggers of 1937*
"The Yam" in *Carefree*
"Can't Help Lovin' Dat Man" in *Show Boat* [1936]
"A Pretty Girl Is Like a Melody" in *The Great Ziegfeld*
"I'm in Love With Vienna" in *The Great Waltz*
"Your Broadway and My Broadway" in *Broadway Melody of 1938*
"Takin' a Chance on Love" in *Cabin in the Sky*
"Under the Bamboo Tree" in *Meet Me in St. Louis*
"The Trolley Song" in *Meet Me in St. Louis*
"Singin' in the Rain" in *Singin' in the Rain*
"Broadway Rhythm" in *Singin' in the Rain*
"The Barn Raising" in *Seven Brides for Seven Brothers*
"Don't Rain on My Parade" in *Funny Girl*
"There's Gotta Be Something Better Than This" in *Sweet Charity*
"Wilkommen" in *Cabaret*

"Tomorrow" in *Bugsy Malone*
"Aquarius" in *Hair*
"Hot Lunch Jam" in *Fame*
Special citation: "The Jitterbug" [deleted from *The Wizard of Oz*]

MOST TANTALIZING LOST FILM:
The Gold Diggers of Broadway

MOST DISTINGUISHED CAST ASSEMBLED FOR ONE FILM:
Show Boat [1936]

LEAST DISTINGUISHED CAST ASSEMBLED FOR ONE FILM:
Show Boat [1951]

BEST NEGLECTED FILM:
Folies Bergère

WORST CELEBRATED FILM:
The Band Wagon

MOST ORIGINAL PREMISE:
Fantasia

LEAST ORIGINAL PREMISE:
Alexander's Ragtime Band

MOST AUTHENTIC BIO:
Yankee Doodle Dandy

LEAST AUTHENTIC BIO:
Look for the Silver Lining

BEST KNOWN HOLLYWOOD ORIGINAL:
The Wizard of Oz

MOST OBSCURE HOLLYWOOD ORIGINAL:
Oh Sailor, Behave!

MOST OBSCURE ADAPTATION FROM BROADWAY:
The Five O'Clock Girl (completed through a rough cut but never released)

LEAST FAITHFUL ADAPTATION FROM BROADWAY:
Sally, Irene and Mary [1938]

MOST ORIGINAL CONCEPTION FOR GENRE:
the RKO dance musical
>**honorable mention:**
>the Warners Berkeley backstager

MOST DARING STUDIO:
Paramount

MOST STRIKING USE OF COLOR:
The Wizard of Oz
>**honorable mention:**
>*Whoopee!*

BEST ARGUMENT FROM THE LEFT:
Gold Diggers of 1935

BEST ARGUMENT FROM THE RIGHT:
The Wizard of Oz

BEST ANARCHIST ARGUMENT:
Hallelujah, I'm a Bum

TAJ MAHAL AWARD FOR MOST IMPRESSIVE DESIGN:
The Wizard of Oz

BURGER QUEEN AWARD FOR LEAST IMPRESSIVE DESIGN:
Honey

OUTSTANDING TRAINED SINGER:
Lawrence Tibbett

OUTSTANDING UNTRAINED SINGER:
Maurice Chevalier

MOST STRIKING ORCHESTRATION AND/OR PLAYING:
Whoopee!

OUTSTANDING COMPOSER:
Harry Warren

OUTSTANDING LYRICIST:
E. Y. Harburg

BEVERLY SILLS AWARD FOR OUTSTANDING CONTRIBUTION
TO SERIOUS MUSIC:
MGM, for capturing the musician's intensity in *Song of Love*

BEST EDITING:
All That Jazz

WORST EDITING:
Little Miss Marker [1934]

MOST WONDERFUL WOMAN:
Rita Hayworth

MOST WONDERFUL MAN:
Fred Astaire

MOST WONDERFUL KID:
Shirley Temple
> **honorable mention:**
> Mitzi Green

MOST BIZARRE PERSON:
Carmen Miranda
> **honorable mention:**
> Milizia Korjus

DULLEST PERSON:
Gordon MacRae
> **honorable mention:**
> Susanna Foster

MOST IMPRESSIVE TEAM:
Astaire and Rogers
> **honorable mention:**
> Garland and Kelly

LEAST IMPRESSIVE TEAM:
Gaynor and Farrell

ONE-TIMER AWARD:
Ethel Shutta in *Whoopee!*
> **honorable mention:**
> Kirsten Flagstad in *The Big Broadcast of 1938*

SURVIVOR AWARD:
Maurice Chevalier
>**honorable mention:**
>Charlotte Greenwood
>**second honorable mention:**
>Pert Kelton

ROD STEIGER AWARD FOR MOST OVERACTED ROLE:
Rod Steiger in *Oklahoma!*

RUBY KEELER AWARD FOR LEAST OVERACTED ROLE:
Yves Montand in *On a Clear Day You Can See Forever*

OUTSTANDING TROUPER AWARD FOR UNBILLED APPEAR-
ANCE:
Glenda Jackson in *The Boy Friend*
>**honorable mention:**
>Jack Benny in *Gypsy*

MOST PRECISE CHOOSER OF ROLES:
Lena Horne

LEAST PRECISE CHOOSER OF ROLES:
June Haver

GALE STORM AWARD FOR LEAST WELL EXPLOITED PERSON-
ALITY:
Fanny Brice
>**honorable mention:**
>Vivienne Segal

VIRGINIA KATHERINE McMATH AWARD FOR MOST VERSA-
TILE PERFORMER:
Jeanette MacDonald
>**honorable mention:**
>Ann Sothern

FERNANDO LAMAS AWARD FOR BEST MALE SINGER BORN IN
ARGENTINA WHO APPEARED IN FOUR JILLS AND A JEEP:
Dick Haymes

Index

Abbott, Bud, and Lou Costello, 172

Alexander's Ragtime Band, 145–46

Ali Baba Goes to Town, 62

Allen, Gracie, 92, 93, 120, 136, 137, 146

All That Jazz, 224–26

Allyson, June, 181, 182

Ameche, Don, 76, 145, 151, 174

American Graffiti, 211

American in Paris, An, 177, 197

Anchors Aweigh, 161, 173

Andrews, Julie, 201–2, 203, 205, 206, 219

Animal Crackers, 138

Annie Get Your Gun, 55, 188

Anything Goes, 97

Applause, 40–41, 79, 99

Arden, Eve, 172, 214

Arlen, Harold, 66, 88, 139, 157, 160, 192

Armstrong, Louis, 197, 207

Astaire, Fred, 43, 67, 70, 71, 74, 75, 79, 81, 89, 108, 110, 111–21, 124, 127, 129, 140, 159, 161, 167, 168–72, 177, 183, 186, 188–89, 190, 197, 198, 200, 206, 224, 228, 230

At Long Last Love, 219

Avalon, Frankie, 202, 214

Babes in Arms, 165, 168

Babes in Toyland (1934), 135

Babes in Toyland (1961), 201

Babes on Broadway, 165

Baby Leroy, 74, 75

Bacon, Lloyd, 44, 48, 85, 89

Balalaika, 132–33

Ball, Lucille, 55, 117, 217

Band Wagon, The, 177, 189

Barkleys of Broadway, The, 120, 183

Barthelmess, Richard, 7, 9, 32, 33

Barty, Billy, 83, 85

Battle of Paris, The, 71

Beach Party, 202

Beatles, The, 209–210, 212

Bedtime Story, A, 74

Bells Are Ringing, 202

Benny, Jack, 22, 92

Berkeley, Busby, 44, 46–47, 48, 63, 76, 81–88, 89, 91, 98, 109–10, 114, 118, 123, 143, 145, 165, 173, 183, 186, 188, 221

Berlin, Irving, 19, 25, 43, 67, 72, 78, 117, 125, 140, 144, 145, 170, 171, 183, 193

Bernstein, Leonard, 181
Best Foot Forward, 162
Be Yourself, 52–53, 140
Bigboy, 51
Big Broadcast, The, series, 92
Big Store, The, 139
Birth of the Blues, 164
Bitter Sweet, 133
Blaine, Vivian, 176, 182, 195
Blessed Event, 92
Blondell, Joan, 81–82, 84, 85, 86–87, 88, 89, 107, 214
Blore, Eric, 113, 115, 116, 123, 127, 136
Blue Angel, The, 60
Blue Bird, The, 151
Blues Brothers, The, 224
Blues in the Night, 163
Blue Skies, 171
Bogdanovich, Peter, 219
Boles, John, 19, 29, 30, 31, 53, 57, 123, 142, 150
Bolger, Ray, 72, 101, 110, 156, 160, 201
Bordoni, Irene, 32, 33, 54, 142
Born to Dance, 71–72, 107, 110
Boy Friend, The, 221
Brando, Marlon, 195
Bremer, Lucille, 170
Brendel, El, 35
Brice, Fanny, 52–53, 65, 100, 101, 125, 161, 206, 230, 231
Brigadoon, 187, 188
Bright Eyes, 149
Bright Lights, 88
Broadway, 18
Broadway Melody, The, 13–16, 17, 18, 32, 72–73, 83
Broadway Melody of 1936, 73, 110
Broadway Melody of 1940, 168–70
Broadway Serenade, 132
Broadway Thru a Keyhole, 89–90
Brown, Joe E., 49, 61, 88, 136
Brown, Lew, 28, 34–35

Brown, Nacio Herb, 15, 28, 63, 72–73, 189
Bruce, Virginia, 72, 101
Buchanan, Jack, 38, 189
Buck Privates, 172
Buddy Holly Story, The, 214
Bugsy Malone, 220, 227
Burns, George, 92, 93, 120, 137, 146, 212
Busey, Gary, 214
Bye Bye Birdie, 209

Cabaret, 60, 221–22, 225
Cabin in the Sky, 176–77
Cagney, James, 85, 174, 187, 202
Cairo, 133, 177
Calamity Jane, 191–92
Call Me Madam, 187, 188
Camelot, 204–5, 207
Can-Can, 204–5
Can't Help Singing, 175
Cantor, Eddie, 5, 43, 61–65, 101, 106, 136, 180, 186, 230
Can't Stop the Music, 231–32
Captain January, 150
Carefree, 140
Carmen Jones, 187
Carminati, Tullio, 94
Caron, Leslie, 197
Carousel, 199
Carroll, Nancy, 17, 21, 28, 54, 60, 61, 80, 142
Cat and the Fiddle, The, 20
Centennial Summer, 175
Charisse, Cyd, 116, 187, 189, 198
Chevalier, Maurice, 31, 37–39, 41–42, 54, 55, 57–59, 61, 65, 74–75, 80, 106, 127, 142–43, 197–98, 204, 231
Children of Dreams, 69
Chocolate Soldier, The, 133
Claire, Bernice, 65
Close Harmony, 17
Coal Miner's Daughter, 224

Cocoanuts, The, 109, 138
Cohan, George M., 15, 27, 69, 125, 174
College Humor, 146
College Love, 28
College Swing, 93
Comden, Betty, 180, 181, 189
Compson, Betty, 22, 49
Connecticut Yankee in King Arthur's Court, A, 181
Connolly, Bobby, 90–91, 139
Coppola, Francis Ford, 206
Coquette, 9
Court Jester, The, 197
Cover Girl, 167, 169
Crawford, Joan, 18, 21, 22, 30, 59, 70, 73, 88–89, 107, 180
Crosby Bing, 43, 65, 80, 92, 97, 126–27, 142, 146–48, 150–51, 160, 162, 164, 170, 171–72, 174, 181, 197, 201, 229, 231
Cukor, George, 38, 192–93, 202
Curly Top, 150

Daddy Long Legs, 197
Dailey, Dan, 168, 182, 193
Dames, 74
Damn Yankees, 198
Damsel in Distress, A, 120–21, 137
Dance of Life, The, 40
Dancing Lady, 88–89, 136
Dancing Pirate, The, 130
Dandridge, Dorothy, 163, 199
Daniels, Bebe, 29, 30, 41, 43–48, 53, 55, 142, 221
Darling Lili, 219
Davies, Marion, 22, 30, 146
Davis, Joan, 107
Day, Doris, 57, 143, 180, 186, 187, 191–92, 198
Deep in My Heart, 187
De Forest, Lee, 8
De Haven, Gloria, 162, 186
Delicious, 67

Del Rio, Delores, 111
Desert Song, The, 19–20, 21, 26
DeSylva, B.G., 28, 34–35, 68
Dietrich, Marlene, 60–61
Disney, Walt, 10–11, 69, 153–54, 188, 201–2
Dixiana, 55
Dr. Doolittle, 205–6
Donen, Stanley, 180, 181, 189, 198, 217, 219
Don Juan, 2–3
Double or Nothing, 147
Down Argentine Way, 162, 168
Downey, Morton, 17, 18
DuBarry Was a Lady, 55, 162
Dubin, Al, 47, 48, 76–78, 81, 85–86, 93, 123
Duck Soup, 138
Dumont, Margaret, 138, 139
Duncan, Vivian and Rosetta, 15
Dunne, Irene, 98–100, 104, 114–15, 135, 140
Durante, Jimmy, 107, 148, 182
Durbin, Deanna, 61, 65, 134, 173, 175, 182, 190, 229, 230–31
Duvivier, Julien, 102–3

Easter Parade, 183
East Side of Heaven, 148
Eastwood, Clint, 117, 207
Ebsen, Buddy, 107, 110, 148, 150, 157
Eddy, Nelson, 59, 67, 71–72, 75, 89, 95–97, 108, 110, 126, 127–33, 173, 182
Erwin, Stuart, 92, 93
Every Night at Eight, 144
Every Sunday, 134

Fame, 222, 226–27
Farrell, Charles, 34–35, 67
Farrell, Glenda, 87
Fashions of 1934, 86
Fay, Frank, 31–33, 54

Faye, Alice, 57, 61, 65, 76, 80, 93, 107, 111, 136, 142, 143–46, 148, 150, 151, 155, 159, 161, 162, 168, 173, 174, 190, 196, 229, 231

Fazenda, Louise, 19, 20, 32, 49

Fiddler on the Roof, 217

Fields, Dorothy, 21, 117, 118, 123, 140

Fields, W. C., 56, 75, 92, 157

Fifty Million Frenchmen, 43

Finian's Rainbow, 206–7

Firefly, The, 131–32

Fitzgerald, Ella, 172

Fleet's In, The, 163

Flying Down to Rio, 70–71, 111–12, 115

Flying High, 27, 34, 35

FM, 212

Folies Bergère, 143

Follow That Dream, 196

Follow the Fleet, 115, 116–17, 118, 119

Follow the Leader, 55

Fontaine, Joan, 121

Footlight Parade, 85

Footlights and Fools, 17

Forman, Milos, 227–28

For Me and My Gal, 165–67

42nd Street, 18, 44–49, 53, 54, 55, 65, 76, 79, 88, 109–10, 126, 221, 226

Fosse, Bob, 60, 187, 198, 208, 221, 224–26

Four Jills in a Jeep, 161

Fox Movietone Follies, The, 22, 73

Frankie and Johnny, 196

Freed, Arthur, 15, 28, 72–73, 170, 177, 180, 183, 189, 198

Freeland, Thornton, 53

Friml, Rudolf, 27, 58, 67, 72, 131

Funicello, Annette, 201, 202

Funny Face, 197

Funny Girl, 206, 230

Funny Lady, 218

Gable, Clark, 88–89, 129

Gang's All Here, The, 173

Garland, Judy, 45, 55, 61, 93–94, 157, 161, 162, 165–68, 177–79, 181, 183–85, 188, 192–93, 230, 231

Garrett, Betty, 181

Gay Desperado, The, 103–4

Gay Divorcee, The, 11, 112–14, 119, 120

Gaynor, Janet, 34–35, 53, 67, 142, 190

Gaynor, Mitzi, 193, 197, 199

Gentlemen Prefer Blondes, 187

George White's 1935 Scandals, 110, 144

George White's Scandals, 143

Gershwin, George, 19, 55, 67, 120, 164, 174, 197, 199

Gershwin, Ira, 19, 55, 67, 78, 120, 167, 176, 192

Gigi, 197–98

Gilbert, John, 10, 22, 57

Gimme Shelter, 210

Girl Crazy (1932), 55

Girl Crazy (1943), 168

Girl Most Likely, The, 225

Girl of the Golden West, The, 128, 132

Glorifying the American Girl, 178, 186

Godspell, 220

Going Hollywood, 146

Going My Way, 168

Goin' to Town, 137

Go Into Your Dance, 77–78

Gold Diggers of Broadway, The, 107

Gold Diggers of 1933, 46, 77, 80, 81–85, 107

Gold Diggers of 1935, 77, 87–88

Gold Diggers of 1937, 88

Golden Dawn, 20

Goldwyn, Samuel, 62–63, 124, 180, 195, 199

Goodman, Benny, 92, 173
Good News (1930), 28–29, 34, 35, 181
Good News (1947), 181
Gordon, Mack, 75–76, 93, 146, 150
Gould, Dave, 70, 115, 143
Grable, Betty, 61, 63, 65, 93, 94, 113, 143, 161, 165, 168, 182, 186, 195
Gray, Alexander, 33, 55, 65, 91
Gray, Lawrence, 15, 55
Grayson, Kathryn, 160, 161, 172, 173, 182, 186, 187
Grease, 212, 213–14, 216
Great Caruso, The, 186
Great Day!, 70
Great Gabbo, The, 22
Great Victor Herbert, The, 100, 103
Great Waltz, The, 100, 102–3
Great Ziegfeld, The, 100–102, 165, 174
Green, Adolph, 180, 181, 189
Green, Mitzi, 60
Greenwood, Charlotte, 27, 65, 168, 194
Griffith, D. W., 6, 9, 79
Guys and Dolls, 194–95
Gypsy, 55, 202–3

Hair, 227–28
Haley, Jack, 75, 93, 145, 150, 157, 190
Hallelujah, 24–26, 40, 66, 72, 79, 176
Hallelujah, I'm a Bum, 69–70, 159, 178
Hamilton, Margaret, 124, 157
Hammerstein, Oscar, II, 12, 19, 20, 69, 74, 91, 97–100, 104, 176, 199, 203
Hans Christian Andersen, 186
Happiness Ahead, 106
Harburg, E. Y., 66, 88, 90, 91, 139, 157–58

Hard Day's Night, A, 209
Harlow, Jean, 117
Hart, Lorenz, 19, 42, 55, 59, 68–70, 71, 78, 89, 130, 133, 147, 152, 162, 175, 181, 198
Harvey Girls, The, 178–79
Haver, June, 174, 182
Haymes, Dick, 169, 176, 182
Hayworth, Rita, 116, 167, 168, 169–70, 198
Hearts in Dixie, 24
Hello, Dolly!, 208, 212
Help!, 209–10, 228
Henderson, Ray, 28, 34–35
Henie, Sonja, 80, 136, 151–52, 163
Hepburn, Audrey, 197, 201, 202
Hepburn, Katharine, 4, 160, 175
Herbert, Victor, 15, 95, 97, 135
Here Is My Heart, 147
Her Majesty Love, 56–57, 140
Higher and Higher, 162
High Society, 197
High Society Blues, 35, 106
High, Wide and Handsome, 104–5, 106, 107
Hilliard, Harriet, 116–17
Hit the Deck, 70
Hold Everything, 61
Holiday Inn, 170
Hollywood Party, 73
Hollywood Revue of 1929, The, 10, 22, 30–31
Holm, Celeste, 182
Honey, 56, 60, 61
Honky Tonk, 18, 125–26
Hope, Bob, 92, 93, 172–73, 201
Horne, Lena, 176, 177
Horton, Edward Everett, 67, 113–14, 115, 116, 127, 136
Hot Heiress, The, 68, 106
Hutchinson, Josephine, 106
Hutton, Betty, 55, 160, 163, 172, 174, 188

I Dream Too Much, 123–24
I'll See You in My Dreams, 187
I'll Take Romance, 124
I Married an Angel, 133
In Caliente, 88
Innocents of Paris, 57
In Old Chicago, 145
In the Good Old Summertime, 183
It's a Great Feeling, 180
It's a Great Life, 15
It's Always Fair Weather, 193
Iturbi, José, 124, 133, 161, 173

Jackson, Glenda, 221
Jailhouse Rock, 195
Jazz Singer, The (1927), 4–6, 7, 9, 17, 50, 52, 133, 230
Jazz Singer, The (1953), 191
Jesus Christ Superstar, 220
Jolson, Al, 4–7, 10, 32, 46, 46–52, 62, 65, 69, 77–78, 86, 89, 142, 175, 178, 191, 230, 231
Jolson Story, The, 142, 175
Jones, Allan, 95, 98, 99, 102, 103, 131–32, 139
Jones, Shirley, 194
Joy of Living, 140
Just Imagine, 35, 37

Kahn, Gus, 59, 63, 70, 132, 187
Kane, Helen, 28
Kaye, Danny, 57, 178–79, 186, 197
Keel, Howard, 65, 126, 187, 188, 190, 191
Keeler, Ruby, 44–48, 77, 81–85, 86–87, 91, 98, 106, 107, 110, 114, 145, 221
Kelly, Gene, 160, 161, 165–67, 168, 175, 177, 180, 181, 183, 184–85, 187, 188–89, 190, 193, 195, 197, 207, 224, 231
Kelly, Patsy, 93, 144, 190
Kern, Jerome, 12, 13, 19, 74, 91, 97–100, 104, 114, 117, 118, 123, 125, 140, 167, 170, 175–76
Kibbee, Guy, 44, 82, 86, 150
Kidd, Michael, 191, 193, 199, 207
Kid From Brooklyn, The, 180
Kid From Spain, The, 43, 62
Kid Galahad, 195
Kid Millions, 62
King, Carlotta, 19–20
King, Charles, 13, 14, 15, 142
King, Dennis, 27–28
King and I, The, 133, 199
King of Burlesque, 144
King of Jazz, 21, 31, 146
King Steps Out, The, 103
Kirk, Lisa, 209
Kismet, 190
Kiss Me, Kate, 187–88
Knickerbocker Holiday, 133
Korjus, Milizia, 102–3

Lady in the Dark, 162
Lady Sings the Blues, 210–11
Lahr, Bert, 27, 61, 136, 157, 158
Lamarr, Hedy, 165
Lamour, Dorothy, 172, 201
Langford, Frances, 107, 144
Lansbury, Angela, 179
Lanza, Mario, 186
Last Waltz, The, 211–12
Laurel, Stan, and Oliver Hardy, 22, 30, 135–36
Lawford, Peter, 181, 182, 183, 189
Lawrence, Gertrude, 65, 71, 162, 206
Laye, Evelyn, 65, 127
Lee, Davey, 6–7, 51
Lee, Dorothy, 30, 135
Lerner, Alan Jay, 197, 204, 208, 218
LeRoy, Mervyn, 81, 98, 157, 203
Les Girls, 197
Lester, Richard, 204, 209–10
Let's Go Native, 58

Let's Make Love, 201
Lewis, Ted, 32, 33, 65
Lightner, Winnie, 32–34, 61, 65, 89, 107
Li'l Abner, 198–99
Lili, 197
Lillian Russell, 174
Lillie, Beatrice, 32, 33
Little Johnny Jones, 27
Little Miss Marker, 149
Little Nellie Kelly, 167
Little Night Music, A, 49, 217–18
Little Prince, The, 217, 225
Loesser, Frank, 66, 195
Loewe, Frederick, 197, 205, 208
Lord Byron of Broadway, 73
Lost Horizon, 219–20
Lottery Bride, The, 58
Love, Bessie, 13, 15, 22, 28, 142
Love Finds Andy Hardy, 165
Love in the Rough, 21, 106
Love Me Forever, 124
Love Me or Leave Me, 187
Love Me Tender, 195
Love Me Tonight, 41–42, 43, 57–58, 68, 71, 79, 106, 120, 183
Love Parade, The, 20, 29, 37–38, 41, 43, 55–56, 58, 59, 139
Loy, Myrna, 19, 20, 32, 42
Lubitsch, Ernst, 20, 26, 31, 37–39, 41, 43, 58–59, 74, 80, 96, 102, 109, 143, 155, 183
Lucas, Nick, 32, 125
Lupino, Ida, 97, 104
Lyon, Ben, 53–54, 56–57, 68, 106

MacDonald, Jeanette, 20, 27–28, 37–39, 43, 55, 58–60, 61, 67, 68, 74, 75, 79, 95–97, 108, 127–33, 142, 145, 172, 177, 182, 229
MacLaine, Shirley, 204, 208
MacMahon, Aline, 81–83
MacRae, Gordon, 186, 194, 199
Mame, 217

Mammy, 51, 66
Mamoulian, Rouben, 26, 37, 40–43, 58, 60, 68, 80, 102, 103–5, 123, 155, 183–84, 198, 199
Man of La Mancha, 217
Marshall, Everett, 55
Martin, Mary, 103, 160, 164, 203
Martin, Tony, 94, 107, 140, 186
Martini, Nino, 103–4
Marx Brothers, 136, 137–40, 162, 230
Mary Poppins, 201–2
Massey, Ilona, 71, 132, 133
Maytime, 128, 130–31
McCarey, Leo, 139
McCormack, John, 122
McDaniel, Hattie, 98–99, 161
Meet Danny Wilson, 191, 192
Meet Me in St. Louis, 177–79, 184
Melchior, Lauritz, 124, 173, 181–82
Melody of Love, 11
Melton, James, 123
Mercer, Johnny, 134, 160, 164, 170
Merkel, Una, 44, 45, 47, 107
Merman, Ethel, 55, 65, 97, 145, 160, 187, 188, 190, 193
Merry Widow, The, 37, 58–60, 109
Metropolitan, 122
Midler, Bette, 229–31
Miller, Ann, 181, 183, 186, 187
Miller, Marilyn, 56–57, 74, 101, 110
Minnelli, Liza, 60, 219, 221–22, 231
Minnelli, Vincente, 171, 177–79, 184–85, 189, 197–98, 218
Miranda, Carmen, 161, 162, 168, 172, 173, 190–91
Mississippi, 147
Monroe, Marilyn, 143, 187, 193, 201
Monte Carlo, 20, 38–39, 74
Moonlight and Pretzels, 90–91, 98, 226
Moore, Colleen, 17–18

Moore, Grace, 4, 58, 94–95, 103, 124, 133, 186
Moore, Mary Tyler, 196, 205
Moore, Victor, 117, 160, 161
Moreno, Rita, 205
Morgan, Dennis, 65, 102, 181
Morgan, Frank, 27, 70, 96, 101, 148, 157
Morgan, Helen, 12, 40–41, 77, 78, 98, 99
Moten, Etta, 84, 111
Mother Wore Tights, 182
Movie Movie, 219
Munshin, Jules, 181, 183
Muppet Movie, The, 223
Murphy, George, 110, 145, 148, 162, 169
Music Man, The, 202
Muscle Beach Party, 202
Music in the Air, 91
My Fair Lady, 201, 202
My Lucky Star, 151
My Man, 7, 52

Nancy Goes to Rio, 190
Naughty But Nice, 133–34
Naughty Marietta, 18, 95–97, 127, 128
Nelson, Gene, 186, 193
New Moon (1930), 26–27, 133
New Moon (1940), 128, 133
Newton-John, Olivia, 213, 231
New York, New York, 219
Night After Night, 137
Night and Day, 175
Night at the Opera, A, 139
Night Is Young, The, 127
No, No, Nanette, 70
Novarro, Ramon, 18, 65, 127, 142
Now I'll Tell, 143
Nype, Russell, 232

Oakie, Jack, 28, 61, 75, 172, 190
Oberon, Merle, 143

O'Brien, Margaret, 178–79
O'Connor, Donald, 147, 189, 190, 193
Oklahoma!, 194
Oliver!, 206
On a Clear Day You Can See Forever, 218
One Hour With You, 39, 43, 58
O'Neil, Sally, 49, 107
One in a Million, 151
One Night of Love, 59, 94–95, 104, 124
One Touch of Venus, 231
On the Avenue, 144–45
On the Town, 181
On With the Show!, 48–49, 83, 163
On Your Toes, 152

Pagan Love Song, 190
Paint Your Wagon, 207–8
Pajama Game, The, 198, 199
Palmy Days, 62
Panama Hattie, 55
Page, Anita, 13, 15
Paramount on Parade, 21–22, 31, 54, 56
Parker, Alan, 220, 226–27
Phantom President, The, 69
Pickford, Mary, 9
Pidgeon, Walter, 53, 142
Pigskin Parade, 93–94, 106, 191
Pinocchio, 154, 157, 188
Pirate, The, 184–85
Pons, Lily, 59, 123–24
Poor Little Rich Girl, 150
Porgy and Bess, 199
Porter, Cole, 19, 71–72, 74, 78, 97, 113, 162, 169, 170, 175, 184, 187, 190, 197, 198, 219
Powell, Dick, 44, 48, 74, 81–88, 92, 106, 126–27, 144–45, 160
Powell, Eleanor, 71, 107, 110–11, 116, 168–69, 224, 225, 231
Powell, Jane, 189, 190, 191

Powell, William, 101
Preisser, June, 168
Presley, Elvis, 195–97, 201
Professional Sweetheart, 111
Puttin' on the Ritz, 55, 79

Quadrophenia, 216
Queen High, 27
Queen of the Night Clubs, 18

Rainer, Luise, 101–2, 103
Rainger, Ralph, 61, 74–75, 123
Raitt, John, 188, 199
Raye, Martha, 92, 93, 147, 161, 172
Raymond, Gene, 111
Reaching for the Moon, 43
Revel, Harry, 75–76, 93, 146, 150
Reynolds, Burt, 219
Reynolds, Debbie, 189
Rhapsody in Blue, 174
Rhythm on the Range, 147
Richman, Harry, 55
Rich, Young and Pretty, 190–91
Ride 'Em Cowboy, 172
Rin-Tin-Tin, 2, 32, 33
Rio Rita (1929), 29–30, 53, 135
Rio Rita (1942), 172
Ritz Brothers, 136, 144, 151
Road to, series, 172–73, 201
Robbins, Jerome, 205
Roberta, 114–15, 119, 120, 140
Robeson, Paul, 98–100
Robinson, Bill, 148, 149, 150, 176
Rock Around the Clock, 195
Rocky Horror Picture Show, The, 222–23
Rodgers, Richard, 19, 42, 55, 68–70, 71, 89, 130, 133, 147, 152, 162, 175, 176, 181, 198, 199, 203
Rogers, Buddy, 17, 54, 56, 74
Rogers, Ginger, 43, 44, 45, 47, 67, 70, 75, 81, 82, 93, 108, 111–21, 127, 129, 140, 159, 162, 183, 200
Rogue Song, The, 27, 125

Romance on the High Seas, 180
Roman Scandals, 62
Romberg, Sigmund, 19, 20, 67, 69, 72, 130, 182, 187
Rooney, Mickey, 161, 165–67, 168, 175, 183
Rosalie, 71–72, 110–11, 132
Rose, The, 17, 211, 228–30, 231, 232
Rose Marie (1936), 128–29
Rose Marie (1954), 190
Rose of the Rancho, 123
Rose of Washington Square, 100, 142
Roth, Lillian, 38, 43, 55–56, 65, 142
Royal Wedding, 189
Ruggles, Charles, 27, 39, 42
Russell, Ken, 210, 221
Russell, Nipsey, 213
Russell, Rosalind, 55, 202–3

Sally, 56
Sally, Irene and Mary, 107
Sandrich, Mark, 113, 119, 170
San Francisco, 129–30, 132, 145
Say It With Songs, 51
Schertzinger, Victor, 38
Scorsese, Martin, 212, 219
Scott, Randolph, 104, 114, 116, 117, 148
Second Chorus, 169
Segal, Vivienne, 20, 59, 142
Sgt. Pepper's Lonely Hearts Club Band, 212, 213
Seven Brides for Seven Brothers, 190–91
1776, 217
Shall We Dance, 67, 111, 119
Shaw, Wini, 87, 98
She Done Him Wrong, 137
She Learned About Sailors, 143–44
Sheridan, Ann, 137, 174
Sherman, Richard and Robert, 202
Shore, Dinah, 181

Show Boat (1929), 11–13, 17, 98
Show Boat (1936), 98–100, 104
Show Boat (1951), 190
Show of Shows, The, 31–34, 54
Shutta, Ethel, 63
Silk Stockings, 198
Silvers, Phil, 188, 204
Sinatra, Frank, 155, 162–63, 180–83, 191, 195, 197, 198, 199, 204–5
Singing Fool, The, 6–7, 10, 13, 191
Singing Kid, The, 142
Singin' in the Rain, 8, 189–90
Sing, You Sinners, 147
Sitting Pretty, 75–76
Skelton, Red, 186
Slipper and the Rose, The, 49, 222–23
Smiling Lieutenant, The, 38, 140
Smilin' Through, 133
Smith, Queenie, 98
Smith, Stanley, 28, 55, 60
Snow White and the Seven Dwarfs, 153–54, 158, 188
Something for the Boys, 162
Sondheim, Stephen, 204, 217–18
Song of Love, 4, 175
Song O' My Heart, 122
Song of the West, 20
Song to Remember, A, 174, 175
Sothern, Ann, 55, 143
So This Is Love, 186
Sound of Music, The, 203–4
South Pacific, 199
Sparks, Ned, 44, 82, 93, 98, 135, 151
Spring Is Here, 55
Stage Door Canteen, 160
Stage Struck, 88
Stand Up and Cheer, 149
Star!, 206
Star Is Born, A, 17, 192–93, 218–19, 230
Stars Over Broadway, 123

Star-Spangled Rhythm, 160
State Fair, 177
Steamboat Willie, 10–11
Steele, Tommy, 206–7
Step Lively, 162–63
Stormy Weather, 176
Story of Vernon and Irene Castle, The, 119–20
Streisand, Barbra, 206–7, 218–19, 230
Strike Me Pink, 62
Strike Up the Band, 165
Styne, Jule, 66, 162, 186
Summer Holiday, 183–84
Summer Stock, 188
Sunny, 56
Sunny Side Up, 34–35, 79, 106
Swannee River, 172
Swanson, Gloria, 40
Swarthout, Gladys, 123
Sweet Adeline, 97–98, 104
Sweet Charity, 207–8, 225
Sweethearts, 128, 132
Sweetie, 28
Swing Time, 111, 117–19
Syncopation, 18

Take a Chance, 66
Take Me Out to the Ball Game, 183
Tashman, Lilyan, 142
Temple, Shirley, 57, 74, 80, 148–51, 157
Thank Your Lucky Stars, 161
That Night in Rio, 162
There's No Business Like Show Business, 193
They Shall Have Music, 124
Thin Ice, 151
Thomas, Danny, 187, 191
Thoroughly Modern Millie, 205
Thousands Cheer, 160–61
Three Little Girls in Blue, 182
Three Little Pigs, The, 69
Three Little Words, 186

Tibbett, Lawrence, 27, 54–55, 57, 122
Till the Clouds Roll By, 175
Tommy, 210, 211
Top Banana, 188
Top Hat, 67, 111, 115, 116, 119
Travolta, John, 213
Tucker, Sophie, 18, 125–26
Twenty Million Sweethearts, 92–93
Twiggy, 221
200 Motels, 210
Two Sisters from Boston, 181–82
Two Tickets to Broadway, 186

Untamed, 73
Up in Central Park, 182

Vagabond King, The (1930), 27–28
Vagabond King, The (1956), 27
Vagabond Lover, The, 55
Vallee, Rudy, 55, 143
Van Dyke, Dick, 201–2
Van Dyke, W. S., 96, 97, 127, 129
Vera-Ellen, 181, 182
Verdon, Gwen, 198, 208, 225
Vidor, King, 10, 24–26, 39, 79
Viennese Nights, 20, 72
Von Sternberg, Josef, 60–61, 103

Wake Up and Live, 93, 191
Waller, Fats, 164, 176
Warren, Harry, 47, 48, 55, 76–78, 81, 84, 85–86, 88, 93, 123, 134, 163, 170, 173
Waters, Ethel, 49, 52, 125, 160, 163, 177
Weary River, 7, 9
Weekend in Havana, 162
Weill, Kurt, 162, 176, 206
We're Not Dressing, 137, 146–47
West, Mae, 80, 108, 137, 138, 207

Westley, Helen, 98, 124, 148, 190
West Side Story, 205
Whale, James, 98–100
Wheeler, Bert, 30, 135, 136
When You're in Love, 124
Where Do We Go From Here?, 176
Whiting, Richard A., 74
Who, The, 210, 216
Whoopee!, 62–65, 72, 136, 180
Wilde, Cornel, 175, 176
Williams, Esther, 183, 190
Williams, Paul, 218, 220
Winninger, Charles, 98, 165, 176, 190
Wise, Robert, 203, 206
Withers, Jane, 149
Wiz, The, 212, 213
Wizard of Oz, The, 18–19, 151, 154–59, 178, 192, 198, 228
Wonder Bar, 85–86
Wonder Man, 180
Woollsey, Robert, 30, 135, 136
Words and Music, 175
Wynn, Ed, 55, 136, 160, 201

Xanadu, 231, 232

Yankee Doodle Dandy, 174–75
Yolanda and the Thief, 170–71, 177
You Can't Have Everything, 76, 145
You'll Never Get Rich, 169–70
Youmans, Vincent, 20, 70
Young Man of Manhattan, 111
You're a Sweetheart, 145
You Were Never Lovelier, 170

Zanuck, Darryl, 43, 44, 80, 91, 151
Ziegfeld, Florenz, 12, 63, 100–102
Ziegfeld Follies, 161, 177
Ziegfeld Girl, 165